Early Years Policy

The impact on practice

How does early years policy impact on practitioners, children, settings and families?

What are the implications of current policy for the future?

How can early years professionals shape and craft practice in ways that genuinely focus on the needs of children and families, rather than the interests of policy makers?

This exciting new text explores the changing context and increasing importance of early years policy. It takes a broad look at policy developments and shows how these have affected children, settings, parents and the early years workforce.

The book is divided into two parts, the first of which examines theoretical perspectives and sets out the early years policy context, looking at issues surrounding accountability, international influences on policy and the Early Years Foundation Stage. The second half of the book directly shows how policy has influenced practice, and considers:

- the up-skilling of the workforce and the impact of this on practitioners
- the development of the learning environment including outdoor provision
- sustained shared thinking and its link to high-quality learning and teaching
- the impact of policy on parents.

Offering a fresh perspective on early years policy, this timely textbook will be essential reading for students on undergraduate and postgraduate Early Years and Childhood Studies courses and those working towards Early Years Teacher Status.

Zenna Kingdon is Senior Lecturer in Children, Young People and Communities Studies and is Education Studies Framework Leader at the University of St Mark & St John, Plymouth, UK.

Jan Gourd is Senior Lecturer in Children, Young People and Communities Studies at the University of St Mark & St John, Plymouth, UK.

Early Years Policy

The impact on practice

Edited by
Zenna Kingdon and
Jan Gourd

Routledge
Taylor & Francis Group

LONDON AND NEW YORK

First published 2014
by Routledge
2 Park Square, Milton Park, Abingdon, Oxon OX14 4RN

and by Routledge
711 Third Avenue, New York, NY 10017

Routledge is an imprint of the Taylor & Francis Group, an informa business

© 2014 Zenna Kingdon and Jan Gourd

The right of the editors to be identified as the authors of the editorial material, and of the authors for their individual chapters, has been asserted in accordance with sections 77 and 78 of the Copyright, Designs and Patents Act 1988.

British Library Cataloguing in Publication Data
A catalogue record for this book is available from the British Library

Library of Congress Cataloging in Publication Data
A catalog record for this book has been requested

ISBN: 978-0-415-62708-5 (hbk)
ISBN: 978-0-415-62709-2 (pbk)
ISBN: 978-1-315-86301-6 (ebk)

Typeset in Bembo and Helvetica Neue
by Florence Production Ltd, Stoodleigh, Devon, UK

MIX
Paper from
responsible sources
FSC   FSC® C013056
www.fsc.org

Printed and bound in Great Britain by
TJ International Ltd, Padstow, Cornwall

Contents

List of contributors   vii
List of abbreviations   ix

Introduction   1
Zenna Kingdon and Jan Gourd

PART I

Theoretical perspectives   **11**

  1 Early years work, professionalism and the translation
      of policy into practice   13
      Sue Lea

  2 Accountability: tensions and challenges   33
      Lisa Spencer-Woodley

  3 The influence of international policy   56
      Jan Gourd

  4 The Early Years Foundation Stage: Tickell and beyond:
      a critical perspective   75
      Zenna Kingdon

  5 Future policy and the impact of societal change   95
      Jan Gourd

PART II

Policy in practice   **115**

  6 Up-skilling the workforce: managing change in practice   117
      Jan Gourd

7 The impact of foundation degrees on practitioners 135
  Zenna Kingdon

8 Policy and the change in the early years learning
  environment 152
  Zenna Kingdon

9 Research-informed policy – myth or reality?
  Sustained shared thinking 173
  Zenna Kingdon

10 How policy has impacted on parents 192
  Michael Gasper

Conclusion 213
  Jan Gourd and Zenna Kingdon

Glossary 219
Index 221

Contributors

Michael Gasper is a published author and early years consultant specialising in leadership. Having completed 27 years in teaching, 17 as a Head, during which he developed early intervention in partnership with colleagues from Social Care and health services, he joined the Centre for Research in Early Childhood, coordinating research into the effectiveness of the Early Excellence Centre programme. He has worked for the last eight years as a mentor, facilitator and assessor on the National Professional Qualification in Integrated Centre Leadership (NPQICL) managed by National College for cohorts delivered by Lancaster University, London University Institute of Education, SERCO and the Centre for Research in Early Childhood (CREC) in partnership with Birmingham City University. His experience over 40 years has provided a unique insight into the planned and unintended effects of policy on practice.

Jan Gourd has been in education for over 20 years and her roles have included Head of Key Stage 1, deputy Head and ten years as a primary Headteacher in Plymouth. Her current role is as a senior lecturer at the University of St Mark & St John in Plymouth. She leads the current EYP graduate entry programme and route leads the BA Primary Education courses. Jan is particularly interested in creativity, children's writing and literacy, early childhood education and policy. Jan currently teaches across a wide range of programmes including the Early Years FdA and Early Childhood 'top-up' courses.

Zenna Kingdon is a Senior Lecturer at the University of St Mark & St John in Plymouth. She is responsible for a range of Education Studies programmes, including BA (Hons) Early Childhood Education.

Her teaching from undergraduate to postgraduate provision focuses on play and pedagogy and the impact that these have on the lives of young children. After her first degree she returned and qualified as a teacher. She specialised in Key Stage 1 and early years. She has also had extensive involvement with the PVI sector. Her current research interests are centred on play, role-play and sustained shared thinking. She is undertaking a PhD at Plymouth University.

Sue Lea is an experienced manager and community educator who has worked across the public, private, voluntary and community sectors. She has extensive experience of educational practice in a range of settings and this informs her relationships with students of early years, youth and community work, and education studies at the University of St Mark & St John in Plymouth. Sue has an eclectic publication record, including such topics as academic literacies, educational inclusion, anti-oppressive educational relationships and critical explorations of educational leadership. The unifying theme of her work is an exploration of how emancipatory and inclusionary practice can be developed when empowered and informed professionals act as policy entrepreneurs to shape and craft their practice to social justice ends.

Lisa Spencer-Woodley worked across a variety of voluntary sector settings with young people in the fields of homelessness, mental health and drugs and alcohol, after graduating with a degree majoring in Psychology in 1995. During this time Lisa completed her Master's in Youth and Community Work with JNC professional qualification. She is Academic Lead in the Department of Children, Young People and Communities at the University of St Mark & St John in Plymouth. She teaches across a wide range of education and welfare programmes, focusing on critical and community psychology, and critical reflective practice and professional development. Lisa is engaged in research exploring the 'teaching' of critical reflective practice for her Education doctorate at Exeter University.

Abbreviations

CAF	Common Assessment Framework
CRB	Criminal Records Bureau
CWDC	Children's Workforce Development Council
DAP	developmentally appropriate practice
DCSF	Department for Children, Schools and Families
DES	Department of Education and Science
DfE	Department for Education
DfEE	Department for Education and Employment
DfES	Department for Education and Skills
DLOs	desirable learning outcomes
ECaT	Every Child a Talker
ECEC	early childhood education and care
ELPP	Early Learning Partnership Project
EPPE	Effective Provision of Pre-school Education
EPPSE	Effective Pre-school, Primary and Secondary Education
EYFS	Early Years Foundation Stage
EYP	Early Years Professional
EYPS	Early Years Professional Status
EYSEFD	early years sector endorsed foundation degree
EYT	Early Years Teacher
FdA	Foundation degree Arts
GDP	gross domestic product
GEP	Graduate Entry Pathway
GNP	gross national product
GPP	Graduate Practitioner Pathway
HE	higher education
HEFCE	Higher Education Funding Council for England

LGA	Local Government Association
MOPSU	Measuring Outcomes for Public Service Users
NCMA	National Childminding Association (now PACEY)
NCSL	National College of School Leadership
NFER	National Federation for Educational Research
NNEB	National Nursery Examination Board
NPQICL	National Professional Qualification for Integrated Centre Leadership
NQT	newly qualified teacher
NVQ	National Vocational Qualification
PACEY	Professional Association for Childcare and Early Years (formerly NCMA)
PICL	Parents Involved in their Children's Learning
OECD	Organisation for Economic Co-operation and Development
QAA	Quality Assurance Agency
QT	Qualified Teacher
QTS	Qualified Teacher Status
REPEY	Researching Effective Pedagogy in the Early Years
SATs	Statutory Assessment Tests
SEN	special educational needs
SST	sustained shared thinking
TA	Teaching Agency
UEP	Undergraduate Entry Pathway
UPP	Undergraduate Practitioner Pathway

Introduction

Zenna Kingdon and Jan Gourd

This text is intended for students at both undergraduate and postgraduate level, as well as practitioners working in the early years sector. All of the contributors have taught both undergraduate and postgraduate students on early years programmes and have extensive experience on early years foundation degrees and Early Years Professional Status (EYPS) programmes, as well as the National Professional Qualification for Integrated Centre Leadership (NPQICL). We have also had comprehensive experience of working with children and families within a range of different roles that include early years and school settings, children's centres, community settings and as researchers.

We all approached this project with a collective concern about social welfare and the impact that policy agendas can have on children and families, particularly where the policy agendas seem to be working in direct antagonism to those that they were initially intended to support. We began to discuss what we thought policy should be enabling children and families to do. It was during early group discussions that we first discussed the term 'flourishing'. We were all agreed that policy should be about supporting practitioners, children and families to flourish. It was as we read further that we engaged with the work of Martin Seligman, an American psychologist. His recent text *Flourish: A visionary new understanding of happiness and well-being* (2011) describes flourishing as an approach that is underpinned by PERMA:

Personal enjoyment: the pleasant life;

Engagement: a flow state in which thought and feeling are usually absent;

(Positive) **R**elationships: relationships are key to the development of all humans;

Meaning: belonging to and serving something that is bigger than the self;

Accomplishment: the pursuit of success, achievement, and mastery for its own sake.

Seligman (2011) suggests that when a person has these five elements in place they are likely to flourish. Beyond this he suggests that these elements may actually be 'one of our best weapons against mental disorder' (Seligman 2008: 5). Likewise, he argues that should you ask parents what they want for their children and that they will discuss issues related to confidence, happiness, self-esteem and contentment. He suggests that what they want for their children is well-being (Seligman *et al.* 2009). When parents are asked what schools provide they will respond with ideas that include literacy, numeracy and thinking skills – what he refers to as 'the tools of accomplishment' (ibid.: 293). What Seligman *et al.* (2009) suggest is that there appears to be no overlap between the two. In order for children to flourish the elements of PERMA need to be provided. As a writing team we felt that we wanted to consider in detail the ways in which policy agendas and the pedagogy of practitioners enable children to flourish. We felt that Seligman's (2011) description of flourishing was the most appropriate to support our writing in this text. We also felt that within current early years policy and practice we were able to identify elements of PERMA. Some examples include: 'personal enjoyment' equates with child-initiated play within the EYFS (DfE 2012); 'engagement' could be seen to have echoes in sustained shared thinking; 'positive relationships' are one of the Key Elements of Effective Practice within the EYFS, where children are supported by a key worker; 'meaning' can be found in partnership working; and 'accomplishment' can be seen among many of the practitioners who engage in aspects of professionalisation.

The book is divided into two sections. Part I looks at policy from a theoretical perspective. Part II looks at policy in practice. Each chapter has summary sections to support your understanding of the themes and ideas that are to be found within the chapter. We have also included a glossary of terms at the end of the book to support your understanding of some of the issues that you will encounter in the text.

Chapter 1, 'Early years work, professionalism and the translation of policy into practice', discusses policy as text and as practice. It explores the hidden theoretical perspectives of policy makers that prove a challenge for early years workers, in that they are unsure of what it is that they are trying to achieve and why they are doing so. The chapter opens with some discussion of the current globalisation of education agenda and how it can lead to the diminishing of social and democratic benefits, particularly given that it is at local level that professionals, children and parents interact. The chapter offers a framework by which early years practitioners can critically interrogate policy. It recognises that workers will be positioned by policy rather than position themselves if they are not enabled to critically reflect and challenge the processes. There is an exploration of the issues that are created, given that the workforce has no underpinning ethics or values. It demonstrates that early years policy and the meaning, purpose and values of early years work are inextricably linked and therefore raise a range of questions. It concludes that if education is genuinely linked to a better world then those involved must be engaged in critically reflective dialogue in order that we can ensure a flourishing future for all children.

Chapter 2, 'Accountability: tensions and challenges', explores how the changes in the early years sector over the last two decades have led to an increase in provision, in the number of practitioners working within the sector and ultimately to the levels of accountability to which the sector is now held. It explores notions of particular kinds of quality that are linked to a top-down bureaucratic model that does not clearly demonstrate how practitioners can flourish. These tensions and challenges can lead to practitioners who fail to flourish, which can mean that they find it difficult to provide a flourishing environment for the children who are in their care. The flourishing of both the practitioner and the children are entwined; it is challenging to have one without the other. There is an exploration of accountability to the taxpayer over the service user, and also a focus on the notion of choice and voice for the consumer. These inevitably often lead to both the justification of rigorous inspection regimes and league tables that in turn can lead to reduced choice for certain groups. The chapter concludes that we are at a pivotal moment within the development of the early years sector, which if appropriately supported will flourish. Equally it will support the flourishing of children and their families.

Chapter 3, 'The influence of international policy', explores the influence that international policy and practice have had on the development of policy in England and Wales. Approaches including the HighScope, Te Whariki, Reggio Emilia and Nordic pedagogies are explored. There is a clear argument that governmental policy is to look to those whom we perceive as doing better than us and in particular to America. This is despite the fact that in the 2007 UNICEF survey of child well-being we were near the bottom, with America only one place above us, while many of our European neighbours were near the top. HighScope was part of Head Start, based on the Perry Pre-school research in the USA. While we draw on the approach, policy makers fail to recognise that it called for up-skilling and training its workforce. Te Whariki is seen to have links to HighScope but where it differs is that it seeks to interweave cultural experiences into the curriculum. Likewise there is little division between early childhood education and schools; practitioners are similarly qualified to teachers, are respected and have parity of pay. Reggio Emilia has been embraced by many practitioners in the UK. Like Te Whariki it can be seen to draw on HighScope; however, there is no specified curriculum with associated targets. Nordic approaches are discussed, particularly Forest School, with its current impact throughout all phases of education. While what is offered in the UK is not true Forest School, it has led to practitioners considering the outdoor environment. Policy approaches appear to be drawn from America but pedagogical influences can be seen to be far broader.

Chapter 4, 'The Early Years Foundation Stage: Tickell and beyond: a critical perspective', traces the development of the EYFS (DCSF 2008; DfE 2012), discussing the impact that policies and reports have had on it. The chapter contextualises early years provision in the UK, by looking back at its initial roots with the provision of nursery education by Robert Owen in 1816 and the beginnings of recognising childhood as a phase in its own right, rather than as a preparation for later life. The Plowden report (1967) clearly formed the starting point for the clear consideration of early childhood education. While comprehensive recommendations were laid out in the report, they were not acted upon until after the Rumbold report (1990). Into the 1990s there was an exponential interest in early childhood education and care. Policies and curricula were developed and delivered to this sector. The Tickell review (2011) impacted and changed the original EYFS (2008). The Nutbrown review (2012) has considered the qualifications of the workforce. What is clear is that the early years sector remains one that is subject to increased interest and that this is set to continue.

Chapter 5, 'Future policy and the impact of societal change', considers how the early years sector has become central to the policy agendas of all political parties. Part of the agenda has been about up-skilling the workforce in order to encourage women back into the workplace. Seemingly many of the women who are accessing childcare facilities are those who are professionally qualified themselves. They want to see that the staff caring for their children are appropriately qualified. The last two governments have, as part of the policy agenda, positioned early childhood education and care as pivotal in changing outcomes, particularly for children who live in social deprivation. It appears that bureaucracy interferes with the quality of provision. Better-qualified staff tend to be burdened with the paperwork, and this need to document takes time away from the children. Along with higher qualifications come different staff–child ratios, where it is possible to have more children to each member of staff, something that can again negatively impact on quality. The Nutbrown review (2012) recommends the strengthening of the level 3 qualification and the conversion of Early Years Professional Status (EYPS) to Early Years Specialist QTS, which signals further change within the workforce. It appears that the early years sector is set to remain in the sights of the political parties – a new Early Years QTS programme is beginning, we may be looking at the deregulation of ratios and an intervention agenda will continue whichever party is in power. Notions of the performativity of services are likely to continue to underpin policy.

Chapter 6, 'Up-skilling the workforce: managing change in practice', considers the ways in which, during the last decade, the early childhood education and care sector in England and Wales has been concerned with up-skilling. The chapter considers how for many practitioners this has been a positive process and has led to their flourishing, but for some it has been exhausting and too demanding to allow them to grow and flourish. There is exploration of the fact that internationally the minimum qualifications to work in the sector are generally higher than those seen in the UK. Nutbrown (2012) suggests that the British system currently remains chaotic given that there are numerous appropriate level 3 qualifications. The minimum qualification to lead a setting remains a level 3, while there is aspiration for full-daycare settings to be led by a graduate. The pace of change has become increasingly rapid since 1997. However, the system of early childcare and education in the UK appears to remain similar to the split systems of France and the USA in which the qualifications differ depending on the sector. Private provision is seen as the lower qualified, while the higher qualified staff seek the better terms and conditions that are afforded in the state sector. The current provision of support to awards reinforces the divide within the sector but also between teachers. In order to gain EYPS candidates only need an ordinary degree rather than the full Honours degree that is necessary in order to gain QTS. The chapter concludes that while the drive to up-skill the sector has been broad it appears that many practitioners and parents do not know what the new EYPS is, or what it means. While this continues, notions of up-skilling and parity with other sectors remain problematic.

Chapter 7, 'The impact of foundation degrees on practitioners', looks at the impact of a specific foundation degree on a group of practitioners. The chapter is contextualised in policy context terms in the light of the Laming report (2003) into the death of Victoria Climbié, the subsequent

Every Child Matters agenda (DfES 2004) and the EPPE report (Sylva *et al.* 2004) into the impact of pre-school provision on educational outcomes. There is some consideration of the massification of higher education that has taken place in a number of countries during the last decade, which has led to the inclusion of non-traditional students entering higher education. It would seem that the majority of the students on foundation degrees would not historically have been able to enter higher education given that they do not have the usual recognised entry requirements. The chapter then explores the experiences of students who followed the programme. Those interviewed here are all women, reflecting the nature of the workforce which is over 90 per cent female. Issues of gender are explored. Many of the women describe entering the early years workforce as a way of being able to earn an income while their own children were young. They then enrolled on the foundation degree because they were coerced by managers. Despite entering the process without their full agreement they usually reported that they found they had flourished through the process, and had developed self-esteem and they discuss how they had become critically reflective practitioners.

Chapter 8, 'Policy and the change in the early years learning environment', traces the development of a play-based curriculum from its early inception to current practice. The impact of the Industrial Revolution on the need for, and development of, universal education is considered. The work of early pioneers, including Friedrich Froebel, Susan Isaacs and the McMillan sisters, is explored with discussion of how their work can be seen to be reflected in the current EYFS (2012). Play as a concept is analysed and critiqued. While many people discuss play, no one appears to be able to give a clear definition of what it actually is. What is play and fun for one person is not necessarily so for someone else. The notions of play, as enshrined in the UN Convention on the Rights of the Child (1989), are discussed. Playful pedagogies as an approach to providing curricula in the early years are explored and there is discussion of what constitutes a playful pedagogy. The chapter explores how different environments support children's ability to flourish. High-quality early years practice is associated with 'enabling environments', in which children are given opportunities to make decisions about their own learning. The current emphasis on the outdoor environment and its associated concepts of risk and challenge are deliberated upon. The chapter concludes that participation and inclusion impact on the child's ability to flourish.

Chapter 9, 'Research-informed policy – myth or reality?: Sustained shared thinking', explores a specific policy initiative that was forefronted by the EPPE research (2004). Sustained shared thinking (SST), when appropriately and proactively pursued, supports the flourishing of the child. SST as seen in EPPE (2004) is associated with graduate-ness. While the term 'sustained shared thinking' was coined by the EPPE research team, the underpinning of such pedagogical practice can be seen to have developed from a rich repertoire of social constructivist theory. The chapter investigates the work of both Lev Vygotsky and Jerome Bruner. Vygotsky's zone of proximal development is considered as well as his discussions of mental functions and psychological systems that he believed were needed in order that a child could learn. Bruner's notion of folk pedagogies and folk psychologies, in which knowledge is co-constructed in a community of learners, is discussed. The parallels in practice between SST and the pedagogical practices of Reggio Emilia are drawn. Early Years Professionals need to be able to demonstrate SST in practice in order to gain their status. A group of practitioners' views of the approach are drawn on in order to consider how SST may support both the quality of the practice and the flourishing of the children who attend. The chapter concludes that this is clearly a research-informed policy; however, while we continue with level 3 practitioners leading practice, there are concerns about their ability to deliver the policy agenda.

Chapter 10, 'How policy has impacted on parents', considers how partnership working as a theme has emerged over time, starting in the 1980s and 1990s. The chapter considers how policy has worked in practice and how the relationships that have been built between practi-tioners and parents have impacted on children. Models of partnership are discussed and the question of whether parents are truly partners is explored. The chapter reveals the ways in which research evidence demonstrates that children attain more highly where parents are partners. It appears that despite notions of partnership invisible boundaries often persist. Parents are perceived as less qualified and less knowledge-able. Many partnerships, even in positive environments, lack equality, which is problematic. Likewise fear of change can negatively impact on individuals' ability to work in partnership. Partnerships are found to be effective in early years settings where they are based on mutual trust. This leads to all parties enjoying opportunities to flourish. Positive partnerships allow parents to demonstrate what specific communities need. The encouragement of parents to become volunteers and am-bassadors has often supported them in returning to the workplace. The chapter concludes that the current austerity measures will impact on children's services' partnership working. The ways in which this will occur are yet to be seen.

Finally, the book draws a number of themes together in the conclusion. These include issues of performativity, economic concerns, professionalisation, deficit models of childhood, policy agendas, political instability, pedagogy and flourishing and flow. Performativity appears to underpin many of the current policy agendas where there is a perceived need to demonstrate measurable outcomes and economic viability. There are clear economic concerns that during times of austerity provision and interventions need to demonstrate value for money – at least in the short term. Professionalisation has been a policy driver within the sector over the last decade, particularly in order to support women returning to the workforce. Professionalisation also links with deficit models of childhood, where interventions are perceived to alleviate societal ills, and concerns that arise for children who are brought up in social deprivation. Political instability impacts on policy agendas as each successive government seeks to demonstrate its approach to early childhood education and care and to advocate an approach that it believes to be better than that which was offered by the opposition. In these games of political football new approaches are not given time to settle and to provide long-term impact. While much of this appears negative, that is not how we view the current situation. We believe that there are opportunities within the sector that allow chances for practitioners to flourish and enjoy a sense of flow within their work. As practitioners flourish they are enabled to support the children and families with whom they work to also flourish. The focus on early childhood education and care over the last decade has enabled a real discussion about positive and appropriate pedagogy for working with our youngest children. Clearly what is now occurring is that practitioners in the sector are engaging with critical reflective practice (MacNaughton 2005) and developing personal pedagogies that enable children to flourish.

References

Department for Children, Schools and Families (DCSF) (2008) *Statutory Framework for the Early Years Foundation Stage*, London: DCSF.

Department for Education (DfE) (2012) *The Early Years Foundation Stage (EYFS)*, London: DfE.

Department for Education and Skills (DfES) (2004) *Every Child Matters: Change for children*, London: DfES.

Laming, Lord H. (2003) *The Victoria Climbié Inquiry: Report of an inquiry by Lord Laming*, London: Department of Health.

MacNaughton, G. (2005) *Doing Foucault in Early Childhood Studies: Applying poststructural ideas*, Abingdon: Routledge.

Nutbrown, C. (2012) *Foundations for Quality. The independent review of early education and childcare qualifications. Final report*, London: Department for Education.

Plowden, Lady B. (1967) *Children and their Primary Schools: A report of the Central Advisory Council for Education (England)*, London: HMSO.

Rumbold, A. (1990) *Starting with Quality*, London: HMSO.

Seligman, M. (2008) 'Positive health', *Applied Psychology: An International Review*, 57: 3–18.

Seligman, M. (2011) *Flourish: A visionary new understanding of happiness and well-being*, New York: Free Press.

Seligman, M., Ernst, R., Gillham, J., Reivich, K. and Linkins, M. (2009) 'Positive education: positive psychology and classroom interventions', *Oxford Review of Education*, 35(3): 293-311.

Sylva, K., Melhuish, E., Sammons, P., Siraj-Blatchford, I. and Taggart, B. (2004) *The Effective Provision of Pre-school Education (EPPE) Project: Final report*, Nottingham: Department for Education and Skills.

Tickell, Dame C. (2011) *The Early Years: Foundations for life, health and learning*, London: Department for Education. Available online at www.education.gov.uk/tickellreview (accessed 26 January 2013).

PART

I

Theoretical perspectives

1

Early years work, professionalism and the translation of policy into practice

Sue Lea

Introduction

This chapter does not seek to describe or analyse current early years policy but to offer a framework by which policy can be critically interrogated by early years practitioners as part of their ongoing professional formation and development. It is concerned primarily with the ways in which central government policy sets out to influence outcomes for children at the local level, and seeks to explore how well-informed early years practitioners and managers can learn to shape and craft the environments in which early years services are delivered within a framework that sets the rights and interests of children at the centre of practice. In order to do this the chapter seeks to highlight some of the different theoretical and value positions that inform policy, including the education and training of early years professionals and the various systems of alternative accountability that operate at the local level. By this broad critical exploration of the policy process, it is hoped that early years workers will be equipped to understand how to interrogate policy aims and objectives in both current and future guises while recognising that they are key actors in the struggle over policy implementation that is always present at the point of local delivery where practice is actively constructed (Apple 2013; Lipsky 2010; Ball 2008).

Interrogating policy

Policy is not abstract. Early years policy sets out to design particular types of interventions into the lives of children, families and communities based often on the hidden theoretical assumptions and value preferences of policy makers. The basic challenge for all professional workers is therefore to understand *what* policy is trying to achieve and *how* it is trying to achieve it. Meaningful explorations of these questions involve examination of both the explicit and implicit assumptions embedded in policy *and* their ultimate impact on the values and purpose of professional practice in early years education. This impact is felt at the local level where the lives of professionals, children and parents intersect, and so it is here that values are negotiated as policy texts are interpreted and translated into practice. It is also at the local level that the evidence of impact of policy implementation on social justice and the potential flourishing of the child can be seen. This chapter therefore explores how early years professionals can move from being mere street-level bureaucrats to become policy entrepreneurs who can 'think globally and act locally' while translating and interpreting policy into practice in ways that enhance the lives of children and contribute to their flourishing through early education.

- Policy sets out to design particular types of intervention.
- Policy is felt at the local level where professionals, children and parents intersect.

The meaning and purpose of education

If early years policy is seen as key to improving the lived experience of children, it is intimately connected to questions about the meaning and purpose of education that are now being constructed from within a global neoliberal economic perspective. MacNaughton (2005) claims that understanding the local micro-practices of power can help us to understand how pedagogical practices are intimately connected to power. Ultimately then, approaches to early years practices involve a local struggle over the 'true' meaning and purpose of education, where practitioners need global analytical frameworks but also values as a guide for their practice. In current times the struggle for emancipatory education is one that often sacrifices the flourishing of the whole child as global educational policy landscapes now emphasise the economic importance of education, while diminishing its social and democratic benefits. Here policy serves to operate as both 'a system of values and a symbolic system' that is used in order to legitimate political decisions (Ball 2008: 13).

These contested understandings and interests are evidenced in policy in a variety of ways set out here. Early years policy impacts disproportionately on the lives of women, particularly poorer and black women. Gender discrimination is clearly evidenced with reference to early years pay, qualifications and workforce development. Early years policy implies judgements about the different parenting styles of different groups of women, often based on 'race', social class (which includes both income and neighbourhood) and age. In terms of child development, policy also assumes a set of developmental 'norms', which are 'raced', classed and gendered. Competing interpretations about the importance, meaning and purpose of play are obscured as curriculum policy; practice guidelines and inspection regimes prioritise measurable outcomes. All of these implicit assumptions are embedded in policy in ways that have the power to directly or indirectly impact on the lived experience of professionals, parents and children.

- Early years policy is linked to questions of the meaning and purpose of education.
- Early years policy implies judgements about a variety of issues in a variety of ways.

Identifying a role: locating yourself in the policy context

Questioning power and values raises different issues from those that emerge from discursively constructed debates about quality and accountability highlighted above. Fundamental questions about policy intentions and the assumptions about the issues that need to be addressed become more obvious from a values perspective. If policy aims at improvement in the lives of *all* children, early years practitioners need to reflect critically on how they might encourage all children to flourish, in a society that offers them unequal opportunities to do so. This requires that practitioners explore their own roles, values and professional responsibilities in relation to improving the lives of the children, particularly through partnership working, where they are often viewed as the least powerful occupational group with the lowest professional status. By acquiring a different understanding of what policy implies in terms of values and power, and by understanding how professionals mediate the interface between the state and the citizen, the early years professional can start to reflect on his or her work in order to make better-informed interventions. It is over 30 years since Lipsky (2010) originally defined the role of welfare professionals in policy as 'street-level bureaucrats' and identified them as important policy makers in their own right. Early years workers need to recognise their potential role in the policy process and to build their professional confidence on a set of values explicitly directed to achieving positive outcomes for children.

Values and the global policy landscape

As informed and empowered professionals early years practitioners can redefine their role and, rather than act merely as conduits for policy makers, can construct themselves as proactive leaders and decision makers who actually translate and interpret policy texts into practice contexts (Lea 2012). Understanding how globalisation changes values is key here and Beck (1992) recognised some time ago the emerging requirement for individuals to engage with education merely to manage personal risk in a globalising world. This potential (mis)use of education for indoc-trination stretches back much further, and Dewey (1916) claimed that education has no meaning unless we define the type of society we want to create. Dewey was writing about a world in which different education systems operated in different countries, but with the process of global-isation we are now entering a situation where it is 'especially striking how some of the central education policy issues transcend national boundaries' (Spillane, in Sugrue 2008: xi). Within this environment of global policy reach, concern is now being expressed about the expansion of neoliberal, market-driven rationalities that weave education into a new global economic base, through current political philosophy and policy making (Bansel 2007).

Collin and Apple (2007) further claim that the consent to a particular notion of globalisation is actively being constructed through schooling and education. They believe that school features prominently as a site of intervention because this is 'where societies develop the human capital necessary for both the running of the informational economy and, relatedly, the steerage of the unfolding processes of globalisation' (ibid.: 433). For this reason Nguyen (2010) claims that we must question the taken-for-granted assumptions about the benefits of global capitalism that are now embedded in educational policies, as we can only fully under-stand their impact if we learn to identify and question their hidden assumptions. By doing this, educators across the life course have a basis on which to reflect on the rationale of league tables, inspections and the private sector management practices being imposed on educational settings. This raises the questions, are we measuring what we value (Biesta 2009) and are the measures we use neutral (Apple 2005)? If managerialism and performativity colonise practice they also colonise values, and diminish the focus on social inequalities in favour of competition and economic purpose. Fairclough (2001: 3) highlights the impact on practice as 'people becom[ing] unconsciously positioned within a discourse', and where the power of the neoliberal discourse has been in its ability to appear natural and normal with no obvious alternative to competition and markets. All educational professionals need to question why and how the hegemonic domination of market philosophies has been imported into education through managerialism, competitive individualism and consumerism. The fundamental challenge for early years professionals is therefore to interrogate their own positions in order that they can consciously (re)position themselves in value terms within policy discourses. This challenge is an intellectual and a value one in both the personal and professional domains *if* the personal is understood to be political.

- Early years professionals can construct themselves as proactive leaders and decision makers.
- There is a need to question the assumptions of the benefits of globalisation.

A neoliberal paradigm

Apple (2013: 6) explains the dangers well. He argues that current educational interventions are designed from within a neoliberal philosophy with 'a vision that sees every sector of society as subject to the logics of commodification, marketisation, competition and cost-benefit analysis'. In the early years, as elsewhere, this market logic and language 'opens a space for certain identities and closes down others' (ibid.: 7), while policy expects the early years worker to become the midwife of the global child who is market ready and discursively formed by education and care. This policy approach ensures that 'no aspect of the child must be left uneducated: education touches the spirit, soul, motivation, wishes, desires, dispositions and attitudes of the child to be educated' (Fendler 2001, in Dahlberg and Moss 2005: 39). For Dahlberg and Moss (2005), this creation of the child as a self-governing subject is the key to participation in the new world order. Apple (2013) concludes that a key question that needs to be addressed by educators is the extent to which they comply with or challenge assumptions about current educational directions as they ask themselves whether or not their educational interventions change society. This question can only be addressed if practitioners are able to recognise and position themselves, and the children they work with, as empowered social actors rather than passive recipients of a policy process that seeks to create them discursively within neoliberal paradigms.

The above claims are significant for practice as they assume a new discourse where global education policy promotes neoliberal economics and market freedoms at the expense of social justice and welfare. If global education policy assumes a global capitalist society, it will embed particular values, dispositions and discursive practices in the minds of future generations. Through education early years workers could unintentionally be indoctrinating children from an early age into a competitive global future where individualism and competition, rather than collectivism and cooperation, are indicated. Neoliberalism is already moving education from a public good to a private commodity in which self-capitalisation for the labour market is indicated and this process is now well under way with the introduction of fees in higher education. A philosophy that assumes that childhood education is merely a preparation for employment is one where economic policy rather than social policy becomes the epistemological driver of policy making. This marks a significant shift in the type of society we are actively creating through education. It is a global society in which social justice and social welfare are sacrificed to global economic competition. Apple (2013: 16) highlights how test scores already 'operate as proxy' for competition, which 'devalues and is deeply disrespectful of the labour of love, care, and solidarity that underpins so much of educational activities'. By developing policy within a neoliberal, market-driven, values context the ideological assumptions of policy makers set out to impose particular solutions on particular definitions of problems. What is radically different from the past is the scope and pace of change in which education policy is now being implemented on a global scale.

Values and the national policy landscape

It has long been the case that ideology and values have impacted on early years policy and this is evidenced in attitudes to both women and children in educational policy making, which continues to be manipulated in line with patriarchal, neoliberal ideology. If we explore early years policy in relation to the role of women we can track changing attitudes to women through policy making. Here, different preferences in relation to women's roles are evidenced, with mothers being viewed as childcarers, home makers or workers, according to the ideological interpretation of policy makers. This positioning has changed in relation to changing national economic priorities and the numbers of nursery places have fluctuated to accommodate ideology. For example, in the Second World War they were expanded to embrace women's participation in the workforce, only to be reduced in the late 1940s following the end of the war. As late as 1967, Plowden proposed limiting full-time nursery places based on the assumption that young children should be with their mothers for part of each day (Baldock *et al*. 2009). This debate is now moving again with government promoting the notion that mothers have a *duty* to work and increasingly this duty is extending to the idea that they ensure their children benefit from the provisions of the Early Years Foundation Stage (EYFS) (DfE 2012) as parents are drawn into education policy through the nursery. Similar positioning is evidenced around play where the findings of the Cambridge Primary Review team were ignored. Having examined over 1,000 written submissions (some as long as 300 pages), over 3,000 publications and 28 published research reports, and having held 240 consultation meetings with children, parents and teachers, their work was summarily dismissed as 'peddling recycled, partial or out-of-date research' (Alexander 2009a: 4). Effectively this rejected the primacy and value of play in early years in favour of a more disciplinary approach to learning in early childhood education.

■   It is possible to track changing attitudes to women through educational policy.
■   The rejection of the Cambridge review appears to reject the primacy of play in early years.

Hidden assumptions

What both cases above illustrate is that patriarchal ideologies have infantilised both women and children in policy terms. Women and children have been denied their rights in practice, based on the power of decision makers who cloak their value decisions in ways that obscure the assumptions embedded within them. Viewing the early years worker as a policy entrepreneur, whose role is to rearticulate and affirm the rights of both women and children to self-determination, appears to be an appropriate recognition of their role. Using both of the above examples, we can understand how, within policy making, hidden assumptions operate that impact on social and economic institutions, on cultural norms and values and most importantly on the psyche of individuals. In order to appreciate fully the impact of power in the policy process, we can explore and reflect on the questions: whose interests are potentially being served, whose are being harmed and whose are being ignored? By reflecting on these questions we can unearth some of the hidden assumptions embedded in policy making and seek to understand the implications of defining issues in particular ways in order to understand, to open up spaces and to create new discourses through policy. So, inter-rogation of policy during the Second World War and immediately afterwards demonstrates how policy served the dominant interests of men and the labour market. This harmed the interests of women workers who found themselves being pulled into, or pushed out of, the labour market for reasons unrelated to their ability to labour.

Childcare provision effectively ignored the rights and interests of children as policy interventions were designed to manage and maintain gendered assumptions about the working population and children's wishes and rights were viewed as irrelevant. Policy served men's interests, potentially harmed the interests of working women and largely ignored children's interests, in a complex policy accommodation that served the interests of post-war reconstruction and the creation of the welfare state on a male-breadwinner model. Similarly and more recently, the Cambridge Primary Review (Alexander 2009b) was marginalised by dominant neoliberal values and the interests of policy makers were served, the interests and reputations of academic researchers/educators were harmed, and once again the interests of children were ignored. The issue of the rights of the child was not debated because the strength of neoliberal hegemony and its economic logic places children and the early years at the disposal of a State that seeks to promote passive learning where the counting and measuring of the population of children takes priority over their flourishing.

The absence of outright conflict in the above examples might lead some to argue that certain issues are 'organised out' of the policy-making process as social actors do not understand their 'real interests' and their beliefs are manipulated to ensure that conflict is minimised (Cairney 2012: 67). This raises important questions about the extent to which a freedom, choice and wider values context can be seen or implied within the development of the early years policy agenda. It also raises issues about the ways in which knowledge and power operate in the policy process, and of whose interests prevail. It is in this exploration that policy becomes both interesting and challenging, because without a clear and explicit values approach to inform what it is we are setting out to achieve in education, policy making and policy interventions can appear to be neutral activities when in fact they are profoundly political.

■ Childcare policy often ignores the rights and interests of children.
■ Policy intervention is often viewed as neutral but it is highly political.

The early years worker as street-level bureaucrat

As society becomes more complex so does the business of translating and interpreting policy into practice. During the implementation of any policy the paradigmatic and theoretical assumptions of policy makers emerge, and often conflict with the perspectives of the street-level bureaucrat and the users of services to which policy is applied. It is at this stage that the different and contested interpretations that underpin 'problem solving' are negotiated. Understanding the policy process therefore offers early years practitioners the potential to deliver better policy outcomes, where 'better' is understood as responsive to local needs and desires (Shulock, in Nudzor 2009: 504). Policy is written text but it is also practice. Policy is text that aims to change practice through setting new values and priorities where both may be essentially contested and serve particular interests at the expense of others. Acquiring a critical understanding of the policy process is therefore a key intellectual challenge for the early years practitioner, who must be clear about the values on which their practice rests if they are to exercise informed professional judgements. Policy is not neutral here either, but is intimately and deliberately woven into the fabric of professional identity and practice through inspection regimes and managerialist ideology, which aims to 'reconstitute social relations, forms of esteem and value, sense of purpose and notions of excellence and good practice' (Ball 2008: 42). Effectively then, policy can set out to define and redefine the values and practices of particular occupational groups. This is obvious and continuous in the active construction of early years policy and practice (Baldock 2011; Baldock et al. 2009; Rodd 2009; Dahlberg and Moss 2005; MacNaughton 2005), but is best understood as part of much broader set of global policy interventions into lifelong learning that extensively documents educational policy change in formal and informal settings and in compulsory and post-compulsory education (Apple 2013; Ball and Junemann 2012; Biesta 2006; Gewirtz 2002; Aronowitz 2000).

In common with other educational professionals early years workers now 'hold the keys to a dimension of citizenship' (Lipsky 2010: 4). In the early years this is particularly important as the negotiations and accommodations of the policy process tend to undervalue the emotional labour that is present at the point at which education, care and the rights of children intersect. Logically then, this requires that early years practitioners are critically informed and able to explore reflexively their own ethical and value preferences as they examine their often taken-for-granted assumptions about the nature and purpose of education, care and the rights of the child. It is argued here that, without a commitment by practitioners to explore the meaning and purpose of their role within these relations of power, the theory upon which early years practice rests can severely compromise the rights of future generations of children. Any critical interrogation of policy must therefore explore the different ways in which interpretative decisions act to potentially serve, harm or ignore the rights and identities of certain groups of children while privileging others.

■ Understanding policy allows the practitioner to deliver better policy outcomes.

■ Early years practitioners need to be critically aware and informed in order that they can reflexively explore their own values and ethics.

Re-constructing childhood

The context in which early years policy is developed is not divorced from broader educational interventions where neoliberalism is now colonising many aspects of educational engagements (Apple 2013; Bansel 2007). 'Education is a site of struggle and compromise. It serves as a proxy as well for larger battles over what our institutions should do, who they should serve, and who should make these decisions' (Apple 2005: 272). It is not unique that the early years represents an educational engagement that is actively reconstructing childhood within a neoliberal ideological form, but what is unique is the remaking of pedagogical practices by policies intimately connected to the 'micro-practices of power' (Gore, in MacNaughton 2005: 63). The possibilities of operating power over children by 'surveillance, normalisation, exclusion, classification, distribution, individualisation, totalisation and regulation' (ibid.) are increasingly present in early years policy, which sets up a panopticon around the child where interventions are specified by policy and enacted by newly endorsed state-sponsored practitioners whose primary role is to lead policy change. The direction of change is specified by policy that combines specified curriculum interventions set out in the EYFS (2012), which assumes implementation by lead practitioners in the early years, who are expected to comply with the centrally determined practice standards set out in Early Years Professional Status (EYPS). Compliance with both centrally imposed demands is achieved by Ofsted inspection.

It has been argued elsewhere that these centrally imposed policy demands are designed and verified from within a neoliberal economic paradigm that is driving the commodification of education from within a competitive and ideological managerial framework (Apple 2013; Ball 2008; Bansel 2007; Gewirtz 2002). The main tool of competition is the league table, which is used as a blunt instrument to rank organisational compliance with policy objectives following a state-sponsored inspection regime by Ofsted that is devised to assist consumers, not citizens, to choose their 'preferred' educational service. This approach potentially transforms the ethical and emotional aspects of the education and care of children into the technical and managerial raising of a future workforce. As such it represents a struggle for the soul of the professional early years educator.

It is over 30 years ago that Lipsky defined the practice context of local workers in the policy process as that of the 'street-level bureaucrat', where they were both practitioner and also local decision maker as they struggled to achieve the implementation of policy (Lipsky 2010). This generated an appreciation by many professionals working within local welfare and education services that they were policy entrepreneurs with a responsibility to empower citizens through local democratic involvement with the design of services. This remains the work of community practitioners, including social workers, who continue to challenge policy implementation at the local level with reference to a clear set of values and the production of local emancipatory ways of knowing set within a values framework of social justice (Shaw 2006; Ledwith 2005; Twelvetrees 2002). The professional formation of social pedagogues, including community workers, youth workers, social workers and schoolteachers, presents similar challenges to that of early years workers where they can view their role as value-neutral or value-engaged. These occupational groups are positioned both 'in and against the state' and have dual accountabilities, both top-down and bottom-up.

Operating as a policy entrepreneur

It is at the point at which policy implementation is sought that the early years occupies both a 'caring' and an educative space that is located within the relationship between the early years professional, the child and the primary caregiver of the child. It is also at the local level that professionals have traditionally sought to respond in creative ways to the demands, constraints and conflicts that policy imposes on working relationships (Lipsky 2010). This is the point at which professional judgements regarding interventions are made and where the potential to (re)form the child through early interventions is often ignored. The early years worker operating as a policy entrepreneur will question the social, political and economic contexts that create the problems that policy sets out to address and make informed decisions based on the local context about what is best for a particular child. It is argued, therefore, that a central aspect of professional formation for all early years professionals is that they recognise their power to not only deliver 'goods' but also to confer or withhold status through their relationships with children (ibid.). Understanding roles in this way not only validates the agentic and decision-making power of the professional working at the local level but also calls on professionals to recognise their potential power to reproduce or challenge dominance (Apple 2013) and to make and remake identities (Dahlberg and Moss 2005).

Policy from this perspective can be understood as a device that weaves together values, theories, policy and practice according to the views of powerful decision makers. The policy entrepreneur will also understand the process as one that seeks to impose particular values on educational relationships and will seek to ensure their role is not that of the garment finisher in the production of the cloak of power. Those persons in the policy process, who are often removed from the visceral effects of poverty on the lives of children, often mis-describe and misunderstand the realities of implementing education, care and the rights of the child in the early years. Early years workers who passively accept policy as neutral or beneficial will often find policy to be imperfect as it carries within it contradictions from wider society that the policy entrepreneur will actively negotiate during implementation. Informed, critically reflective early years professionals who increasingly commit to developing a clear values base to their work will find that a values base for practice can assist in clarifying and understanding how 'educational settings are also part of the cultural apparatus of society', where certain identities are promoted at the expense of others (Apple 2013: 21) and where educators are doomed to be partisan, as 'not choosing is itself a choice' (Counts, in Apple 2013: 53).

> ■ Early years inhabits both a caring and educative space, where the child, the main carer and the practitioner meet.
> ■ Early years workers who simply passively accept policy as neutral or even beneficial in all situations will often find policy to be imperfect.

The early years worker as policy entrepreneur

To understand that decision making by professionals at the local level is necessary *in order to* deliver policy is important, but where this is required those decisions and the operation of power by professionals must also be based on some notion of legitimacy or clear criteria. Policy makers do face elections and so have a democratic mandate to carry out policy making and so, as street-level bureaucrats, workers in the early years need to develop a clear basis for operating professional discretion. A set of professional values or ethics normally underpins professionalism, but no such values guide, or ethical statements, exist in the early years in England. Early years workers in England need not look far, however, to seek a guide to practice that demonstrates a values approach to early years work that has implications for work with children, parents and the wider community and the society in which they practise. Once workers have a firm values foundation on which to rest their responsibilities for education, care and the rights of children, they will be in a position to make informed judgements about preferred solutions and resolutions to policy dilemmas.

In Scotland (www.ltscotland.org.uk) four key principles have been developed for generating positive outcomes and providing the best start for children. They begin with the rights of the child, and move through developing relationships, responsive care and respect for children. Each of these areas takes a broad values perspective as a guide to what can be expected when children enter early education. While it could be argued that there are broad similarities between the four key principles of EYFS (2012) in England and Scotland, the explicit emphasis on respect for children and the rights of the child distinguish the two sets of principles linguistically and conceptually. Together the notion of respect and rights forms a strong values context as a basis for early education particularly as a broad spectrum of rights is defined. These encompass political, social, economic, cultural and civil rights, which are honoured in respectful relationships that respond to care needs where children's rights to their community and cultural beliefs are acknowledged. As principled commitments, the explicit articulation of values is essential in creating an ethical context that acknowledges that education and care play important roles in defining the life of the child in a way that enables the formation of a positive personal identity.

A values framework

While global forces transform identities, economies and the politics of knowledge (Moreton 2009, in Apple 2013), it is at the local level that this transformatory project achieves intimacy through educational relationships and relationships of care within a rights-based value context. The absence of an explicit values dimension in the training and education of early years professionals is of great significance as it is precisely in the early years that the foundation of children's moral and cognitive development is grounded, so both policy makers and professionals bear a crucial responsibility for the values they espouse and encourage (Powell 2010). Powell argues that, despite repeated reference to particular values in policy documentation, there is a vague, limited, contradictory demonstration of what this might mean in terms of the values, belief systems and dispositions of the early years worker, and goes on to claim that there is also little direct reference to aspirations about the kinds of people it is hoped that young people will become. Indeed, as noted by Dahlberg and Moss (2005: 11), 'ethics hardly figures in current discourses about the preschool . . . and it occupies a very marginal place in national policies'. Powell (2010) further questions the adequacy of the notion that an absence of criminal conviction is a sufficient demonstration of suitability to work with children and claims there is no direct reference to what constitutes suitability beyond this mechanism.

The translation of values into practice could and should be clearly visible within both the professional requirements of EYPS and the Practice Guidance of the EYFS (2012). Other occupational groups set out the conduct expected by fieldworkers, and there is a long tradition in community development learning that explicitly links social justice and anti-oppressive practice to empowering ways of working (www.fcdl.org.uk). In fact the Practice Guidance in the early years hints at values but does so in a way that marginalises the dispositions of practitioners while emphasising the diversity and individuality of work with children. The mix of 'explicit statements and implicit messages' (Powell

2010: 223) contains a range of messages to early years workers that cannot easily be reconciled in practice. It is for this reason that questions about the future of the early years policy are inseparable from questions about the meaning, purpose and values of early years work. Effectively, workers in the early years will have to interpret policy at the point at which they translate policy documents into living practice. This choice *will* inevitably involve value judgements as 'different conceptions of education are inextricably linked to different conceptions of the good society' (Carr and Hartnett 1996: 29) and so early years workers are forced to make choices about the lives of children. The choices made may be consciously or subconsciously promoting a particular view of the type of future society they believe in, and the type of education and curriculum they wish to promote, and this will be practised in a context where the lives, voices and aspirations of children are often ignored or taken for granted. The broader social, political and economic structures and widespread social and economic inequality may be seen as core or marginal to their practice despite early years being the first place where various interests intersect as evidenced by the complex policies that are now directed towards the private sphere of the family (Vandenbroeck *et al.* 2010).

As the implementers of policy, early years workers are an important part of a process that connects policy intentions to practice interventions. For this reason practitioners need to take a position, rather than be positioned by policy. This profound concern for the future of the early years is most clearly expressed by Dahlberg and Moss (2005: 12) when they ask 'What ethics? What politics? What sort of practices?' Informed and critically reflective practitioners need to reach an informed decision about whether they are satisfied to be merely a conduit through which policy makers exercise their intentions, or whether they understand their role to be that of a translator and interpreter of policy, with a responsibility for shaping and crafting practice in the pre-school environment. Dahlberg and Moss (2005) highlight how ethical rather than legal considerations feature minimally in national policies and this is consistent with the notion that social and economic problems are natural and normal and that policy is required to re-form the subject, in this case the child, through policy intervention.

- There is currently no values base for early years workers that other professions have.
- Questions about the future of the early years policy are inseparable from questions about the meaning, purpose and values of early years work.

Demands, constraints and choices in early education and care

The educational philosophy that currently underpins policy making is significant as it implies a particular definition of childhood, it carries particular definitions of the rights of children, and it assumes the particular form of professional practice set out within the requirements of EYPS. There is now an increasing recognition that the education of educators must prepare them to meet the challenges of unmasking the power that is always present in educational encounters in a globalising world. De Lissovoy (2010) claims that educators have a special task in relation to democratic globalism. He says this can only be achieved 'in the context of a recognition of the relations of power that have shaped history, and in particular the political, cultural, economic and epistemological processes of domination' (ibid.: 279). He proposes nothing less than a curriculum for a new way of living that challenges previous dominative power and is committed to building an ethical globality in which educators actively create community by confronting the previous oppressions.

This approach may seem far removed from the baby room, but the interplay between the global and the local will be of increasing importance in understanding future policy developments. It has been argued by both Walkerdine (1992, in MacNaughton 2005) and MacNaughton (2005) that early childhood pedagogies constitute a regime of truth that currently reproduces and supports inequalities. De Lissovoy (2010) highlights the fact that practitioners in education can no longer ignore the practical and political challenges of globalisation and explores how the logic of capitalism is now colonising education. Dahlberg and Moss (2005) demonstrate how discourses in the early years are now being created that obscure the broader political philosophy and neoliberal values deeply embedded in both policy and practice interventions. This is where power is operated from within new discursive formations that displace and sacrifice the ethical, in favour of the managerial. With the underlying, hidden epistemologies that are driving policy and practice interventions comes the potential to redefine the meaning and purpose of early years education and care. These redefinitions obscure the political, social and economic assumptions, intents and meanings that are placing demands and constraints on practice and limiting professional discretion. 'Discourses are the exercise of power. They are practices . . . that govern how we think and act' (ibid.: 141).

New discursive regimes

These new discursive regimes organise the ways in which practitioners view the world and so policy implementation is always a battle because educators are discursively constructed through policy. Practice and values are shaped by policy and by the truth claims made by policy, which now defines specific forms of intervention into the lives of children. In the name of education and care, the child is counted, measured and observed and then disciplined to govern the self to historically and culturally specific definitions of what counts as 'normal'. Even as the child is taught to self-govern, so is the practitioner who learns to self-monitor practice against organisational and occupational standards. The early years professional, in common with other educators, is expected to perform within the discursive frameworks of quality and accountability. This practice takes place within the discipline of the managerial panopticon of inspection, regulation and league tables. Policy, 'works in very practical and material ways through the installation of policy devices or technologies, such as choice performance management and competition' (Ball 2008: 13). The move from government to governance (or self-government) is key to understanding the various ways in which power is changing and new relationships are emerging in the forms of networks that often centralise resources and power while devolving responsibility and accountability.

This is evidenced in the creation of academies and free schools as the boundaries between private and public business are being blurred and the ideology of managerialism as 'new' public management is being extended. This change is a profound shift in the values base of education and boundaries are further blurred by a 'new' philanthropy, sometimes called 'philanthrocapitalism' (Ball and Junemann 2012). In many cases new mixed forms of organisation are being developed where social, political and business relationships are intertwined and where it is difficult to research relationships that operate while hidden from public view (ibid.). Given the mixing of the various different types of organisations in formal schooling, which is moving to replicate the mixed economy of the early years, it appears likely that the involvement of philanthrocapitalism is likely to continue to extend its reach into the early years through network governance. One of the ways in which central control can achieve this extension of power is through the development of common leadership programmes. This is already happening through pre-service training of teachers and is currently being extended through EYPS. The National College of School Leadership (NCSL) plays a central role in post-service training and was extended to include Children's Services at the end of the last government and, although some reversal was imposed following the 2010 election, the NCSL is still heavily involved in the training of leaders and managers across educational domains. Combined with involvement of the State in the specification of curriculum across formal and informal educational domains from birth to 19, control of access and student numbers in higher education, the specification of training of a range of graduate professions who work with children and young people, and preferred leadership programmes for educational professionals, there is now indicated a set of policy demands and constraints that operate within policy networks to limit the choices available to leaders of learning (Lea 2012).

- Practitioners are constructed through policy that defines particular types of interventions in children's lives.
- There has been a shift in the values base in education; national standards lead to policy demands and constraints that limit choice.

Conclusion

If education is linked to a vision of a better world, a shared understanding of its meaning and purpose can only be achieved by genuine dialogue, openness to the ideas of others, and critical reflection aimed at developing a genuine understanding of the role of values in the policy process. In this way real choice and real freedom about how to promote global human flourishing through early interventions may be possible. If our interest in the early years is centred on an ethic of care that aims to enhance respect, resilience and freedom of thought through education, we will need to invest in an early years education policy that values the local professional as policy entrepreneur in an inclusive and democratic policy process. Here the early years professional will seek to value every child equally by attempting to redress systemic social and economic injustice in order to move towards a flourishing global future for all children.

REFLECTIVE QUESTIONS

■   How can you be supported to become a critically reflective practitioner?
■   Why is it important that early years workers are enabled to interrogate policy?
■   What are the implications of policy being understood as political rather than being neutral?

References

Alexander, R. (2009a) *Plowden, Truth and Myth: A warning*. Available online at www.primaryreview.org.uk (accessed 20 November 2012).

Alexander, R. (ed.) (2009b) *Children, their World, their Education: Final report and recommendations of the Cambridge Primary Review*, London: Routledge.

Apple, M.W. (2005) 'Doing things the 'right' way: legitimating educational inequalities in conservative times', *Educational Review*, 57(3): 271–93.

Apple, M.W. (2013) *Can Education Change Society?*, Abingdon: Routledge.

Aronowitz, S. (2000) *The Knowledge Factory: Dismantling the corporate university and creating true higher learning*, Boston, MA: Beacon Press.

Baldock, P. (2011) *Developing Early Childhood Services: Past, present and future*, Maidenhead: Open University Press.

Baldock, P., Fitzgerald, D. and Kay, J. (2009) *Understanding Early Years Policy* (2nd edn), London: Sage.

Ball, S.J. (2008) *The Education Debate*, Bristol: The Policy Press.

Ball, S.J. and Junemann, C. (2012) *Networks, New Governance and Education*, Bristol: The Policy Press.

Bansel, P. (2007) 'Subject of choice and lifelong learning', *International Journal of Qualitative Studies in Education*, 20(3): 283–300.

Beck, U. (1992) *Risk Society: Towards a new modernity*, London: Sage.

Biesta, G. (2006) 'What's the point of lifelong learning if lifelong learning has no point? On the democratic deficit of policies for lifelong learning', *European Educational Research Journal*, 3: 3.

Biesta, G. (2009) *Good Education: What it is and why we need it*. Available online at www.ioe.stir.ac.uk (accessed 13 January 2013).

Cairney, T. (2012) *Understanding Public Policy: Theories and issues*, Basingstoke: Palgrave Macmillan.

Carr, W. and Hartnett, A. (1996) *Education and the Struggle for Democracy*, Milton Keynes: Open University Press.

Collin, R. and Apple, M.W. (2007) 'Schooling, literacies and biopolitics in the global age', *Discourse: Studies in the Cultural Politics of Education*, 28(4): 433–54.

Dahlberg, G. and Moss, P. (2005) *Ethics and Politics in Early Childhood Education*, Abingdon: RoutledgeFalmer.

De Lissovoy, N. (2010) 'Decolonial pedagogy and the ethics of the global', *Discourse: Studies in the Cultural Politics of Education*, 31(3): 279–93.

Department for Education (DfE) (2012) *The Early Years Foundation Stage (EYFS)*, London: DfE.

Dewey, J. (1916) *Democracy and Education: An introduction to the philosophy of education*, New York: The Free Press.

Fairclough, N. (2001) *The Dialectics of Discourse*. Available online at www.ling. lancs.ac.uk /profiles/263 (accessed 13 January 2013).

Gewirtz, S. (2002) *The Managerial School: Post-welfarism and social justice in education*, London: Routledge.

Lea, S. (2012) 'Are youth work leaders free to lead? An exploration of policy constraints', in Ord, J. (ed.) *Critical Issues in Youth Work Management*, Abingdon: Routledge, pp. 60–71.

Ledwith, M. (2005) *Community Development: A critical approach*, Bristol: The Policy Press.

Lipsky, M. (2010) *Street-level Bureaucracy: Dilemmas of the individual in public service*, New York: Russell Sage Foundation.

MacNaughton, G. (2005) *Doing Foucault in Early Childhood Studies: Applying poststructural ideas*, Abingdon: Routledge.

Nguyen, T.X.T. (2010) 'Deconstructing education for all: discourse, power and the politics of inclusion', *International Journal of Inclusive Education*, 14(4): 341–55.

Nudzor, H.P. (2009) 'Re-conceptualising the paradox in policy implementation: a post-modernist conceptual approach', *Discourse: Studies in the Cultural Politics of Education*, 30(4): 501–13.

Plowden, Lady B. (1967) *Children and their Primary Schools: A report of the Central Advisory Council for Education (England)*, London: HMSO.

Powell, S. (2010) 'Hide and seek: values in early childhood education and care', *British Journal of Educational Studies*, 58(2): 213–29.

Rodd, J. (2009) *Leadership in Early Childhood* (3rd edn), Maidenhead: Open University Press.

Shaw, M. (2006) *Community Development – Everywhere and Nowhere? Rediscovering the purpose and practice of community development*. Available online at www.ed.ac. uk/schools-departments/education/ (accessed 14 January 2013).

Sugrue, C. (ed.) (2008) *The Future of Educational Change: International perspectives*, Abingdon: Routledge.

Twelvetrees, A. (2002) *Community Work* (3rd edn), Basingstoke: Palgrave.

Vandenbroeck, M., Cousee, F. and Bradt, L. (2010) 'The social and political construction of early childhood education', *British Journal of Educational Studies*, 58(2): 139–53.

Accountability
Tensions and challenges

Lisa Spencer-Woodley

Introduction: a contradictory space

This chapter aims to explore the tensions, debates and challenges that the culture of accountability imposes on early years practitioners. As an educator in higher education who teaches early years practitioners, both highly experienced and new to the sector, and at undergraduate and postgraduate levels, my aim is to maintain a high level of critical engagement, to support students to position themselves through knowledge, understanding and praxis, and to always be working towards widening participation, social justice and anti-oppressive practice. This creates a tension as I, and the students I work with, are working and learning within a top-down imposed set of ideas of what quality looks like and feels like, and a top-down imposed set of professional standards that they must demonstrate. This leads to my experience, and the experience of the students I teach, being a *living contradiction* (Whitehead 1989) of 'holding educational values and the experience of their negation' (ibid.). Ball (2003) uses Lyotard's (1984) concept of the *law of contradiction* and Blackmore and Sachs' (1997) concept of *institutional schizophrenia* to explore where practice energy is, and values are, focused. The effort and energy of accounting and accountability can overtake and take over practitioners' reserves and levels of energy and significantly affect practitioners' ability to maintain their personal values, and experience and knowledge-based practice. On top of this, 'not infrequently the requirements of such systems bring into being unhelpful or indeed damaging practices, which nonetheless satisfy performance requirements' (Ball 2008b: 50). The question then arises of whether these top-down imposed processes of accountability and professionalisation actually damage the very thing that, rhetorically at least, they aim to achieve, that is: high-quality early years provision and practice.

As a critical theorist who draws on post-structural theory, as a professional who holds my values central to my practice, and as an anti-oppressive practitioner, I am highly critical of policy, discourse and ideology that, I believe, impedes children's ability to flourish. I do however hope, through my critical investigations in this chapter, to offer some possible ways forward through the tensions and dilemmas inherent in such a period of change. I hope these possibilities enable practitioners to position themselves (Edwards 1997) in the debates, rather than be positioned by a policy infrastructure (Ball 2008a) that is highly destabil-ising, even more so in the context of a global economic situation that increases fear of financial insecurity and decreases self-confidence in people's own professional stance. As Vincent (2011) suggests, as 'ideology literally becomes the common sense of a society . . . [and] masquerades as the only acceptable reality . . . we need to relearn how to rigorously criticise those who manage or govern us – in all walks of life'.

- Accounting and accountability can negatively affect practitioners' ability to maintain their values.
- Critiquing policy should enable practitioners to position themselves rather than be positioned.

The policy context

For anyone with any connection to the early years sector in the UK it is impossible to have missed the period of great change over the last 15 or so years, change that has included funded places for specific groups of children, clearly defined minimum baselines for expectations around qualifications, a plethora of policy initiatives of varying scales – some specific to early years and others more general in relation to children and their families and the development of the children's workforce, and the introduction of a graduate professional status for early years practitioners (Early Years Professional Status, EYPS) (for a useful overview of policy developments in the sector relating to professionalisation of the work-force, see Owen and Haynes (2008)). This agenda has been imposed within the more general governmental policy context of increasing managerialism, and the rhetoric of globalisation and the need to 'com-pete' in a global economy, all within the clear neoliberal ideological foundation of successive governments since the 1970s.

This period of change has led to an increase in the number of early years places, including free places for specific groups of children, and an increase in the number of early years settings. For example, all three- and four-year-olds in England are entitled to 15 hours a week of free early education and it is planned to increase the number of two-year-old children eligible for up to 15 hours of free early education to '20 per cent of the least advantaged two-year-olds' (DfE 2012a) from September 2013. According to government statistics released in 2012, the number of three- and four-year-old children who access some form of free early education in England is 96 per cent, which has remained relatively stable within one percentage point over the last five years (DfE 2012b). As Dahlberg and Moss (2005: vi) highlight, this growth is not without risk:

> increasing institutionalisation of childhood may lead to greater and more effective governing of children. This may happen in particular when early childhood institutions are understood as enclosures for the effective application of technologies to produce predetermined and standardised outcomes – a very common way of thinking today.

- A plethora of policy initiatives has led to enormous change in the early years sector.
- There has been rapid expansion of early years provision.
- The pace of change is not without risk and challenge.

Accountability and education

In turn this has led to increasing levels of required accountability and 'more uniformity and normalisation of thought and practice' (Dahlberg and Moss 2005: vi.). This is embedded within a dominant discourse of a particular kind of 'quality' and has followed on from similar changes to how practice is governed in the wider education sector. I do not locate early years provision solely within the field of education; however, as early years increasingly moves towards an education and preparation for school model (DfE 2011) many of the changes are similar. I will therefore draw on these changes and subsequent analysis, alongside my own 'subject position' as an education professional (Ball 2008a: 50). I work within higher education in the UK, where 'private sector management techniques, and their accompanying free market ideological beliefs, in their present perverse hybrid form, are now in the process of driving a coach and horses through academic freedom' (Vincent 2011: 334).

Recognition for the early years sector

Practitioners, researchers and writers in the early years sector have argued for the sector and early years practitioners to get equal recognition of the importance of early years practice for children, and their families and carers, as schools do. However, in calling for this recognition there is a risk of mirroring the 'de-professionalisation' (Beck 2008; Schön 1983) experienced by teachers over the past 40 years.

Moss (2008: 122) asks:

> why does British society seem to take for granted that work with young children (but also, at the other end of life, elderly people) should largely depend on poorly qualified workers earning, on average, not much above the minimum wage?

He suggests four reasons:

1   That children are seen as 'incomplete human beings', and as such 'simple formulas' can be applied to their development.

2   That 'care' work is perceived as largely the, biologically essentialist, natural role of women, and therefore is not in need of payment or practice development.

3   The increase in private provision as a result of neoliberal, free-market ideologies has led to a competitive wage minimisation.

4   Early childhood is viewed by the State in a 'positivistic paradigm', which simply 'calls for technicians trained in the right answers'.

> (ibid.)

In arguing for more recognition of the importance of early years practice, it is therefore imperative that it is clear what is meant by 'recognition', and if this does include a focus on professionalisation, that the ideological and epistemological perspectives are also clear and transparent.

Questioning 'accountability'?

The perspective I put forward here is not one that questions whether the, at least more historical, concept of accountability is good or bad; after all, as Strathern (2000: 3) points out, '[a]s an instrument of accountability . . . audit is almost impossible to criticise in principle – after all, it advances values that academics generally hold dear, such as responsibility, openness about outcomes and widening of access'.

Indeed, one of my deeply held values is that I am accountable to the very people with whom I work; not because they are the tax-paying public, but rather because they are deserving of a service that is of benefit to them.

This is also not an account that suggests who early years workers should be accountable to, although my position I think will be explicit; rather, this is a recognition and analysis of the ideological positions and their associated discourses, and an exploration of ways in which early years practitioners might be able to survive within their *living contradictions*; to meet externally imposed requirements, alongside accountability to their own values and to those for whom they provide an important service.

It is the current State-imposed construction of accountability that I critique. The discourse of successive neoliberal governments, that those who through their professional practice 'spend' taxpayers money must be accountable for 'their' spending, has its deep roots in a particular ideological position. A new social construction, or culture of accountability as a meeting of 'financial and moral' (ibid.: 2) requirements, has meant that accountability to the State and taxpayer takes primacy over accountability to the people who use the services provided. For example, the Measuring Outcomes for Public Service Users (MOPSU) three-year government project, while in its title giving primacy to service users, had as its core aim to 'inform value for money decisions by developing new, and examining existing, measures of outcomes' (ONS 2010). This project included a research focus on early years, the final report of which states that, 'Underpinning the project is the idea that value for money should determine who delivers public services' (Hopkin *et al.* 2010).

- ■ Deferring to one's own value base is important in being held accountable.
- ■ State-imposed accountability justifies the use of taxpayers' money.

Value for money

As Biesta states:

> 'Value for money' has become a guiding principle in the transactions between the state and its taxpayers. This way of thinking is at the basis of the emergence of a culture of accountability that has resulted in tight systems of inspection and control and ever more prescriptive educational protocols.
>
> (2006: 19)

Professional practice becomes open to scrutiny by the State on behalf of those who pay tax to the State and therefore the very parameters by which society judges professional practice becomes constructed by the State:

> These policies [performativity, privatisation and a move from government to governance] do not just change the way teachers work and how they are employed and paid, they also change who they are, how we judge them and how we define a good teacher.
>
> (Ball 2008a: 50)

Ideology becomes absorbed into the everyday language of current service providers (Vincent 2011) and thus 'professional accountability' becomes common sense (Beck 2008) and hegemonic (Vincent 2011). Biesta (2009) argues that the common-sense view of what education is actually for, as academic achievement in language, science and mathematics, is relied on as an explanation because of an 'absence of explicit attention'. While there is, relative to before the last 15 or so years, a plethora of attention in early years, this attention has been focused, unsurprisingly given the neoliberal ideology, on developing evidence-based practice within a modernist, positivistic, scientific paradigm, and holds a methodological fundamentalist position that gives absolute primacy to randomised experiments (House 2005), and is itself in danger of becoming hegemonic (Smith 2008). The notion of value for money through accountability to the State and the notion that the benchmarks that 'value' is measured against are evidence based through modernist methods, both become a 'common sense'. It is so 'common sense' that it is 'forgotten' that ideology, which is contestable and questionable, underlies it. As Vincent (2011: 336) argues, 'this can, in some contexts, be a profoundly menacing form of ideology since it masquerades as the only acceptable reality and pervades deeply into human lives, being largely unquestioned'.

Common-sense ideas and practices that have developed from ideological positions are clearly embedded within power structures that serve the interests of particular groups of people (Biesta 2009). As much as the proponents of modernist, positivist, scientific research would argue for the objectiveness of the randomised experimental approach, post-structural, post-modern and some critical theorists, researchers, writers and practitioners have argued for multiple truths and interpretive approaches to research. The Foucaultian notion of a 'regime of truth' is useful here. A regime of truth is where truths that 'naturalise existing regimes of power' (MacNaughton 2005: 20), where the powerful maintain what truth is (Atkinson 2003) and where discourse 'frame[s] how we think, feel, understand and practice' (MacNaughton 2005: 20). The discourse of saving taxpayers' money, based on practices that prepare children to become 'economically viable units' that put in to, as opposed to take out from, the State informs a highly powerful regime of truth. This is based on the 'truth' that, within the current global economic climate, this is the only option.

Stakeholders – voice and choice?

The past four decades of neoliberal reform of the education sector in the UK have seen a greater focus on the choice and voice of the 'consumers' of education. Likewise, as I have previously suggested, the democratic 'voice' of the recipients of education providers can be very valuable in challenging inequality. However, alongside other education and welfare provision, the notion of voice in relation to education services for children has been translated into a notion of 'choice' for parents in relation to where their children go to gain their education. This 'choice' mechanism is enabled through the development of league tables and the publishing of 'inspection' results, and is often used as a prevailing reason for rigorous inspection and measurement regimes.

The Conservatives introduced the notion of parental 'choice' during the 1980s (Ball 2008b), and this has been developed by New Labour with a focus on the active role of the stakeholder (Whitty 2008). Increasing the 'voice' of parents and children is clearly positive if its aims are to genuinely empower and challenge issues of social injustice, however it is more 'a reflection of neo-liberal concern to restrict the voice of the teacher' (ibid.: 29). The voice becomes an individual 'consumer choice' mechanism with a very limited reality of choice given the reliance of many choices on economic capacity to travel or buy and move house, for example.

'Most professionals are now employed, or at least regulated, by governments' (ibid.: 32), and as practitioners and settings in the early years sector become increasingly regulated government becomes one of the major stakeholders. The rhetoric of 'accountability' to taxpayers and to parents and children is joined by notion of having to ensure the UK can compete economically in a global arena:

> the setting of national targets is also indicative of the recon-ceptualisation of the education system as a single entity and as a fundamental component of national economic competitiveness . . . The way in which reform objectives, particularly the 'raising of standards', were tied to the economic necessities of international competition.
>
> (Ball 2008b: 113 and 114)

This in turn is processed through the production of economically viable units. Individuals have to become and continue to act in an economically viable way to ensure minimum reliance on the State, maximum performance in a global free market, and maximisation of economic global competitiveness.

> [T]his discourse offers a regime of truth about early childhood education and care as a technology for ensuring social regulation and economic success, in which the young child is constructed as a redemptive agent who can be programmed to become the future solution to our current problems.
>
> (Dahlberg and Moss 2005: vii)

According to Ball (2008b: 132–3), there is also a considerable body of evidence that 'choice systems in themselves promote inequality . . . the possibility of choice available to parents and to schools [is] taken advantage of differently by different social groups'. This is also reproduced in early years settings. Variable fees, variable availability of free places and the targeting of particular stratified groups of parents, such as single parents, black and minority ethnic parents, parents living in poverty and parents living in 'disadvantaged areas', by specified 'children's centres' and the mixed economy of private, local authority and third sector early years settings mean that, for those people most disadvantaged, choice is highly restricted, if it exists at all.

The notion of choice is also highly challenging in relation to the 'content and purpose' (Biesta 2009: 23) of early childhood education and care. Content and purpose are cornerstones of professionalism and professional practice; however, the focus on 'learning' and 'developmental goals' means that early years practice emulates what has happened in education. The notion of 'meeting the predefined needs of the learner' (ibid.), where it is assumed that the children and parents know what it is they need to learn or develop, is inherent in consumer choice models and 'suggests a framework in which the only questions that can meaningfully be asked are *technical* questions, that is questions about the efficiency and effectiveness of the educational *process*' (ibid.; emphasis in original). So, this ideological cycle, which defines both what needs to happen to children – they need to become economically viable, and that the only mechanism of measuring this and of working out what this should be measured against is informed by the exact same ideological position that the status quo maintains, in turn maintains the powerful in their elevated positions of power (Biesta 2009). The consequence of this is the appearance of good practice in that a 'choice' has been offered, and therefore responsibility is with the 'chooser' if there is failure. This is, in its own way, far more pervasive and powerful than the individualistic neoliberal arguments that 'taking out from' the State is a personal choice and individual failing as opposed to a structural or systemic one. It is more pervasive and powerful because believing that there is a 'choice' in where you send your child to be 'educated' in the 'correct' ways is far more likely to go unquestioned than accusations of 'choosing' to receive some form of welfare.

So not only is the concept of choice, at least in this context, based on highly contestable truths, the content of the choice system is also highly contestable. The 'choice' system relies on information about what the experience of the child in that setting might be. This information is presented through the publishing of inspection results and then comparisons of different settings being able to be made. The inspection regimes use measurements that give primacy to 'developmental truths' (MacNaughton 2005: 24), which are based on white, western, minority world ideas of universal developmental stages, and propagate truths about quality. Dahlberg *et al.* (2007: 105) caution against using the term 'quality' as a benchmark at all. They state:

> The 'problem with quality' cannot be addressed by struggling to reconstruct the concept in ways it was never intended to go. If we try to make accommodation with, for example, subjectivity or multiple perspectives, then an increasingly desperate search for quality will prove to be an increasingly desperate wild goose chase. For the concept of quality in relation to early childhood intuitions is irretrievably modernist.

- The notion of children's voice is often mistranslated as parental choice with regard to the type of education that their child receives.
- The concept of choice is often political rhetoric rather than reality.
- Choice can promote rather eradicate inequality.

The processes of accountability

If we are serious about being committed to children flourishing, the people who work with those children also need to flourish. The problem is that flourishing requires autonomy (White 2006), positive emotion, engagement, relationships, meaning and accomplishment (Seligman 2011), all of which are either undermined by, determined by or indeed actively derided by the current culture of accountability, and so accountability is directly in opposition to flourishing:

> We are required to spend increasing amounts of our time in making ourselves accountable, reporting on what we do rather than doing it. And there is a particular set of skills to be acquired here – skills of presentation and of inflation, making the most of ourselves, making a spectacle of ourselves. We become transparent but empty.
>
> (Ball 2008a: 56)

The early years sector and practitioners are held accountable and 'are sanctioned and systematised by government, by professional associations and by the academy' (MacNaughton 2005 29–30). A complete detailed analysis of all the processes of accountability would take up a very large volume; I will therefore focus on two of the mechanisms through which accountability is performed: professionalisation and performativity.

Professionalisation

The notion of professions, the professional and the process of pro-fessionalisation has a long history. Crook (2008: 11–12) offers a useful overview of the history of the concepts of profession and profession-alisation and traces them back to the Middle Ages, with 'Churchmen ... being the most prominent group', the development of semi-professionals such as 'a barber supplementing his normal work . . . [with] surgical procedures and teeth extractions', and the 'so-called classical pro-fessions of medicine, law and theology'. He suggests that the professions started to broaden in the mid-nineteenth century to include, among others, civil servants and academics.

Tobias (2001) puts forward three perspectives on what a professional is. The first concerns attributes. A biologically essentialist perspective continues to play a role in defining the attributes needed in the early years sector, particularly around the role of women in providing services for children. However, the dominant ideas put forward through policy review and reform, particularly as early childhood education and care veers more towards the education side of 'learning' and preparation for school, is that of a 'clear, rigorous system of qualifications' that are 'effective in developing the necessary skills, knowledge and understanding to work with babies and young children' (Nutbrown 2012: 17). In other words, the attributes are skills based and 'learnable'. Nutbrown, in her report for the government entitled *Foundations for Quality: Independent review of early education and childcare qualifications* (2012), goes on to extensively list and discuss what she believes are the necessary skills, knowledge and understanding. However, she sets aside a relatively minimal sentence highlighting the need for 'those working in the early years [to be] carers as well as educators, providing the warmth and love children need to develop' (ibid.: 19). Interestingly the report does not, as with the other aforementioned skills-based attributes, discuss whether this is to be 'learned' by the early years practitioner, which may indicate a more essentialist perspective towards this particular 'attribute'.

The second perspective, Tobias (2001) suggests, concerns a process of professionalisation. This is a process where individuals can aspire to 'occupational mobility provided they are willing to undertake the necessary schooling and hard work' (Tobias 2003: 447) and other occupations can become professional 'provided that they are willing to become more selective, self-regulating and self-motivated, raise the quality and quantity of their work and of course continue their work related learning' (ibid.: 448). These ideas have been imposed on the education sector and educational professionals for many decades now through a variety of means. Through the process of 'professionalisation' of the early years sector these are now imposed on early years practitioners and providers. As Nutbrown (2012: 5) states:

> The role of Government is to ensure the necessary standards are being met, but the sector must play a role in determining how these can be achieved as it strives for excellence. The sector is becoming more professional, and Government must support this diverse sector to make its own improvements.

The third perspective concerns issues of power and the market. The first two perspectives are functionalist and although the second orientates itself to process 'it remains very difficult to pose critical questions about the fundamental social, economic and political nature of the profession-alisation process' (Tobias 2003: 448). Tobias suggests that 'power and legitimacy' (ibid.: 449) are the primary drivers of professionalisation, located in 'the increasing commodification of goods and services which was necessary to the rise of capitalism' (ibid.), and this has been established in the neoliberal reforms of the New Right and New Labour and, I argue, is continuing under the current Coalition.

Schön (1983) describes a crisis in the confidence afforded to the professions during the 1960s and 1970s. He suggests that there had been a public loss of confidence following discreditation of professionals – a 'disposition to blame professionals for their failures' (ibid.: 4). Whitty (2008: 33–4) states that, 'from the mid 1970's . . . there were swingeing attacks on public sector professionals, including teachers, who were accused of abusing their autonomy to the detriment of pupils and society'. The 'teaching profession' has had more regulation by the State (ibid.) than the 'major' professions such as medicine (Schön 1983). What is interesting more recently is that the major professions are also increasingly, albeit slowly, becoming more regulated; for example, medical doctors are now being required to take part in annual appraisal systems alongside collecting and producing evidence for their five-yearly revalidation of their medical practice registration (GMC 2011).

State interference in England in the form of the 'modernisation project' (Whitty 2008) has de-professionalised rather than re-profession-alised teachers (Beck 2008). Schön (1983: 13) notes 'a trend towards de-professionalisation' as a result of a move away from teachers being 'autonomous managers of their own careers' towards being 'workers in a bureaucracy'. Teachers have been discredited and in turn made more accountable (Beck 2008); this discreditation has been described by Ball (1990) as *discourses of derision*.

> [The] liberal educational establishment' . . . came to be regarded by governments as left-leaning and favouring what in their view were highly questionable 'progressive' or 'child centred' approaches . . . lack of competitive discipline and 'progressive' teaching methods were blamed for a levelling down of standards.
>
> (Whitty 2008: 34)

Among a myriad of policy initiatives, one of the most important of this time was the 1988 Education Reform Act and alongside this the introduction of the National Curriculum, which took away teachers' autonomy in developing the curriculum (Beck 2008; Whitty 2008).

- The concept of what constitutes a professional dates from the Middle Ages.
- Tobias suggests three perspectives on professionalism: attributes, process, and power and the market.
- During the 1960s and 1970s there was a crisis of confidence afforded to the professions.

Performativity

New Labour continued the neoliberal focus through a model of 'managerialism', increasing the surveillance of professional practice (Beck 2008; Whitty 2008) through top-down performance management (Ball 2008b) and increasing regulation and control (Brock 2006). While there is a multiplicity of critiques of the National Curriculum in schools, the introduction of the Early Years Foundation Stage (EYFS) (DCSF 2008) under New Labour, which is effectively a curriculum for the early years, has received relatively minimal critique. The EYFS (2008) outlines the content and expected outcomes of early years provision, and is grounded in a developmental psychology perspective. These 'ideas about universal, age-related stages have produced widely held truths about children's development and learning' (Lenz Taguchi 2010: 7), which act as a 'grand narrative' that informs early years policy (Dahlberg *et al.* 2007). As MacNaughton (2005: 1) comments, the EYFS has 'settled so firmly in the fabric of early childhood studies that its familiarity makes it just seem "right", "best" and "ethical"'.

This culture of accountability through professionalisation stems from the same 'discursive construction of a "crisis" in education' where 'early childhood services are widely represented as failing to meet the needs of children and families' (Osgood 2006: 6). Osgood suggests that in the early years sector reforms have deregulated and reregulated to 'meet the economic and social needs of society' (ibid.). Morgaine (1999: 7) suggests that, in the professionalisation of early years practitioners, 'we are predicting that children can be better served by controlling workers through training, education and observable actions'.

- New Labour continued and increased regulation and control of the early years sector.
- The need for professionalisation has arisen from a perceived crisis in early years education and care.

The challenge for professionalism from within the sector

The state is not alone in pushing for professionalisation in the early years, indeed for many years professionalisation of the workforce has been argued for by the early years sector itself (Brock 2006; Owen 2006). This is not surprising given the lack of recognition, particularly through poor terms and conditions, wages and status, of the important and highly skilled role of the early years practitioner. Osgood suggests that 'Advocates for the professionalism agenda believe that professionalisation could lead to a strengthened position and increased respect for those who work in ECEC [early childhood education and care]' (2006: 5). Indeed, professions, and therefore professionals, are perceived to hold a higher status in society; however, this is often because of 'the professional claim to extraordinary knowledge in matters of great social importance' (Hughes 1959, cited in Schön 1983: 4).

In return, we grant professionals extraordinary rights and privileges. Hence professional careers are among the most coveted and remunerative, and there are few occupations that have failed to seek out professional status (ibid.).

Within the early years sector there has been a recognition that quality provision requires 'adequate training and fair working conditions' (Moss 2008: 123), a position that has not yet been achieved. Whitty (2008: 23) suggests professional status 'is typically dependent on the sort of bargain an occupation has struck with the state – what is sometimes called its professional mandate'. The government, rather than focusing on the status of early years practice through working conditions, has instead focused on regulating and controlling the workforce through 'officially sanctioned truths that govern normal and desirable ways to think, act and feel' (MacNaughton 2005: 29–30). This is within a positivistic ideological paradigm that:

> values certainty and mastery, linearity and predetermined outcomes, objectivity and universality, and believes in the ability of science to

reveal the true nature of a real world, giving one right answer for every question. This paradigm calls for technicians trained in right answers, not professionals trained to reflect and question.

(Moss 2008: 125)

Professionalisation and qualifications

The process of professionalisation can often include the development of new qualifications as part of the 'professional mandate'. EYPS was developed in 2006 and envisaged a graduate EYP in every setting by 2015. A focus on higher levels of qualification is not unjustifiable, after all research into the early years has continued to demonstrate more positive outcomes and experiences for young children in relation to care and development (Peeters and Vandenbroeck 2012). However, as these authors point out, 'this does not mean qualifications can be considered in isolation, nor that the professionalization of the workforce is in itself sufficient to predict the quality of provision' (ibid.: 100). The EYPS is focused on leaders (Miller 2008), so a whole swathe of the workforce is ignored through this qualification process. The Nutbrown review (2012: 5) has called for 'A new long-term vision . . . for the early years' workforce, with a reformed system of qualifications to help achieve this'. At the time of writing this has yet to be acted on or responded to but there is at least hope that this may be a move towards 'making the quantum jump from a low qualified/poorly paid workforce to a workforce on a par to that in school, taking young children as seriously as we take school children' (Moss 2008: 121). The risk though that arises from reviews that highlight failings, such as Nutbrown's, is that, as Osgood suggests, they contribute to a 'discursive construction of "a crisis in ECEC" [that] provides sufficient justification for regulation and control' (2009: 740). This justification not only justifies existing accountability mechanisms, but also justifies further and more extensive mechanisms.

Performativity or professionalism?

Performativity is taking over the traditional ideas of professionalism (Ball 2003: 216); it is 'a technology, a culture and a mode of regulation'. We all 'perform' in our various roles in life – that is not in question; what is in question is how we are measured, what we are measured against, who controls and decides on these processes and how these processes of 'incentive, control, attrition and change – based on rewards and sanctions' (ibid.) are implemented.

The reductionist approach, which reduces educational and care practice to a level that is measurable in quantifiable ways, is based on a positivistic scientific paradigm, and set in a dominant discourse of 'what works' (Dahlberg and Moss 2005: vii). The notion that there is 'one truth', that there is one 'best way' of practising, reduces the parameters of creative practice.

Performativity as measured and judged against a set of standards is sweeping the education sector and is constant and ongoing (Ball 2008b). The standards come in a myriad of different forms, from professional qualification standards, to 'quality' assurance standards, such as Ofsted and the Quality Assurance Agency for Higher Education (QAA), to competency frameworks, to curriculum and attainment frameworks, and the list goes on. As well as reflecting a neoliberal government agenda of what is a good and, therefore, what is a bad standard of practice (Anning *et al.* 2004), all of these are designed to subject practitioners to 'a myriad of judgements, measures, comparisons and targets. Information is collected continuously, recorded and published, often in the form of league tables. Performance is also measured eventfully, by peer reviews, site visits and inspections' (Ball 2008b: 50). The end result is a different meaning to being an early years practitioner and 'the power elite (government and its agencies) act as regulator of the behaviours of the subordinate (the ECEC workforce)' (Osgood 2009: 740).

Ball (2008a) discusses the 'first-order' and 'second-order' effects of performativity. First-order effects include the reorienting of 'pedagogical and scholarly activities towards those that are likely to have a positive impact on measurable performance outcomes' (ibid.: 54), which inevitably leads to activities that are not so easily measured being dropped, even if this is against practitioners' judgement. This once again ensures practitioners are located in *living contradictions*. This leads in to the second-order effects, which 'change the way in which they [teachers]experience their work and the satisfactions they get from it – their sense of moral purpose and of responsibility for their students is distorted' (ibid.).

- Performativity can be seen to diminish the concept of professionalism by the ways in which measurement occurs.
- Practitioners are located in living contradictions that impact on the ways in which they experience their work.

Resistance

Simpson (2010) argues that the 'constructionist' perspectives of pro-fessionalisation, performativity and hence accountability, which attempt to take account of agency (he specifically uses the example of the work of Osgood), do not make clear where 'an EYP starts and ends in relation to the discursive context' (Simpson 2010: 7). He suggests they are represented as 'cultural dupes' (ibid.), and that 'dominant government discourse of professionalism is inappropriately privileged above any other discursive and social forms as an explanatory factor in shaping EYPs' orientations' (ibid.). He defines two perspectives of early years professionalism: '(1) those that represent early years' professionalism as largely socially constructed and determined; and (2) those that represent EYPs as more active and reflexive agents' (ibid.: 6). I do not see these so distinctly, after all social construction, with appropriate 'tools' to challenge the power differentials, leads to the possibility of deconstruction and reconstruction, where agency, as defined by the agent, is absolutely key. Agency as a concept therefore does not, and should not, enable the defining of where 'an EYP starts and ends'.

In his findings from research with EYPs, Simpson found that 'the pervasive nature of official discourse connected to regulatory frameworks was visible in the narratives of the interviewees but it became clear it was not determinant in shaping what interviewees thought their professionalism is about' (ibid.: 9). This is very encouraging, but as the sector becomes increasingly regulated and continues towards an education and preparation for school model, the power balance will continue to change and, as Brock cautions, 'professionals working in the early years will interpret the standards as they are stated; people will endeavour to meet them exactly . . . this has certainly been the case in primary education' (2006: 6).Therefore if early years practitioners' own agency is to become more enabled, then resistance needs to be supported through the development and implementation of practices that enable practitioners to use agency effectively. Miller (2008) suggests that it is possible for practitioners to do so within a regulatory framework; I would agree if the higher and further education institutions that educate early years practitioners are entrusted to do this. The problem is, as I suggested in the introduction, that education professionals from all education sectors are subject to the same increasing regulation and reform.

The importance of this resistance cannot be stressed highly enough as the negative consequences of performativity are serious. The conse-quences of inequality for children and families I have previously discussed, and these come alongside the challenges within our living contradictions where values are being 'challenged or displaced' (Ball 2008b: 51). There is a growing 'ontological insecurity: both a loss of a sense of meaning in what we do and of what is important in what we do' (Ball 2008a: 54). Perhaps more seriously there can also be a direct impact on well-being: 'Performativity comes to be inscribed on our bodies as well as our minds, making us anxious, tired and stressed and sometimes ill' (ibid.: 56).

Reconstruction and positioning

In critiquing Ebbeck (2003), who argues that post-structuralist critique is not useful as it does not suggest how to 'act', an early years practitioner suggests that:

> Ebbeck's argument can only be valid if we accept that teaching is simply a technical task, and that in understanding this task, teachers can know how to act. My experiences tell me the opposite – that teaching is unknowable, complex, contextual, unpredictable, contra-dictory, messy and intently personal.
>
> (Barnes 2005: 15)

As a post-structuralist who recognises the value of multiple truths, I would not venture to suggest 'how' early years practitioners 'do' their work; as Albon (2012) suggests, this would be indicative of a *metanarrative*. A metanarrative as described by Lyotard (1979) as a universal truth and has similarities to Foucaultian notions of a regime of truth. However, I would like to suggest some possible ways in which practitioners can survive and flourish in their work – ways that enable them to improve their practice, ways that enable them to position themselves in the debates, and ways that may support them in resisting the 'regulatory gaze' (Osgood 2006) of performativity. I give no detail here, first because others have given some detail within this edited collection, second because these ideas are ones that I have found useful in my own resistance and in learning about them I have developed my own interpretation and used my own knowledge and agency to adapt them for my own perspectives and practices, and finally because I argue against meta-narratives and agree with Albon (2012) that Lyotard's (1979) notion of *micro-narratives* is useful for settings to develop their own appropriate practice narratives – not as prescriptive performance management tools for practitioners, but rather as geographically and, hence, (multi)culturally and socio-economically specific practice frameworks. As Cromby and Nightingale (1999) suggest, relativism, which is associated with postmodern and post-structural perspectives, and realism, which is associated with modernist, positivistic scientific perspectives, are often deployed morally and politically, and as such I, like Siraj-Blatchford (1994: 54), do not want to fall 'into the abyss of total relativism where inequality itself could not be grounded'.

Tools for resistance

I have found the work of Brookfield (1995) on critical reflective teaching really useful; he puts forward a model with four lenses: 'autobiographies, students' eyes, theoretical literature and colleagues experiences' (ibid.: 29–30). This model is adaptable to early years practice; for example, by changing the students' lens to that of children and their families or carers, it also values agency, both through the autobiographical lens and through the notion of lenses, which both are interpreted by and inform the active practitioner. While I have found the four lens model extremely valuable because, as Edwards (1997: 5) suggests, 'Positioning oneself and being positioned in certain discourses becomes . . . the basis for personal self-identity', as such I argue that, in addition, a policy lens with which I can contextualise my position and also the position of my colleagues and the service users is essential.

My second suggestion is that of pedagogical documentation, a method that has developed within European early years contexts. Pedagogical documentation is more than 'recording' practice in documents. While the tools used to do this are important in themselves, it is the process that is used to develop and then 'use' those documents that allows for the creation of 'reflective and democratic practice' (Dahlberg *et al.* 2007: 145). By creating the activity, space (ibid.) and artefacts (Fleet *et al.* 2006) with which to hold critically reflective conversations with colleagues and students (ibid.), it is possible to reconstruct pedagogical activity (Dahlberg *et al.* 2007), challenge taken-for-granted assumptions (Brookfield 1995) and oppose and resist the 'knowledge–power nexus, those regimes of truth which attempt to determine for us what is true or false, right or wrong, and what we may or may not think and do' (Dahlberg *et al.* 2007: 144).

Conclusion

The suggestions I put forward are not new ideas; they have been, and continue to be, debated, discussed and developed both in the wider education sector and specifically in early years. I argue that they actively support the elements of flourishing put forward by White (2006) – autonomy, and Seligman (2011) – positive emotion, engagement, relationships, meaning and accomplishment.

Within the early years sector in the UK we are at a pivotal moment in the flourishing of children, their families and early years practitioners. The enormous change in the early years has led to some concerning developments, particularly in the culture of accountability that continues to be imposed, yet we have opportunities now as never before. There will hopefully continue to be increases in the number of practitioners (re-)entering further and higher education, alongside a continuation in the growth of academic and practice debates, and academic and practitioner research. We must embrace this moment; if we do we will enjoy witnessing the flourishing of a highly valued sector of UK education and care provision.

REFLECTIVE QUESTIONS

- How does the performativity agenda directly affect your work as a practitioner in the early years sector?
- Do you feel that you should be accountable to government, society, parents, the child, yourself or any other organisation or individual?
- Does public expenditure on professionalisation need to be justified in terms of performativity?
- How do you position yourself as a professional within the performativity and accountability agenda?

References

Albon, D. (2012) 'Postmodern and poststructuralist perspectives on early childhood education', in Miller, L., Drury, R. and Cable, C. (eds) *Extending Professional Practice in the Early Years*, London: Sage.

Anning, A. Cullen, J. and Fleer, M. (eds) (2004) *Early Childhood Education: Society and culture*, London: Sage.

Atkinson, E. (2003) 'Education, postmodernism and the organisation of consent', in Satterthwaite, J., Atkinson, E. and Gale. K. (eds) *Discourse, Power and Resistance: Challenging the rhetoric of contemporary education*, Stoke on Trent: Trentham.

Ball, S.J. (1990) *Politics and Policy Making in Education*, London: Routledge.

Ball, S.J. (2003) 'The teachers' souls and the terrors of performativity', *Journal of Education Policy*, 18(2): 215–28.

Ball, S.J. (2008a) 'Performativity, privatisation, professionals and the state', in Cunningham, B. (ed.) *Exploring Professionalism*, London: Institute of Education, University of London.

Ball, S.J. (2008b) *The Education Debate*, Bristol: Policy Press.

Barnes, S. (2005) 'Unsettling and resettling pedagogical knowledges', vignette in MacNaughton, G. (2005) *Doing Foucault in Early Childhood Education: Applying poststructural ideas*, Abingdon: Routledge.

Beck, J. (2008) 'Governmental professionalism: re-professionalising or de-professionalising teachers in England', *British Journal of Educational Studies*, 56(2): 119–43.

Biesta, G.J.J. (2006) *Beyond Learning: Democratic education for a human future*, Boulder, CO: Paradigm.

Biesta, G.J.J. (2009) 'Good education in an age of measurement: on the road to reconnect with the question of purpose in education', *Educational Assessment, Evaluation and Accountability*, 21: 33–46.

Blackmore, J. and Sachs, J. (1997) *Worried, Weary and Just Plain Worn Out: Gender, restructuring and the psychic economy of higher education*, paper presented at the AARE annual conference, 1–4 December, Brisbane.

Brock, A. (2006) *Dimensions of Early Years' Professionalism: Attitudes versus competences? A paper from Training Advancement and Co-operation in Teaching Young Children* (TACTYC). Available online at www.tactyc.org.uk/pdfs/Reflection-brock.pdf (accessed 20 November 2012).

Brookfield, S. (1995) *Becoming a Critically Reflective Teacher*, San Francisco CA: Jossey Bass.

Cromby, J. and Nightingale, D.J. (1999) 'What's wrong with social construction', in Nightingale, D.J. and Cromby, J. (eds) *Social Constructionist Psychology*, Buckingham: Open University Press.

Crook, D. (2008) 'Some historical perspectives on professionalism', in Cunningham, B. (ed.) *Exploring Professionalism*, London: Institute of Education, University of London.

Dahlberg, G. and Moss, P. (2005) *Ethics and Politics in Early Childhood Education*, London: Routledge.

Dahlberg, G. Moss, P. and Pence, A. (2007) *Beyond Quality in Childhood Education and Care: Languages of evaluation* (2nd edition), Abingdon: Routledge.

Department for Children, Schools and Families (DCSF, replaced by Department for Education) (2008) *The Early Years Foundation Stage*, Nottingham: DCSF.

Department for Education (DfE) (2011) *Government Sets Out Reform of Early Learning and Children's Centres*, London: DfE. Available online at www.education.gov.uk/childrenandyoungpeople/earlylearningandchildcare/a00191829/government-sets-out-reform-of-early-learning-and-childrens-centres (accessed 13 January 2013).

Department for Education (DfE) (2012a) *Early Education for Two year Olds*, London: DfE. Available online at www.education.gov.uk/childrenandyoungpeople/earlylearningandchildcare/delivery/free%20entitlement%20to%20early%20education/b0070114/eefortwoyearolds (accessed 13 January 2013).

Department for Education (DfE) (2012b) *Provision for Children Under Five Years of Age in England*, London: DfE. Available online at www.education.gov.uk/rsgateway/DB/SFR/s001074/sfr13-2012.pdf (accessed 13 January 2013).

Edwards, R. (1997) *Changing Places? Flexibility, lifelong learning and a learning society*, London: Routledge.

Fleet, A. Hammersley, M. Patterson, C. Schillert, L. and Stanke, E. (2006) 'Five voices: interrupting the dominant discourse', in Fleet, A. Patterson, C. and Robertson, J. (eds) *Insights Behind Early Childhood Pedagogical Documentation*, Sydney: Pademelon Press.

General Medical Council (GMC) (2011) *The Good Medical Practice Framework for Appraisal and Revalidation*, Manchester: GMC. Available online at www.gmc-uk.org/GMP_framework_for_appraisal_and_revalidation.pdf_41326960.pdf (accessed 14 November 2012).

Hopkin, R. Stokes, L. and Wilkinson, D. (2010) *Quality, Outcomes and Costs in Early Years' Education*, London: National Institute of Economic and Social Research.

House, E.R. (2005) 'Qualitative evaluation and changing social policy', in Denzin, N.K. and Lincoln, Y.S. (eds) *The Sage Handbook of Qualitative Research* (3rd edn), London: Sage.

Lenz Taguchi, H. (2010) *Going Beyond the Theory/Practice Divide in Early Childhood Education*, London: Routledge.

Lyotard, J.F. (1979) *The Postmodern Condition: A report on knowledge* (trans. G. Bennington and B. Massumi), Manchester: Manchester University Press.

MacNaughton, G. (2005) *Doing Foucault in Early Childhood Education: Applying poststructural ideas*, Abingdon: Routledge.

Miller, L. (2008) 'Developing new professional roles in the early years', in Miller, L. and Cable, C. (eds) *Professionalism in the Early Years*, London: Hodder Education.

Morgaine, C. (1999) 'Alternative paradigms and professionalizing childhood care and education: the Oregon example', *Child and Youth Care Forum*, 28(1): 5–19.

Moss, P. (2008) 'The democratic and reflective professional: rethinking and reforming the early years' workforce', in Miller, L. and Cable, C. (eds) *Professionalism in the Early Years*, London: Hodder Education.

Nutbrown, C. (2012) *Foundations For Quality: The independent review of early education and childcare qualifications. Final report*, London: Department for Education.

Office for National Statistics (ONS) (2010) *Measuring Outcomes for Public Service Users: Final report*, Newport: ONS. Available online at www.ons.gov.uk/ons/about-ons/what-we-do/programmes-projects/completed-projects-and-reviews/measuring-outcomes-for-public-service-users/mopsu-reports-and-updates/index.html (accessed 13 January 2013).

Osgood, J. (2006) 'Deconstructing professionalism in early childhood education: resisting the regulatory gaze', *Contemporary Issues in Early Childhood*, 7(1): 5–14.

Osgood, J. (2009) 'Childcare workforce reform in England and "The Early Years' Professional": A critical discourse analysis', *Journal of Education Policy*, 24(6): 733–51.

Owen, S. (2006) 'Training and workforce issues in the early years', in Pugh, G. and Duffy, B. (eds) *Contemporary Issues in the Early Years* (4th edn), London: Sage.

Owen, S. and Haynes, G. (2008) 'Developing professionalism in the early years: from policy to practice', in Miller, L. and Cable, C. (eds) *Professionalism in the Early Years*, London: Hodder Education.

Peeters, J. and Vandenbroeck, M. (2012) 'Childcare practitioners and the process of professionalization', in Miller, L., Drury, R. and Cable, C. (eds) *Extending Professional Practice in the Early Years*, London: Sage.

Schön, D. (1983) *The Reflective Practitioner: How professionals think in action*, London: Maurice Temple Smith.

Seligman, M.E.P. (2011) *Flourish: A new understanding of happiness and well-being and how to achieve them*, London: Nicholas Brealey.

Simpson, D. (2010) 'Being professional? Conceptualising early years' professionalism in England', *European Early Childhood Education Research Journal*, 18(1): 6–14.

Siraj-Blatchford, I. (1994) *Praxis Makes Perfect: Critical educational research for social justice*, Ticknall: Education Now.

Smith, R. (2008) 'Proteus rising: re-imagining educational research', *Journal of Philosophy of Education*, 42(S1): 182–98.

Strathern, M. (2000) 'Introduction: new accountabilities', in Strathern, M. (ed.) *Audit Cultures: Anthropological studies in accountability, ethics and the academy*, London: Routledge.

Tobias, R. (2001) *Continuing education and professionalization: travelling without a compass*, paper presented at SCUTREA 31st annual conference, 3–5 July 2001, University of East London.

Tobias, R. (2003) 'Continuing education and professionalization: travelling without a compass', *International Journal of Lifelong Education*, 22(5): 445–56.

Vincent, A. (2011) 'Ideology and the university', *The Political Quarterly*, 82(3): 332–40.

White, J. (2006) 'Autonomy, human flourishing and the curriculum', *Journal of Philosophy of Education*, 40(3): 381–90.

Whitehead, J. (1989) 'Creating a living educational theory from questions of the kind, "how do I improve my practice?"', *Cambridge Journal of Education*, 19(1): 41–52. Available online at www.actionresearch.net/writings/livtheory.html (accessed 7 November 2012).

Whitty, G. (2008) 'Changing modes of teacher professionalism: traditional, managerial, collaborative and democratic', in Cunningham, B. (ed.) *Exploring Professionalism: The Bedford papers*, London: Institute of Education, University of London.

3 The influence of international policy

Jan Gourd

Introduction

This chapter will explore the influence that international early years policy and practice have had on policy and its interpretation within England. The chapter will draw comparisons between the EYFS (DfE 2012a) and the approaches found within the HighScope programme in America, the Reggio Emilia philosophy in Italy, Te Whariki in New Zealand and the Nordic approaches, particularly the influence of the Forest School as seen within England and the success in the percentage of female employment of Iceland. A number of threads within policy will be considered, particularly enabling environments, the place of child-initiated play, the pursuit of quality and assessment and performativity.

The global context

The issue of early years education and care is one that is receiving unprecedented global attention. The Organisation for Economic Co-operation and Development (OECD 2006) documents the fact that it is the desire to increase the women's labour market that has largely fuelled this policy. Added to this, the demographic challenges of an ageing population, lower fertility rates and educational inequality seem to be international issues (Plantenga and Remery 2009). Given that a country's 'economic prosperity depends on mainstreaming a high employment/ population ratio' (OECD 2006: 78), it is this that can be seen to drive policy. Oberhuemer (2005: 30) suggests six reasons for growing political interest internationally in early years curricular policy:

1   Within the context of a global economy, education is taking on a new significance as a valuable resource in so-called knowledge societies. Regulating the curriculum is seen as a proactive contribution towards acknowledging the early years as an essential foundation for individual learning biographies, and towards raising the status and visibility of early childhood institutions.

2   Recent neuroscientific research on brain development in the early years has contributed to a sharpened perception by policy makers of the educational potential of high-quality early childhood provision, although it must be added that the implications of this research for the curriculum debate are still unclear.

3   Within the context of national decentralisation policies resulting from new forms of public management, curricular frameworks are seen as a necessary goal-steering device and as a public accountability measure within the education system as a whole.

4   In countries with a pre-school sector traditionally representing diverse community and cultural groups and different pedagogical and philosophical approaches, curriculum guidelines are regarded as establishing a shared framework of guiding principles, providing these are developed in collaboration with the major stakeholders in the field.

5   In countries intent on significant expansion of a poorly resourced sector, mandatory guidelines are seen as a quality improvement and equity measure.

6   Finally, curricular guidelines are considered to provide early childhood professionals with a common framework for enhancing communication between staff in the centre and with parents.

While it is clear to see how five of the points apply to the English context, it is difficult to see that point 3 is relevant as in England control of early years was always at local level and it is only with the introduction of the EYFS (DCSF 2008) that the control was centralised.

International influence

In our effort to try to retain supremacy Britain has a history of always looking elsewhere at those it perceives to be doing better. Once education became politicised the idea of being better than anyone else became paramount. Indeed, famously the school starting age was decided by politicians in this vein (Penn 2011).

It is indeed in early childhood education that political targets, including economic policies (e.g. women's labour participation); social policies (e.g. the elimination of poverty); immigration policies (e.g. the management of ethnic diversity); and educational policies (e.g. bridging the educational gap) not only meet, but also intersect within the intimacy of the daily life of families (Vandenbroeck *et al.* 2010: 139).

The problem lies with the simplistic model of application that is envisaged; it is the failure to recognise the complexity of individual societies that means that the current view of policy as social antagonist is bound to fail. Dealing with complexity is difficult and requires a philosophical ability to theorise that is not easily formulated into policy directive and measurable targets.

Rather than necessarily looking, for our lead, at successful countries as measured by how children flourish, politicians seem to be drawn to the Anglo-American relationship and consider this as the first solution in a series of fixes. This is possibly because the performativity agenda and the deficit view of children and families are nearest to the philosophical stance of our politicians regardless of political party.

In the Unicef (2007) survey on children's well-being the UK came bottom as an average of all six dimensions, with the USA being one position above. The Nordic countries, Spain and Italy come nearer the top of the table. A follow-up report comparing Sweden, Spain and the UK, published in 2011, found that inequality, consumerism, the time that parents spent with their children and the availability of stimu-lating (often outdoor) activity seemed to be significant factors in the different scores on child well-being (Nairn 2011). Children from the UK flourished less well than their counterparts because in the main our society works differently and has had different historical experiences in terms of both financial and political stability. The study uses Bronfen-brenner's (1979, cited in Nairn 2011) social ecological model to try to contextualise the findings.

Rarely are the social conditions, cultural differences and political stability taken into account when politicians seek solutions abroad. They fail to contextualise the solutions they hijack and rebrand using their own party political stamp. Glass (2001, cited in Baldock *et al.* 2013: 165) suggests that 'caution needs to be applied if there is an unquestionable assumption that what works in other countries can be directly applied in UK contexts'. He goes on to suggest that any policy appraisal needs to ask the question, 'what is worth doing for children?' (ibid.) This is a question often forgotten when political gains are to be made from the headline policy initiative.

■   Policy directives cannot be imported from one country to another without considering the differing cultures of donator and recipient

International ideas welcomed by practitioners

The Te Whariki and Reggio Emilia influences are seized upon by practitioners and educationalists as alternatives to policy directives constructed by civil servants who have often no practical knowledge of the educational context of the proposed policy. The gains for children of these approaches can be seen by those with practice experience. Indeed, the policy maker's simplistic view of education is criticised by Dalhberg (in Moss 2013: 76), who suggests that in order to make meaningful change we must consider the 'whole learning chain and all its components; the goals and results, but also the pedagogical process – and the frame factors'. Early childhood education and care (ECEC) in Britain, and I would suggest in America, on whom we seem to rely for our solutions, sits outside the world of critically reflective pedagogical experience but firmly within the fiscal system and the performativity agenda. There is a tacit attempt at research-informed policy but the research base is seen by many to be highly questionable and often commissioned and manipulated to suit the already defined solution (Cunningham 2012). Practitioners are drawn to approaches that seem to put well-being ahead of performance. The whole context of flourishing seems to be encompassed within models that practitioners are drawn to. But even then Baldock *et al.* (2013: 106) suggest that 'There is always a risk that contact with foreign models will be used to generate "recipes" for new practice without an understanding of the local circumstances that produced them.'

Baldock (ibid.) then cites Johnson (1999), who describes English-speaking countries' attempts to raid the Reggio Emilia experience and to produce 'ill-digested ideas torn out of context'. This seems to be a phrase that could sum up the UK experience of early years policy development – a series of raids, the subjects of which are based merely on political whim. A comprehensive look at services and how we enable a generation of children to flourish and move us from the bottom of the child well-being survey are the philanthropic actions needed of politicians who sadly focus instead on seeking to further their political careers. This can be seen clearly in the initial cross-party positive reaction to the publication of *The Spirit Level* (Wilkinson and Pickett 2010), which was quickly forgotten by high-profile politicians as soon as the ideologically driven think tanks regained control of political thought.

■   Practitioners recognise that lessons can be gained from international policy, but it is the approaches that come from the bottom up that are more readily recognised as valid.

Closing the gap

In recent years many policy initiatives have been put in place under the auspices of closing the gap between the most and least successful in society in monetary policy terms. In terms of well-being it is doubtful whether the deficit model of early childhood that the UK seems to be subscribing to can actually promote well-being and flourishing. The lowest ranking within the child well- being survey has not really been contextualised holistically. The inequality agenda has been recognised but through a deficit lens. Nairn (2011) suggests that what matters most to a child's well-being is the quality of the relationships that he or she has. Children in the UK talked about good days as being those when predominantly parents had time for them. Children within the UK as well as in Spain and Sweden overwhelmingly subscribed to family relationships as being dominant in their feelings of well-being. The human emotional labour required to engender well-being of children in the family home is also an important factor in ECEC. Moss (2013) unpacks this view, suggesting that human technologies defined as 'good quality' are seen as the panacea of provision. He suggests that:

> ECE seems to offer a modern day philosopher's stone that can achieve fundamental transformations through applying human technologies (usually described under the heading of 'good quality') at an early age, obviating the need to tackle directly deep-rooted inequalities and other injustices.
>
> (2013: 10)

Moss and Dahlberg (2008: 3) previously offered this definition of what quality means: '"Quality" is generally understood as an attribute of services for young children that ensures the efficient production of predefined, normative outcomes, typically developmental or simple learning goals.'

In order to tackle the inequalities and other injustices we need to look again at how we nurture our children and strip quality of its performativity agenda in order to create a new order of a flourishing society and services within it. MacNaughton (2005) suggests that creating a professional critically reflective workforce, which works with our youngest children in an ethically determined manner, might be the starting point for tackling all of those issues of fairness, injustice and inequality that seem to predetermine our place at the bottom of well-being surveys.

The Labour governments (1997–2010) saw the early years agenda both as a vote winner and as a legitimate attempt at socialist policy. 'Readiness for school' became an overt aim of policy, again harking back to the supremacy ideal of earlier politicians. If our children are 'ready for school', we might once again regain our dominance of, for example, world trade. The Marxist ideal continues to dominate societal aims and most closely aligns us with America. Indeed, Field (2010), a Labour MP, has written extensively on the subject of compensatory early years education. Field (2010) and Allen (2011) are cited by government as justification for the paper, *Developing a New Vision for the Early Years* (DfE 2012b). Allen (2011) starts with the child and family as deficit models that need 'normalising' through intervention programmes aimed at raising attainment against age-related norms. The efficiency of this normalising is one of his main concerns and he lists his 19 most effective programmes in meeting this agenda. He calls the early childhood phase, 0–5 years, the 'readiness for school' phase and suggests that the primary years are the 'readiness for secondary' phase and the secondary phase is 'readiness for life'. Thus the child is positioned as always preparing for something else. This conception of the child is important in locating UK policy within an international context, as the dominant ideas behind policy obviously shape its construction and ultimately its outcomes. It is interesting to note that Allen (2011) called for opinions from leading experts on early intervention and invited four academic groups to join the team to look at the evidence for early intervention. Of those four, three were from American universities (ibid.). The American influence then has been dominant in policy decisions made on early attainment. The debate as to whether an approach that has been perceived as success-ful in one culture is necessarily advantageous in another does not seem to have been fully considered. Certainly, in the European Commission's report on childcare strategies across the European Union, the cultural perspective on the issues is highlighted when a description of the available services is given (Plantenga and Remery 2009).

> ■ Professional practitioners need to employ critical reflective practice when deciding on what is right for the children and families with whom they work.
> ■ Developmentally appropriate practice needs to be considered by practitioners at all times.

The influence of America on British government policy

The notion of compensatory education seems to be a largely Anglo-American idea. Politicians seem to be determined to try to 'fix' what they see as an ill society. Indeed, the 'problem' with society, parents and children, as well as childhood, has been the subject of the popular press for the past decade. Sue Palmer's (2007) 'toxic childhood' idea has gained much publicity and has led to a plethora of literature and TV series that set out to 'fix' deviant parenting. The Marxist system of monetary policy operated in these economies is always going to cause inequality and opportunities will therefore be unequal. However, schemes such as the American Head Start programme, which seeks to address children's health, nutrition and deficit parenting, are cited as 'bearing out the biological determinism thesis' (Miller and Hevey 2012: 63). Indeed, the rhetoric of disadvantaged children that has dominated American thought since the 1960s takes a very simplistic view of disadvantage. Roopnarine and Johnson (2012: 14) state:

> The term *culturally deprived* was used extensively in the early education literature of the 1960s. This term referred primarily to poor, urban, mostly black children and families. In actuality, the children were not usually deprived of their family culture, and often they resided in communities that contained numerous cultural institutions, but not necessarily those of Euro-American culture.

Head Start programmes are designed to 'enable disadvantaged groups of young children to gain greater advantage from their schooling' (Pound 2011: 139). Thus we have 'school readiness' – a concept James Callaghan alluded to in his Ruskin College speech of 1976. It seems even in the 1970s and 1980s, despite the 1967 findings of Plowden, which were highly regarded internationally, we were already 'trashing' our own thinking, which was the envy of the world at the time. Instead we were already looking to America for better solutions. Maybe this has something to do with economic recession as in times of economic crisis we seek quick-fix solutions to maintain economic viability.

> ■ The economic state of a nation influences childhood policy as children are viewed as the key to future economic improvement.

The HighScope approach

HighScope was one of the Head Start programmes developed in the USA and was part of the Perry Pre-school Project. This project started in 1962 and sought to recruit a number of families to participate in longitudinal research to try to determine the life benefits of a particular programme of pre-school education. A control group who did not access the programme was also formed. The programme was developed by David Weikart, who was trained as a school psychologist (Holt 2010). Pound (2011) notes that the emphasis within the programme on the training and up-skilling of the staff who delivered it is often forgotten when the influence of HighScope is explored. Indeed, many of the antecedents of recent English early years policy can all be seen to have been influenced by this 1960s' American model. HighScope, being the subject of longitudinal research, fulfils all the politicians' requirements for research-based policy, a term that gained favour with politicians in order to justify policy decisions from around 1988 onwards. Claims made for HighScope included that, 'for every dollar invested in high quality early childhood education, seven dollars could be saved. This in turn engaged politicians and led in England to the development of Sure Start' (Pound 2011: 169).

The HighScope approach is based on Piagetian theory around ages and stages of development (Pramling Samuelsson and Asplund Carlsson 2008). Epstein *et al.* (in Miller and Pound 2011) see the adults' role within HighScope as supporting Vygotsky's *zone of proximal development*, however the curriculum manuals do suggest certain activities at certain ages, so overall I would suggest the approach generally draws more heavily on the work of Piaget. The approach is dependent on a 'Plan, Do, Review' model whereby the children have agency to choose the activities they will undertake, planning them with a practitioner, carrying out the activity and then evaluating the outcomes again with a practitioner leading the feedback. The HighScope approach, like the EYFS (2008, 2012), focused on achieving goals and the activities are created with this firmly in the practitioner's mind. The Plan, Do, Review activities are balanced with group time that is practitioner led and clearly directed towards achievement goals. These group times are often didactic in nature (Epstein *et al.*, in Miller and Pound 2011). This balanced approach is seen as an advantage by some and a 'selling out' to an objectives-led, performativity-led curriculum by others. Similarities with the projects in the Reggio Emilia approach could be drawn, except that the HighScope Plan, Do, Review sessional approach is for short-term activities whereas the Reggio approach to projects is much longer term. HighScope is dependent on an enabling environment. The equipment for the chosen activities has to be readily available to the children and organised in such a way as to be accessible. In the nursery class in England that I observed using the HighScope approach, the equipment was organised in themed areas (role-play, construction, art etc.) and each box of equipment had a velcro label attached that the children put on a central planning board when they had decided that was what they were going to do. A group of children could then stick their velcro name tab underneath to show that they were engaging within that specific activity. The way in which the children engaged with the Plan, Do, Review model was impressive. The routine was clearly taken on board by these children; however, time was organised in rigid time slots and there was little room for flexibility, but this might have been because the nursery class was part of a mainstream school and thus subject to the school's timetabling. Children in this situation were not able to continue their play beyond the allocated hour for that activity and so many opportunities to extend and develop the play were missed.

HighScope requires interaction between practitioner and child. The practitioner is listening to the child's ideas and responding. In this respect it is very like the Reggio philosophy, except that in the HighScope approach the practitioner is viewed as the capable and confident superior partner, the power relationship being clear, whereas in Reggio, with its emphasis both on the child as competent and on learning together, the power relationship, although present, is much less specific. What the routine of the HighScope approach does is almost guarantee that the children get adult interaction, the one-to-one dialogue that is seen to be essential to children's progress (Tizzard and Hughes 1984) but is often missing in large childcare contexts. This dialogue is also true within the Reggio Emilia and Te Whariki approaches but is far less specific within the EYFS (2008, 2012), that is, it is not part of a structured routine although it is implicit in the guidance on sustained shared thinking.

We need to ask why, though, we seem to base all early years policy on an American scheme that addresses performativity and the measurable outcomes of a childhood but fails to address adequately the flourishing of the child.

- HighScope requires a highly organised and structured environment for the children to access.
- HighScope does not offer obvious development of play themes over a sustained period of time.

The Nordic approach

I am taking the Nordic approach to mean the northern European countries of Denmark, Sweden, Finland, Iceland and Norway. Iceland is interesting as an agenda of schoolification of pre-school has been taking place since the late 1990s. This is described as the downward pressure of the curriculum and has been felt in the early years sector. Schooling is seen as a continuum, with the pre-school being the first stage (Einarsdottir 2006). Pre-schools in Iceland were originally established for the children of the poor in order to provide them with food and hygiene. A National Curriculum for this phase was introduced in 1999. Pre-school teachers are now graduate level. The school starting age decreased from seven to six in the 1990s. In Iceland the pre-school curriculum uses playful pedagogy, while the primary curriculum emphasises subject learning. This is a contentious issue for some of the first-grade teachers (ibid.).

An EC study in 2009 compared childcare provision across 30 European countries; Iceland was seen to have a high overall employment rate and a high female employment rate, the overall rate being 85.1 per cent (Plantenga and Remery 2009). Iceland also has the highest fertility rates of the countries in the study showing an average of just over two children per woman. Thus with Iceland you see a country with high female employment of just over 80 per cent and high fertility rates. The UK has lower female employment at 62 per cent and lower fertility at around 1.8 children (ibid.). What can also be seen from the EC's report is that a much higher percentage of children over three years of age spend over 30 hours in childcare arrangements (80 per cent) than do those in the UK, where the majority of children spend less than 30 hours in childcare, with only about 26 per cent spending over 30 hours. The cost of childcare in Iceland is cited as being 'relatively high' (ibid.: 41). Iceland could then be seen economically to be very strong with high participation rates in employment despite the cost. The adult-to-child ratio for childminders in Iceland was 1:4 with no statistics on other provision available. The demand for pre-school educators is high:

> Pre-school teachers and staff responsible for the pedagogical care are required to obtain a university degree, which means a 3-year education programme. Demand for pre-school educators has consistently exceeded supply, leading to most pre-primary schools having to rely on unskilled employees.
>
> (ibid.: 46)

In terms of child well-being Iceland also scores highly (OECD 2006), with the risk of poverty being low. Indeed, despite being at the centre of a Banking System collapse in 2008 the Icelandic economy seems to be one of the fastest moving out of recession and the actions taken (including nationalising the banks) seem to have hastened the recovery (White 2012).

In Norway the curriculum has been in existence since 1996. It is a detailed plan of goals, content and methods to be employed with children from one to six years old. Similarly a curriculum for one- to six-year-olds has been in existence in Sweden since 1998. Here children do not start formal schooling until seven. The curriculum in Sweden offers goals and guidance but does not specify method (Alvestad and Duncan 2006). Norway is second only to Iceland in terms of female employment and has the fourth highest fertility rate (Plantenga and Remery 2009).

School readiness is not part of the expectation of ECE within the Nordic countries in general, bar Iceland where it has crept up the political agenda (Bennett, cited in Moss 2013; Einarsdottir 2006). Indeed, the school educators showed respect and recognition of the role of early childhood pedagogy. This, Bennett suggests (cited in Moss 2013), is due to the high profile given to early childhood services as part of the welfare state.

The Forest School experience hailed from Sweden in the 1950s and also became dominant in Denmark (Blackwell and Pound, cited in Miller and Pound 2011). Forest School philosophy seeks to foster a sense of personal worth and self-esteem among the participants as well as fostering a sense of adventure and risk-taking. The woodland setting should offer a sense of place and space to encourage individual exploration. They are also chosen to nurture a sense of awe and wonder at the natural environment and a responsibility towards maintenance of the ecosystem. The provision within these countries has been seen to offer many benefits (Tovey 2007); however, it needs to be noted that in these countries provision is well established and offers day-long experiences. The benefits of the Forest environment are seen to be through the conquering of differing terrain, for example learning how to walk through mud, across bramble and over fallen trees, thus adding a physical challenge dimension not found elsewhere. Alongside this comes the free creativity encouraged by an environment of 'loose bits' (ibid.) to create places that are anything you want them to be. Indeed, the den-building aspect of Forest Schools has been an influence on many settings in out-door environments. Maybe this is the greatest influence that the movement has had on the early years curriculum in this country, not so much the true Forest School experience but the way in which early years practitioners have reconsidered the place of outdoor play in response to the Forest School movement and tried to enhance the provision to offer more child-initiated learning and more physical challenge. It seems that the greatest influence may have been on reversing the trend to sanitise the early years environment at all costs. Indeed, the 'risk averse society' (Gill 2007) debate seems to be having an impact throughout education, not just within the early years, with many primary schools and even the secondary sector giving the Forest School movement credence. As there has been little research to draw upon within the UK other than the small-scale Murray and O'Brien studies cited in Miller and Pound (2011), it is hard to determine the scale of the influence or the benefits that provision is indeed promoting. The experience within the UK is set, as with all the early years policies discussed here, within an entirely different cultural heritage from where it originated and, as such, will have a different pedagogy dependent on the values, experience, belief, training, knowledge and situation of the leaders. For example, our climatic tolerance as practitioners may be different. Indeed, many aspirant EYPs on our courses talk of the reluctance of practitioners to participate in outdoor activity. How then will this influence the quality of the experience offered?

The true Forest School experience requires significant extended engagement with the outdoor environment that is not negatively influenced by prevailing weather conditions. Forest School experiences within the UK are often specially arranged and timetabled events over a minimum period of 12 weeks. Very few settings are literally within large open spaces allowing free access. Ideally the Forest School experience has an extended time frame and is a regular opportunity.

More generally the influence of this approach can be seen in the outdoor access that all early years settings are to provide. The emphasis on the outdoor environment seeks to counter concern for sedentary indoor childhoods. Louv (2008) illustrates an American concern for the continuing demise of access to outdoor space. Whether our adoption of the approach has been endorsed because it is a bottom-up attempt, for example at Bridgwater College, Somerset (from the mid-1990s), to provide a creative dimension to learning, or whether politicians have endorsed it because of similar American ideals is difficult to determine. The need for outdoor play has, however, made its way into statutory regulation by Ofsted through policy decisions.

- In studies of child well-being by the OECD, the Nordic countries generally top the tables in terms of child well-being.
- The cultural integration of outdoor experiences is perceived to be greater in Nordic countries than others.

New Zealand – Te Whariki

This curriculum has a social constructivist approach and so fits neatly with the aims of HighScope, Head Start and Sure Start programmes. Where it differs, however, is that it takes children's own culture and seeks to weave it through the curriculum. It sees the social context of the child as of prime importance and does not view the localised culture as deficit but integral to the child's self-concept and identity.

Carr and Lee (2012) acknowledge the difficulties we face globally in terms of aligning fixed outcomes to the qualities that we wish to nurture in young children. They suggest that 'assessment for learning plays a powerful role in the construction of a learner identity' (ibid.: 1). It is therefore essential that we find a way of charting progress that develops from the desirable qualities we wish to nurture in early childhood rather than constructing a fixed ability proforma that defines the child.

The Te Whariki curriculum embodies a play-based approach but acknowledges teacher responsibility to extend play (Synodi 2010). The division between early childhood practitioners and teachers has all but disappeared, as since 1988 both have been following equivalent three-year courses that have become the benchmark qualification in registered early childhood services (Dalli 2008). This has eventually led to equal pay – a process that has taken some 20 years to achieve (ibid.).

- The Te Whariki curriculum is integral to the local culture.
- The division between early childhood teachers and those teachers working in statutory schooling has disappeared.

Reggio Emilia

The Reggio philosophy has found many advocates among early years practitioners within the UK, although it is hard to see that it has influenced policy makers rather than just policy implementers. The Reggio emphasis on the environment goes further than any other approach, giving it a central place as the child's third teacher. Because Reggio is focused on the environment in this way it could be argued that the concept of enabling environments has its roots in the Reggio philosophy. However, a strict adherence to statements of expected achievements and a specified curriculum couldn't be more adverse to Reggio practice. In Reggio settings the environment with its provocations could be said to help create the curriculum. The emphasis on the arts within the Reggio philosophy, with the prominence of the *atelier* and *atelerista*, creates a unique focus that could be considered as a cultural priority. Indeed, the attention to the development of the senses through the environment provided, the kitchen being central and the smells creating a sense of anticipation of the meal, seems to be culturally important to its Italian roots. The Reggio approach sees the child as a highly competent activist within his or her own learning.

In contrast to HighScope the Reggio approach draws more on Vygotskian theory than Piagetian. The practitioner is there to guide the child and to learn with them, there is an acknowledgement of the reciprocity of learning, and learning is seen as a continuous journey. The story of the learning from provocation, the initial stimulus, to outcome, the end of the interest, is charted through story. A narrative of the learning is created. This narrative can be viewed by others and aims to be shared documentation of the experience between the children and the practitioners. This has many parallels with the Te Whariki learning stories. The EYFS (2008, 2012) Learning Journey could be seen to have been influenced by these approaches; however, most Learning Journeys that I have seen have been heavily practitioner led and overtly annotated with the outcomes of curricular targets. Learning Journeys tend to be the justification from the curriculum rather than an explanation of how the curriculum has been shaped by the child, the performativity agenda being clearly foregrounded in the Journey documentation.

The new requirement to test two-year-olds against a range of explicit targets also completely distances the Reggio philosophy from England's ECE practice.

It would be fair to say that the Reggio Emilia approach carries great weight with those who seek to operate developmentally sound practice but would not be quantitative enough in outcomes for our politicians who see education as a commodity. Indeed, New (2013) suggests that in America Reggio Emilia seems a mirage rather than a real possibility.

- Reggio Emilia has a strong philosophical basis on which practice is based.
- It relies heavily on the environment as the 'child's third teacher'.
- It is an approach that has come from the bottom up; that is, from those who live and work in the region.

Conclusion

The introduction by the Coalition of the political Big Society idea would seem to offer political will to enable those who seek more local collective solutions to services to operate outside of central control, as is the case of the population of Reggio Emilia in determining the direction of their childhood services. Bamfield (2012: 161) suggests that 'The Big Society is therefore based on the twin goals of decentralising and limiting state power, on the one hand, and enabling and extending civic and democratic engagement, on the other.'

Just as Reggio Emilia settings are at the heart of their communities, so too are many children's centres in the UK. Indeed, it could be said that Labour had become very successful in creating the beginnings of a Big Society by creating umbrella centres where communities could gather. Their success in harnessing local support was evident in the protests at the closure of some of these centres when the Coalition came to power – a Coalition that Baldock et al. (2013: 24) suggest soon started 'chipping away at the changes the Labour Party had introduced'. Bamfield (2012) gives the example of a user of a children's centre explaining that it had been like her family, a place where the communities meet and individuals build bridges with one another. It is ironic then that, in decentralising finance to local authorities to make decisions on local need a part of the passing of control for services from central to local government, the Coalition could have actually inadvertently destroyed the very networks that the Big Society needs in order to be seen as successful. Given that the Labour government over its last ten years had been seen by the middle classes as very successful in building up support for parents and children, these are the very people who are being alienated by the closure of centres in areas that are not deemed to be deprived. The Coalition insists that the closures are down to local authorities, who with restricted budgets find themselves having central targets to meet on deprivation and therefore targeting those at the expense of universal provision. Funds are limited and choices hard to make, but authorities have been passed the difficult decision making under rhetoric of flexibility and responding to local need. The Department for Education suggested:

> The Early Intervention Grant (EIG) replaced a number of centrally directed grants to support services for children, young people and families. The grant is not ring-fenced, allowing greater flexibility and freedom at local level, to respond to local needs, drive reform and promote early intervention more effectively.
>
> (DfE 2013)

The cynic would suggest that this is the 'buck passing' of difficult decisions to the local level so that blame is deflected from central government and they are not implicated in making the specific decision. Reggio Emilia is a local initiative – services for local people administered at the local level, however it is a local community that has had stable political influence for over 40 years. Baldock *et al.* (2013: 106) suggests that:

> it is clear that politicians of all parties are inclined to look abroad mainly for models that confirm the validity of their own approaches, rather than to examine what is happening elsewhere in ways that might challenge their preconceptions.

Critical reflective practice it seems is not within the skill set of a politician; perhaps as they live with constant job insecurity they are themselves unable to flourish at any point in their tenure. Baldock *et al.* (2013) further the argument by suggesting that less than intelligent use has been made of reports from international agencies such as the OECD and EC, who provide regular review and analysis of the failures and successes of each country's policies. Indeed, if the evidence had been analysed with an open mind and by abandoning political dogma, we might have seen our policy decisions shaped by the obvious successes of our northern European neighbours rather than replicating the failure to allow families and children to flourish that America seems to have achieved through its obvious levels of inequality.

REFLECTIVE QUESTIONS

■ Do you think that UK early years policy makers appropriately consider international evidence when determining policy direction?

■ Have you seen evidence of international policy in your work or in settings that you have visited?

■ How do you make sure that you offer children developmentally appropriate experiences?

References

Allen, G. (2011) *Early Intervention: The next steps*, London: Department of Work and Pensions. Available online at www.dwp.gov.uk/docs/early-intervention-next-steps.pdf (accessed 2 July 2013).

Alvestad, M. and Duncan, J. (2006) '"The value is enormous – it's priceless I think!" New Zealand preschool teachers' understandings of the early childhood curriculum in New Zealand: a comparative perspective', *International Journal of Early Childhood*, 38(1): 31–45.

Baldock, P., Fitzgerald, D. and Kay, J. (2013) *Understanding Early Years Policy* (3rd edn), London: Sage.

Bamfield, L. (2012) 'Beginning the Big Society in the early years', *The Political Quarterly*, 82(s1): 158–77.

Carr, M. and Lee, W. (2012) *Learning Stories: Constructing learner identities in early education*, London: Sage.

Cunningham, P. (2012) *Politics and the Primary Teacher*, London: Routledge.

Dalli, C. (2008) 'The new teacher in New Zealand', in Miller, L. and Cable, C. (eds) *Professionalism in the Early Years*, London: Hodder Education.

Dalli, C. (2011) 'A curriculum of open possibilities: a New Zealand kindergarten teacher's view of professional practice', *Early Years: An International Journal of Research and Development*, 31(3): 229–43.

Department for Children, Schools and Families (DCSF) (2008) *Statutory Framework for the Early Years Foundation Stage*, London: DCSF.

Department for Education (DfE) (2012a) *The Early Years Foundation Stage (EYFS)*, London: DfE.

Department for Education (DfE) (2012b) *Developing a New Vision for the Early Years*. Available online at www.education.gov.uk/childrenandyoungpeople/early learningandchildcare/delivery/a0074569/developing-a-new-vision-for-the-early-years (accessed 25 January 2013).

Department for Education (DFE) (2012c) www.education.gov.uk/childrenand youngpeople/earlylearningandchildcare/delivery/funding/a0070357/eig-faqs (accessed 4 September 2013)

Einarsdottir, J. (2006) 'From pre-school to primary school: when different contexts meet', *Scandinavian Journal of Educational Research*, 50(2): 165–84.

Field, F. (2010) *The Foundation Years: Preventing poor children becoming poor adults: The report of the Independent Review on Poverty and Life Chances*, London: Cabinet Office. Available online at www.nfm.org.uk/component/jdownloads/finish/74/333 (accessed 2 July 2013).

Gill, T. (2007) *No Fear: Growing up in a risk adverse society*, London: Calouste Gulbenkian Foundation.

Holt, N. (2010) *Bringing the HighScope Approach to your Early Years Practice*, Abingdon: Routledge.

Louv, R. (2008) *Last Child in the Woods: Saving our children from nature deficit disorder*, Chapel Hill, NC: Algonquin Books.

MacNaughton, G. (2005) *Doing Foucault in Early Childhood Studies: Applying poststructural ideas*, Abingdon: Routledge.

Miller, L. and Hevey, D. (2012) *Policy Issues in the Early Years*, London: Sage.

Miller, L. and Pound, L. (2011) *Theories and Approaches to Learning in the Early Years (Critical Issues in the Early Years)*, London: Sage.

Moss, P. (ed.) (2013) *Early Childhood and Compulsory Education: Reconceptualising the relationship (contesting early childhood)*, London: Routledge.

Moss, P. and Dahlberg, G. (2008) 'Beyond quality in early childhood education and care', *New Zealand Journal of Teachers' Work*, 5(1): 3–12.

Nairn, A. (2011) *Children's Well-being in UK, Sweden and Spain: The role of inequality and materialism*, London: Ipsos MORI Social Research Institute.

New, R. (2013) 'Reggio Emilia in the 21st century', in Roopnarine, J. and Johnson, J. (eds) *Approaches to Early Childhood Education* (6th edn), Upper Saddle River, NJ: Pearson.

Oberhuemer, P. (2005) 'International perspectives on early childhood curricula', *International Journal of Early Childhood*, 37(1): 27–37.

Organisation for Economic Co-operation and Development (OECD) (2006) *Starting Strong II: Early childhood education and care*, Paris: OECD.

Palmer, S. (2007) *Toxic Childhood: How the modern world is damaging our children and what we can do about it*, London: Orion.

Penn, H. (2011) *Quality In Early Childhood Services: An international perspective*, Maidenhead: Open University Press.

Plantenga, J. and Remery, C. (2009) *The Provision of Childcare Services: A comparative review of 30 European countries*, Luxembourg: Office for Official Publications of the European Communities.

Pound, L. (2011) *Influencing Early Childhood Education: Key figures, philosophies and ideas: Key themes, philosophies and theories*, Maidenhead: Open University Press.

Pramling Samuelsson, I. and Asplund Carlsson, M. (2008) 'The playing learning child: towards a pedagogy of early childhood', *Scandinavian Journal of Education Research*, 52(6): 623–41.

Roopnarine, J. and Johnson, J. (2012) *Approaches to Early Childhood Education* (6th edn), Upper Saddle River, NJ: Pearson.

Synodi, E. (2010) 'Play in the kindergarten: the case of Norway, Sweden, New Zealand and Japan', *International Journal of Early Years Education*, 18(3): 185–200.

Tizzard, B. and Hughes, M. (1984) *Young Children Learning: Talking and Thinking*, Oxford: Blackwell.

Tovey, H. (2007) *Playing Outdoors: Spaces and places, risk and challenge*, Maidenhead: Open University Press.

Unicef (2007) *An Overview of Child Well-being in Rich Countries*, Florence: UNICEF.

Vandenbroeck, M., Coussée, F. and Bradt, L. (2010) 'The social and political construction of early childhood education', *British Journal of Educational Studies*, 58(2): 139–53.

White, D. (2012) 'The economic return of Iceland has proved that the joke was on us', *Independent: Ireland*, 16 December.

Wilkinson, R. and Pickett, K. (2010) *The Spirit Level: Why equality is better for everyone*, London: Penguin Books.

4 The Early Years Foundation Stage

Tickell and beyond: a critical perspective

Zenna Kingdon

Introduction

This chapter will critically evaluate how the Early Years Foundation Stage (EYFS), comprising both the original (DCSF 2008) and the newly revised (DfE 2012) versions of the curriculum, was developed. It will consider the impact of policies and reports that have influenced its development over a number of decades. The EYFS was implemented from September 2008. It was intended to provide a framework that would improve outcomes for children from birth to five. The EYFS (2008) drew together a number of other policies and frameworks into one document. On 6 July 2010, less than two years after its introduction, the then Children's Minister, Sarah Teather, asked Dame Clare Tickell, Chief Executive of Action for Children, to carry out an independent review of the EYFS (2003) to consider how this could be less bureaucratic and more focused on supporting children's early learning. The review reported on 30 March 2011 with a view to implementing any changes from September 2012 onwards. This fast-paced change has been a feature of the early years sector over the last decade, and this is explored in some detail.

The curriculum will be contextualised both in world terms and within England and Wales. England and Wales were not alone in developing a curriculum framework for the youngest children. This appears to be fuelled by a recognition that we have moved into knowledge economies in which children need to be able to learn and contribute.

The roles and responsibilities of practitioners who deliver the EYFS (2008, 2012) will be considered, including some discussion of the Nutbrown review (2012) and other discussions of qualifications.

Finally, the chapter will consider the future, for which of course there are no certainties.

Early years curricula

The EYFS (2008, 2012)is one of many examples of curricula that are intended to support the learning and development of young children. From the late 1990s onwards governments in countries from England to Australia and New Zealand, including many European countries, developed curriculum frameworks and regulated at national level what occurred in the early years sector (Oberhuemer 2005). Oberhuemer (2005) suggests that there were a number of reasons for the increased interest in early years education and these included recognition of the status of education in a knowledge economy, recent developments in neuroscience research that demonstrated the impact of high-quality early years provision, and the provision of a framework in which there could be clear communication between parents and settings. These curricula took a number of different constructs and were from overarching guidance through to prescriptions of what should be taught and assessed. Hedges *et al.* (2011: 185) suggest that 'curriculum is a highly contested construct'. However, they argue that much of the literature suggests that these curricula should be focused on children's interests and their needs. Pascal and Bertram (2002: 92) caution that we live in an 'audited society where that which is measurable is seen as significant'. They further argue that narrow focuses on literacy and numeracy may impact on children's deeper attitudes to learning. Curricula such as Te Whariki focus on notions of well-being and belonging with clear references to children's feelings that are affirmed through their pre-school experiences, approaches that curricula in the UK seem less keen to adopt (Soler and Miller 2003). Pascal and Bertram (2002: 93) additionally suggest that, in order for children to become effective learners they need to develop three elements: 'dispositions to learn; social competence and self-concept; emotional well-being'. While in many of the curricula there is a focus on literacy and numeracy, these three strands are also seen in many of the early years curricula that have been developed, along with recognition that children engage more fully where the adults demonstrate awareness and concern for their interests (Hedges *et al.* 2011).

Contextualising the EYFS

In order to understand where the EYFS (2008, 2012) has come from it is important to have some understanding of the history of early years provision in the United Kingdom. While the roots of nursery education go back to Robert Owen in 1816, who advocated free and unstructured play, there was little evidence of it on a large scale. Prior to 1990 there was little interest in early years education, among other reasons because it was not seen as a political priority. One of the first occasions when early years provision was mentioned in any detail was in the Plowden report (1967). In 1963 Lady Bridget Plowden was asked by the then chair of the Central Advisory Council for Education (England), Sir Edward Boyle, to 'consider primary education in all its aspects' (Gillard 2011). This was the first major report into primary education since the Hadow reports of the 1930s. Plowden's report was considered to be firmly based in Piagetian theory (ibid.). Chapter 2 of Plowden (1967), 'The children, their growth and development', is seen as providing the psychological basis for the report. The report can be seen not only as being of its time but also as a new approach to education. Gone was the learning by rote and here was an approach that for the first time in England advocated a child–centred approach to education:

> At the heart of the educational process lies the child. No advances in policy, no acquisitions of new equipment, have their desired effect unless they are in harmony with the nature of the child, unless they are fundamentally acceptable to him [sic].
>
> (Plowden 1967: 7)

The notion of allowing children a say in their education was new. Necessarily, alongside an approach that advocated child–centred learning was recognition that children are individuals and that they would need treating as such: 'Individual differences between children of the same age are so great that any class, however homogeneous it seems, must always be treated as a body of children needing individual and different attention' (ibid.: 25).

Plowden advocated an approach that recognised children as individuals with different needs and desires as well as different interests. This is something that is promoted in the EYFS (2012) today. Its routes can clearly be traced back to Plowden (1967).

While discussions of childhood were not new, a recognition that children should be given opportunities to live as children rather than their future selves was new in educational terms. It was Jean Jacques Rousseau

(1712–78) (Nutbrown *et al.* 2008) who first established the notion of childhood as a specific phase rather than simply as a preparation for adulthood and work. He argued against the Christian tradition, suggesting that children should be allowed to respond to nature, particularly during their early years of life. Discussions within the Plowden report (1967) of an individualised approach to learning were the first time that such notions had been recognised within the education system.

Plowden was essentially a report of recommendations. While the report focused on primary schools and was to answer the question of at what age children should transfer to secondary education, it also looked at provision prior to compulsory education. Chapter 9 of the report focused on nursery education with the last paragraph being a list of 13 recommendations. Focusing on those recommendations it is possible to divide them into three groups, those of their time, those of relevance now and those that are still to come to fruition. The Plowden report had a significant impact on primary education for more than two decades and continues to be discussed today. It also had a significant impact on early years education. Plowden (1967) was the first to discuss qualifications in the early years. She recommended that nursery groups should be ultimately under the supervision of qualified teachers and that nursery assistants should have completed a two-year qualification. Parallels can be drawn with the continuing debates that have led to the introduction of the Early Years Professional Status (EYPS) and the recommendations of the Nutbrown review (2012), in which there is a call for strengthening of the level 3 qualification.

- Rousseau first introduced the notion of childhood as a phase in its own right, while Plowden (1967) clearly put children at the centre of the educational process.
- The Plowden report (1967) was the first report of its kind since the Hadow reports of the 1930s and was to have influence for decades.
- Many of Plowden's recommendations for nursery education can be seen to be relevant in early years provision today.

From Plowden to Rumbold

After Plowden (1967) the role of early years education was not significantly discussed until the Rumbold report (1990). In 1972 Margaret Thatcher had put forward a white paper on education – a framework for expansion, in which she stated that over the next ten years free nursery places should be made available for all three- and four-year-old children who wanted them. This promise was unfortunately not fulfilled due to the economic recession of the 1970s and 1980s (Kwon 2002). Later Thatcher appointed Sir Keith Joseph as her first Secretary of State for education, and he advocated that pre-school provision had an important role to play for children from poorer families (Baldock 2011). However, little was done about it until much later. In 1996 free nursery places for four-year-olds began to be introduced, but it was not until the twenty-first century that we saw universal provision for three- and four-year-olds.

The Plowden report (1967) and subsequent white papers were set against a backdrop of non-intervention in education by governments and ministers. The Ruskin College speech, as it has become known, made by the then prime minister James Callaghan in October 1976, was a significant turning point in the direction and politicisation of education in England and Wales (Phillips and Harper-Jones 2002). While in the early part of the twenty-first-century intervention in the direction of education policy by both the media and politicians is considered to be the norm, this was not the case prior to 1976. Traditionally, the role of Secretary for Education was not considered to be high profile and was given by successive prime ministers to token women MPs within the cabinet, including Margaret Thatcher (1970–4) (Batteson 1997). The 1970s had been a decade that had seen the greatest decline of the country after the Second World War. This was coupled with growing concerns about the effectiveness of schooling. For example, there had been the William Tyndale affair, in which one North London school was identified as being out of control and which had subsequently involved the Inner London Education Authority (ILEA) in a protracted investigation that led to the sacking of the Headteacher, deputy and five other members of staff (Davis 2002). The affair gained notoriety in the press at a national level. When Callaghan made his speech he knew that what he was doing was unprecedented, but at the same time he had concerns that schooling, particularly secondary education, was not meeting the needs of industry nor including parents (Phillips and Harper-Jones 2002; Batteson 1997). There was a further decade before significant changes were seen in education. In 1988 the National Curriculum was introduced. Its introduction could be argued to be the most significant event in the history of education in England and Wales.

Like Plowden (1967), the Rumbold report, *Starting with Quality* (1990), was a report of recommendations, however it focused solely on the youngest children and their specific needs. The discussions within the report were linked to discussions that demonstrated an awareness that the National Curriculum (1988), which had recently been introduced for all pupils in compulsory education, would not be appropriate for younger children. Rumbold (1990) recommended a specific curriculum for children under the age of five. She stated that it should be 'coherent in terms of the child's existing knowledge, understanding and skills, and that it should be experienced in an environment which fosters the development of social relationships and positive attitudes to learning' (ibid.: 9).

The report demonstrated an awareness that play is central to the way in which young children learn and experience the world. She drew on a previous government report to evidence that play that was purposeful and well planned was pleasurable for children and supported their learning in a number of areas. Rumbold (1990) recognised that a focus on formal individual subject-based learning was inappropriate and that younger children experienced the world and their learning in broader terms. She stated that those in government should develop clear guidelines for providers that demonstrated how the curriculum should be planned and organised and how it would ensure progression to a curriculum for older children. She also went on to say that appropriately designed high-quality experiences needed to be supported by appropriate resources. Linked to notions of quality she indicated that 'parental involvement does not merely contribute to quality but is essential if early education is to be successful' (ibid.: 13). The notion of partnership with parents was a feature of the time. The 1989 Children Act had just established the idea that parents did not have rights, but responsibilities. It further aimed to ensure that those who had responsibility for a child's welfare, be that statutory or voluntary agencies as well as the parents, worked together and that there was greater cooperation that would lead to better outcomes for children.

Alongside discussions of quality Rumbold (1990) raised questions about suitable qualifications for practitioners working with young children and discussed notions of career development. She suggested that many of the qualifications that were recognised within the sector were not actually accredited and lacked academic rigour and currency. She argued that the qualifications did not provide a basis for a career structure, which she felt was necessary within the early years sector. She felt that the National Nursery Examination Board (NNEB) qualification, which was the most widely recognised within the sector, carried no academic currency, which she felt was particularly problematic. In 1990, 250,000 four-year-olds were being educated in Reception classes in schools.

She advocated that teachers who were responsible for children under the age of five should have some appropriate training for working with such young children. Rumbold (1990) predicted that the numbers of four-year-olds in schools would rise. Now in 2012 it would seem that there some five times that number in Reception classes. Here the EYFS (2012) is delivered often by staff who have no training in working with our youngest children. The private, voluntary and independent sector was only beginning to come under tighter regulation in 1990. It was not until Ofsted took over responsibility for the registration and inspection of daycare and childminding in 2001 and the introduction of the Care Standards Act in 2000 that there became a legal minimum qualification for running such services. This minimum qualification remains currently as a level 3 (Nutbrown 2012). Rumbold (1990: 15), like Plowden before her, felt that 'considerable value can be gained from the employment of teachers in day nurseries'. She clearly recognised that those staff who were to work with our youngest children needed to be appropriately qualified and respected for their professionalism.

In order to meet the needs of these youngest children, Rumbold (1990) called for an appropriate curriculum for children in the pre-school phase. She drew upon research that demonstrated that during the phase from birth to five, children develop rapidly both physically and intellectually. She recognised that the 'advent of the National Curriculum for children of compulsory school age clearly has implications for the work of those who are responsible for children up to that age' (ibid.: 8). Therefore she felt that it was necessary to be concerned with an appropriate curriculum for children under five. Her report was successful in ensuring that children under the age of five were not included in the National Curriculum, something that many working in the early years sector felt was highly inappropriate for children of their age (Baldock 2011). Instead, younger children were to have a curriculum that recognised their age phase and their requirements. Unfortunately that was not how the first curriculum was received by the early years community.

- Rumbold (1990) was the first to advocate a specific curriculum to meet the needs of children under the age of five.
- She was concerned with notions of quality and saw play as key to an appropriate curriculum for the youngest children.
- Rumbold was the first to suggest that effective partnerships with parents were part of what ensured quality experiences for young children.

Curriculum development: desirable learning outcomes of the EYFS (2008)

The first curriculum was introduced in 1996. The full title of the document was *Nursery Education: Desirable outcomes for children's learning on entering compulsory education* (SCAA 1996), although usually it was simply referred to as the DLOs (desirable learning outcomes). This initial curriculum was closely linked to the nursery voucher system and was concerned with school readiness. Settings that wished to accept the vouchers had to be able to demonstrate that they were supporting children in making progress towards the DLOs on entering school (Kwon 2002). This curriculum was short-lived. It was considered to be in conflict with a view of childhood that was held by many within the sector and their view of what an early childhood curriculum should look like (Soler and Miller 2003). Concerns were raised about the nature of the curriculum. David (1998) contrasted the DLOs, in which there was an emphasis on literacy and numeracy, with their Welsh equivalent, which suggested that early childhood was a time for adventure and discovery and clearly advocated play. She argued, echoing the work of Sylva (1997, cited in David 1998) that the DLOs were narrowly focused on cognitive outcomes and failed to acknowledge creativity and in particular personal and social development. She further discussed the importance of emotions in learning, recognising that self-esteem impacts on children's achievement in other areas, including literacy and numeracy.

In 1997 the newly elected Labour government wanted to change the way in which early years education was funded. Alongside these changes came a change in the curriculum. In September 2000 *Curriculum Guidance for the Foundation Stage* (DfEE 2000), for children aged three to five, was launched. Children who were within the age group were considered to be part of the Foundation Stage. The curriculum was developed in collaboration with the early childhood community. While it continued to focus on learning goals, there was also an emphasis on describing learning opportunities and experiences that would meet the needs of young children. The curriculum was delivered through six areas of learning: personal, social and emotional development; communication, language and literacy; mathematical development; knowledge and understanding of the world; physical development; and creative development. Children were expected to make their way through the curriculum following a series of stepping stones that described their learning until they reached the learning goals. This curriculum began to demonstrate an awareness of research into child development and was developed in consultation with members of the early childhood community (Soler and Miller 2003). One of the key features of the curriculum was the focus on partnership with parents. They were described as the 'children's first and most enduring educators' (QCA 2000: 9). This recognition of the significant role that parents play in young children's lives was decisive in influencing the future direction of the sector. Baldock (2011) would argue that this was one of the important steps taken by the Conservative government of 1979–97. They made radical reforms of regulations within the 1989 Children Act. These reforms included changing from parental rights to parental responsibilities, and Section X considered the regulation of daycare and childminding, extending the range of services that needed to register and making the age range 0–8 as opposed to 0–5 (ibid.).

Many within the early years sector saw the introduction of *Birth to Three Matters* (DfES 2002) as a positive step. It was developed by Lesley Abbott and colleagues at Manchester Metropolitan University as part of a DfES-funded project (Baldock *et al.* 2005). The curriculum was not statutory but was offered to all providers working with the youngest children. It provided guidance on what was considered to be good practice for those working with these very young children. Unlike *Curriculum Guidance for the Foundation Stage* (DfEE 2000), which discussed requirements and what practitioners should and must do, *Birth to Three Matters* (DfES 2002) adopted an approach that stressed the importance of relationships (Duffy 2010). This curriculum was felt by many to have adopted approaches that experts such as Elinor Goldschmied, Sonia Jackson and Peter Elfer had argued for, for many years (Baldock *et al.* 2005). These approaches had been adopted in the best settings and were a demonstration of high-quality practice. *Birth to Three Matters* (DfES 2002) was a clear recognition, sanctioned by government, that the needs of the youngest children and the ways in which they learn were different from the learning styles and needs of older children.

It quickly became apparent that there was a mismatch in both language and approach between the *Curriculum Guidance for the Foundation Stage* (DfEE 2000) and *Birth to Three Matters* (DfES 2002). The latter had only been written two years later but there had been a shift in emphasis and approach. The person-centred approach and language was a reflection of the *Every Child Matters* agenda (DfES 2004), which had been developed in response to the death of Victoria Climbié and the subsequent report by Lord Laming (2003). There was an increasing recognition of the importance of quality provision in the early years (Duffy 2010). These led to the decision to create a single framework that would incorporate the two curricula and the *National Standards for Under Eights Day Care and Childminding* (DfEE 2001). In September 2008 the Early Years Foundation Stage became the statutory curriculum for anyone delivering care or education to any child from birth through to the end of the Foundation Stage.

The introduction of the EYFS

The EYFS (2008) was broadly welcomed by the early years community. It created a distinctive phase for children that was considered to be developmentally appropriate, advocating a play-based curriculum that also merged notions of education and care (Roberts-Holmes 2012). Historically within the UK there had been a separation of these two aspects of early childhood and values were attributed to those working within the different sectors. The EYFS (2008) was referred to as a principled approach and was arranged around four broad themes: A Unique Child, Positive Relationships, Enabling Environments, and Learning and Development. This curriculum advocated a play-based, child-centred approach, in which planning was developed in response to children's interests. The six areas of learning remained, along with 69 early learning goals that children were expected to work towards. Concerns continued to be voiced about both curricula and the practitioners who were being asked to deliver them.

The EYFS (2008) was predicated on a sociocultural theoretical approach in which children are seen as effective co-constructors of knowledge (Roberts-Holmes 2012). There is a clear expectation that the curriculum will be delivered through a play-based experiential approach. However, 'a legislative emphasis on play as an appropriate medium of learning has not necessarily guaranteed its successful implementation' (Howard 2010: 91). Howard (2010) goes on to note that, while the legislation may support a play-based approach, there was a danger that the reality could be something different. Time and resources often mean that there is a risk of practitioners focusing narrowly on educational basics and on the defined outcomes (ibid.). She goes on to discuss the psychological barriers to play, noting that these may include practitioners' knowledge and their confidence in providing a play-based approach as well as parental attitudes (ibid.). Roberts-Holmes (2012) highlights the divide within early years: 78 per cent of nursery places are within the private, voluntary and independent sector while only 22 per cent of Foundation Stage provision is delivered within the maintained sector. Current research into experiences of practitioners delivering the EYFS

(2008) appears to focus on those in the maintained sector, which gives a slanted view of the experience of delivering the curriculum. Howard (2010) and Roberts-Holmes (2012) have conducted research that investigates practitioners' experiences of play and of delivering the EYFS (2008) respectively. However, this research is located in the maintained sector. Here staff demonstrated concerns about their lack of training in both child development and play. It appears that many within the maintained sector are working in the Foundation Stage without any formal qualifications for this age phase (Roberts-Holmes 2012; Howard 2010). Howard (2010) notes that even where they hold relevant qualifications they appear to have significantly less play training than other professionals such as play therapists, play-workers and hospital play specialists. She suggests that this lack of appropriate training can have a negative impact on the ability of practitioners to provide appropriate play opportunities. Instead, they become prone to more formal approaches that are easier to plan and assess, and that meet parental expectations for academic achievement. Furthermore, Wood (2010: 16) suggests that the EYFS (2008) draws on the Effective Provision of Pre-school Education (EPPE) project (Sylva et al. 2004) and locates play within a 'discourse of effectiveness'. This suggests that the play that is encouraged within the EYFS (2008) is a form of play that is in some way measurable. She further argues that, while the EYFS (2008) advocates planned and purposeful play, this could be open to interpretation. The threat is that play could be misinterpreted in practice and lead to adult planning being privileged over children's planning (Wood 2010). Brooker (2011) discusses the fact that both EPPE (2004) and *Researching Effective Pedagogy in the Early Years* (REPEY – Siraj-Blatchford et al. 2002) have had a significant impact on both policy development and practitioner understanding. The result appears to be that practitioners and policy makers feel that they can comment with some assurance on what works for young children. Play is considered to be the most effective vehicle for young children's learning. Historically, play was seen by those within the early years sector as vital. Both the need and the right to play are advocated in western cultures, underpinned by decades of research. Vygotsky (1978: 102) stated that play:

> creates a zone of proximal development of the child. In play a child always behaves beyond his [sic] average age, above his daily behaviour; in play it is as though he were a head taller than himself.

Brooker (2011) argues that play pedagogy appears to bring together two disparate approaches to early childhood: on the one hand there is the eighteenth-century Romantics notion of play as a natural part of childhood and, on the other, the twentieth-century developmentalists' approach, which suggested that play was the most effective way for young children to learn. Both EPPE (2004) and REPEY (2002) supported this through their research in which they discovered that children in high-quality settings were offered appropriate opportunities to engage in a play-based curriculum and had their learning supported by the practitioners through episodes of sustained shared thinking. These seemingly contradictory approaches to play have come together within the EYFS (2008). Within the statutory advice, 'there is the affirmation of play as the expression of children's natural inclinations . . . there is the view, supported by research, that play is the means to achieve curricular learning outcomes' (Brooker 2011: 142). The EYFS (2008) was a complex curriculum that recognised the salience of early childhood as a distinct phase in child development and the need for a broad curriculum that demonstrated a balance of adult-led and child-initiated learning experiences based on close observation of the child and delivered through a play-based approach.

- The EYFS (2008, 2012) is a play-based curriculum, however research evidence suggests that those who deliver it have little play training.
- Play as an approach to early years is embedded in both the Romantics' and developmentalists' approaches.
- The EYFS (2008, 2012) advocates a broad and balanced curriculum that allows children to develop through their own natural curiosity.

The Tickell review

The EYFS (2008) had been delivered for less than two years when Sarah Teather, the then Minister for Children and Families, appointed Dame Clare Tickell, Chief Executive of Action for Children, to carry out an independent review of the EYFS (2008) to consider how this could be less bureaucratic and more focused on supporting children's early learning. The review, *The Early Years: Foundations for life, health and learning* (Tickell 2011), was to cover four main areas: scope of regulation – whether there should be one single framework for all early years providers; learning and development – looking at the latest evidence about children's development and what is needed to give them the best start at school; assessment – whether young children's development should be formally assessed, at a certain age, and what this should cover; and welfare – the minimum standards to keep children safe and support their healthy development. The review reported on 30 March 2011 with a view to implementing any changes from September 2012 onwards.

In total Tickell (2011) made 46 recommendations about changes that should be made to the EYFS (2008). She recommended that personal, social and emotional development, communication and language, and physical development are identified as prime areas of learning in the EYFS. Alongside the three prime areas she proposed four specific areas in which the prime skills would be applied: literacy, mathematics, expressive arts and design, and understanding the world. She further recommended that the government investigate as a matter of urgency how the development of children's English language skills could be effectively supported and assessed. She commented that she also recommended that playing and exploring, active learning, and creating and thinking critically should be highlighted in the EYFS as three characteristics of effective teaching and learning (Tickell 2011).

Initially the review was welcomed by the sector. The 69 goals were to be slimmed down to just 17. Tickell had consulted widely and included the views of parents and practitioners in her recommendations (Gaunt 2011). Representatives of the Pre-school Learning Alliance, The National Day Nursery Association and the National Childminding Association all commented positively on the document. They felt that it was a thoughtful and considered review that had clearly listened to the voices of many within the sector and recognised that the EYFS (2008) was valued by practitioners (ibid.). Thomson (2011) commented that the revised curriculum focused on how, rather than what, children should learn and this was seen as a positive move. Concerns were raised about how the EYFS (2008) and its methods of working with children were shared with the parents, as parents continued to be concerned about the lack of formal teaching in the early years. Langston (2011) argues that the EYFS sits at the heart of a number of government policy agendas. During the summer of 2011 the government published its document, *Supporting Families in the Foundation Years* (DfE 2011). This brings together the Field review (2010), which looked at poverty and life chances, the Allen review (2011), which was concerned with early intervention, and the Tickell review (2011) and gives detailed responses to these reports, with a clear direction of travel. These plans were mostly met with a positive response from within the early years sector. However, more detailed analysis of the new EYFS (2012) document raised some areas of concern. The introduction to the document focuses on school readiness, in order that children have a solid foundation for future progress both within school and throughout their lives. This is in many respects to be expected, however Langston (2011: 17) points out that it is not what is said, rather 'what is omitted, which is that early childhood should be valued in its own right'. That early childhood is a specific phase has long been a central tenet of the early years sector and any undermining of this will be met with justifiable concern. At the time of writing the new EYFS (2012) has been implemented for a very short time. It is therefore impossible to comment on the effectiveness of the changes that have been made. Positive attributes of the new curriculum can be identified as: the recognition that, when children are playing and exploring, when they are engaged in active learning, and when they are creating and thinking critically, effective teaching and learning will be occurring; the focus on three prime areas, including personal, social and emotional development, physical development, and communication and language; and the recommendation of a reduction in unnecessary paperwork and the encouragement of staff to spend more time with the children. It is to be hoped that these changes will have a positive impact on children's life chances and support them in flourishing as individuals.

The Nutbrown review

Tickell (2011) made comment about the qualifications of the staff working within the early years sector. She advocated a minimum level 3 qualification for all staff and recommended that the government maintained an ambition of having a graduate-led workforce. The government commissioned Professor Cathy Nutbrown to review early education and childcare qualifications. The final report with 19 recommendations was published in June 2012. Like the Tickell review (2011), the Nutbrown review (2012) was broadly welcomed by the early years sector. However, for some, the recommendations did not go far enough and those with EYPS were left feeling that they were no longer valued as much as they had previously been told they would be. Nutbrown (2012) recommended a strengthening of qualifications for those working at level 3. This included suggesting that the level 3 qualification itself should be full and relevant and include study of both child development and play. She also suggested that only staff with a level 3 qualification should be included in ratios. Recommendations 17 and 18 are in some ways the most controversial. In 18 she called for the government to consider how it could maintain and increase graduate pedagogical leadership in the sector. New Labour had committed to a graduate in every full daycare setting by 2015, but the Coalition referred to this as an aspiration rather than a commitment and this aspirational rather than committed approach is reflected in the Nutbrown review. In 17 she advocates that anyone with EYPS should be given an opportunity to access routes to Qualified Teacher Status (QTS) as a priority. Gaunt (2012) comments that there are now some 10,000 EYPs who are wondering where they fit into Nutbrown's *Foundations for Quality* (2012). There are members of the early years workforce who hold full Master's degrees, having chosen EYP over QTS, given that they felt that it better prepared them for being a professional within the early years sector. Grenier (2013) suggests that some are misinterpreting Nutbrown and that she is rightly calling for an end to the divide between those working with children under three and those working with older children and who are recognised as teachers. Swarbrick (2012), in his blog, responded to Grenier's comments and likewise demonstrated concern with the role of EYPs, stating that, until 'the sector bites the bullet and calls teachers teachers (and pays them accordingly), and recognises that expertise, we will continue to have this rather odd and too-casual up-skilling of some of the most important people in our society'. Research evidence, particularly from EPPE (2004), demonstrates that the early years of a child's life are key and impact on long-term life chances. It would therefore seem imperative that, in order for us to support children in flourishing and reaching their full potential, we have a system for appropriately qualifying those who are going to work with them. While Nutbrown (2012) has called for a more appropriate, full and relevant level 3 qualification, there does not appear to be the same call for a graduate-led workforce that many working in the sector had hoped there would be.

The future of early years and free schools

Since 1976 and the politicisation of education, change has become more rapid and has often occurred in direct relation to which political party is in power. That has been seen particularly clearly over the last decade. New Labour certainly saw education as a key driver for eliminating a number of social ills, including child poverty (Baldock *et al.* 2005). The Coalition elected in 2010 continues to demonstrate concern with child poverty and social exclusion, and the publication of *Supporting Families in the Foundation Years* (DfE 2011) can be seen as testament to this. However, the ways in which this government is prepared to support children and their families are different from those of the previous administration and impact on the EYFS (2012). The clear commitment to graduates within the sector is diminishing, and while funding for EYPS continues to be available for a number of candidates there is little direct financial support for graduate salaries within the sector. O'Sullivan (2012), in her opinion piece for the National College for School Leadership, comments that while the government is driving forward a programme of encouraging schools to become academies, and is advocating the setting up of free schools, nurseries are excluded from this. Nursery schools cannot become academies under the current Academies Bill. She recognises that, while continuing research demonstrates that what happens in the earliest years of life has the most significant long-term impact, particularly on children's participation in education and their economic viability, the current government is seemingly ignoring this in the drive to reform education. The Economist Intelligence Unit has undertaken a review of early childhood education in 45 countries. Its report, *Starting Well: Benchmarking early education across the world* (EIU 2012), states that early education continues to be the area of least interest for policy makers. In England and Wales the early years sector has enjoyed unprecedented interest in the last decade, and it appears to remain in the sights of the current government. While the sector does not possess the same status as schools, the continued interest is bound to lead to further changes in the future.

Conclusion

This chapter set out to look at the Early Years Foundation Stage (EYFS) (2008, 2012) to consider where it had come from and where it is likely to be going. It is not possible to say with any degree of certainty what is likely to occur in the future. What is evident is that until relatively recently early years education was not prioritised by governments. Recent policy contexts and drivers have impacted on early years curricula and practice. Research, particularly the EPPE report (2004), has demon-strated that what happens in the early years has repercussions for the rest of a child's life; it can prevent social exclusion and support children in finding ways out of poverty as they become adults. While the development of an early years curriculum had already begun prior to the publication of the first stage of the EPPE report, its findings strengthened the position of those in the early years sector who were calling for recognition of the phase as being important in its own right.

Concerns for the early years sector were identified by Plowden (1967). Some of her recommendations can be seen to be coming to fruition now, nearly 50 years after the publication of the report. Early years were often seen as little more than childminding and therefore little attention was paid to this sector of education. Within England and Wales the politicisation of education and the more recent focuses on knowledge economies have meant that the early years have come to the fore in many western countries. This focus has led to a recognition that young children need an appropriate curriculum that meets their needs at the stage they are at and supports them in building foundations for the future in order that they can flourish as individuals.

In order to support these youngest children research evidence continues to demonstrate that they need appropriately qualified staff with knowledge of both child development and play. While research continues to demonstrate this, there appears a lack of political will to ensure that the workforce is both suitably qualified and remunerated. The recent Academies Bill fails to include nursery schools, which again suggests that successive governments are failing to recognise the importance of the early years sector and the impact that it has on children's lives in both the short and long term.

The early years sector clearly enjoys more prominence now than it ever has done but with that prominence comes closer scrutiny and the discussion of how provision should be delivered. It would however seem that, while the rapid change of the last decade may now slow, change will be a feature of the sector for the future as it has been drawn into the education sector with its associated politicised consequences.

REFLECTIVE QUESTIONS

- Why do you think it appears that nearly 50 years after the Plowden report (1967) we are still looking to have some of the recommendations met?
- How do you think the rapid change over the last decade impacts both positively and negatively on the early years sector?
- Why do you think play provides such a fundamental part of the early years curriculum?
- How do you think the EYFS (2012) will develop over the next few years?

References

Allen, G. (2011) *Early Intervention: The next steps*, London: Department of Work and Pensions. Available online at www.dwp.gov.uk/docs/early-intervention-next-steps.pdf (accessed 2 July 2013).

Baldock, P. (2011) *Developing Early Childhood Services: Past, present and future*, Maidenhead: Open University Press.

Baldock, P., Fitzgerald, D. and Kay, J. (2005) *Understanding Early Years Policy*, London: Paul Chapman.

Batteson, C. (1997) 'A review of politics of education in the "moment of 1976"', *British Journal of Education Studies*, 45(4): 363.

Brooker, L. (2011) 'Taking children seriously: an alternative agenda for research', *Journal of Early Childhood Research*, 9(2): 137–49.

David, T. (1998) 'Learning properly? Young children and desirable outcomes', *Early Years*, 18(2): 61–6.

Davis, J. (2002) 'The Inner London Education Authority and the William Tyndale Junior School Affair, 1974–1976', *Oxford Review of Education*, 28(2/3): 275–98.

Department for Children, Schools and Families (DCSF) (2008) *Statutory Framework for the Early Years Foundation Stage*, London: DCSF.

Department for Education (DfE) (2011) *Supporting Families in the Foundation Years*, London: DfE.

Department for Education (DfE) (2012) *The Early Years Foundation Stage (EYFS)*, London: DfE.

Department for Education and Employment (DfEE) (2000) *Curriculum Guidance for the Foundation Stage*, London: DfEE.

Department for Education and Employment (DfEE) (2001) *National Standards for Under Eights Day Care and Childminding*, Nottingham: DfEE.

Department for Education and Skills (DfES) (2002) *Birth to Three Matters*, London: DfES.

Department for Education and Skills (DfES) (2004) *Every Child Matters: Change for children*, London: DfES.

Duffy, B. (2010) 'Art in the early years', in Moyles, J. (ed.) *The Excellence of Play* (3rd edn), Maidenhead: Open University Press.

Economist Intelligence Unit (EIU) (2012) *Starting Well: Benchmarking early education across the world*, London: EIU.

Field, F. (2010) *The Foundation Years: Preventing poor children becoming poor adults: The report of the Independent Review on Poverty and Life Chances*, London: Cabinet Office. Available online at www.nfm.org.uk/component/jdownloads/finish/74/333 (accessed 2 July 2013).

Gaunt, C. (2011) 'EYFS review is welcomed by the sector', *Nursery World*, 7 April.

Gaunt, C. (2012) 'EYPS wonder where they fit into the Nutbrown Vision', *Nursery World*, 25 June.

Gillard, D. (2011) *Education in England: A brief history*. Available online at www.educationengland.org.uk/history (accessed 23 November 2012).

Grenier, J. (2013) 'Feeling a bit offended by the Nutbrown review'. Available online at http://juliangrenier.blogspot.co.uk/2012/06/feeling-bit-offended-nutbrown-review.html#more (accessed 3 January 2013).

Hedges, H., Cullen, J. and Jordan, B. (2011) 'Early years curriculum: funds of knowledge as a conceptual framework for children's interests', *Journal of Curriculum Studies*, 43(2): 185–205.

Howard, J. (2010) 'Early years practitioners' perceptions of play: an exploration of theoretical understanding, planning and involvement, confidence and barriers to practice', *Education & Child Psychology*, 27(4): 91–102.

Kwon, Y. (2002) 'Changing curriculum for early childhood education in England', *Early Childhood Research and Practice*, 4(2).

Laming, Lord H. (2003) *The Victoria Climbié Inquiry: Report of an inquiry by Lord Laming*, London: Department of Health.

Langston, A. (2011) 'A guide to the revised EYFS: part 1 an overview', *Nursery World*, 6–19 September.

Nutbrown, C. (2012) *Foundations for Quality: The independent review of early education and childcare qualifications. Final report*, London: Department for Education.

Nutbrown, C., Clough, P. and Selbie, P. (2008) *Early Childhood Education: History, philosophy and experience*, London: Sage.

Oberhuemer, P. (2005) 'International perspectives on early childhood curricula', *International Journal of Early Childhood*, 37(1): 27–37.

O'Sullivan, J. (2012) 'Getting the foundation years right in an academy model: Opinion piece', NCSL. Available online at www.nationalcollege.org.uk/docinfo?id=184840&filename=getting-the-foundation-years-right-in-an-academy-model-june-o-sullivan-opinion-piece.pdf (accessed 23 November 2012).

Pascal, C. and Bertram, A.D. (2002) 'Assessing young children's learning: what counts?', in Fisher, J. (ed.) *Building Foundations for Learning*, London: Paul Chapman.

Phillips, R. and Harper-Jones, G. (2002) 'Whatever next? Education policy and New Labour: the first four years, 1997–2001', *British Education Research Journal*, 29(1): 125–32.

Plowden, Lady B. (1967) *Children and their Primary Schools: A report of the Central Advisory Council for Education (England)*, London: Department of Education and Science.

Qualifications and Curriculum Authority (QCA) (2000) *Curriculum Guidance for the Foundation Stage*, London: QCA/DfEE.

Roberts-Holmes, G. (2012) '"It's the bread and butter of our practice": experiencing the Early Years Foundation Stage', *International Journal of Early Years Education*, 20(1): 30–42.

Rumbold, A. (1990) *Starting with Quality*, London: HMSO.

School Curriculum Assessment Authority (SCAA) (1996) *Nursery Education: Desirable outcomes for children's learning on entering compulsory education*, London: SCAA and Department for Education and Employment.

Siraj-Blatchford, I., Sylva, K., Muttock, S., Gilden, R. and Bell, D. (2002) *Researching Effective Pedagogy in the Early Years (REPEY)*, Research Report No. 356, Norwich: Department for Education and Skills.

Soler, J. and Miller, L. (2003) 'The struggle for early childhood curricula: a comparison of the English Foundation Stage curriculum, Te Whariki and Reggio Emilia', *International Journal of Early Years Education*, 11(1): 57–68.

Swarbrick, N. (2012) 'Grenier on Nutbrown'. Available online at http://nicktomjoe.brookesblogs.net/2012/06/27/grenier-on-nutbrown/ (accessed 2 January 2013).

Sylva, K., Melhuish, E., Sammons, P., Siraj-Blatchford, I. and Taggart, B. (2004) *The Effective Provision of Pre-school Education (EPPE) Project: Final report*, Nottingham: Department for Education and Skills.

Thomson, R. (2011) 'EYFS review prioritises how children learn', *Nursery World*, 6 April.

Tickell, Dame C. (2011) *The Early Years: Foundations for life, health and learning*, London: Department for Education. Available online at www.education.gov.uk/tickellreview (accessed 26 January 2013).

Vygotsky, L. (1978) *Mind in Society: The development of higher psychological processes*, London: Harvard University Press.

Wood, E. (2010) 'Developing integrated pedagogical approaches to play and learning', in Broadhead, P., Howard, J. and Wood, E. (2010) *Play and Learning in the Early Years*, London: Sage.

5 Future policy and the impact of societal change

Jan Gourd

Introduction

This chapter explores the policy discourse related to early years provision current within England at the time of writing. The last ten years have been momentous in terms of the early years policy agenda and significant and rapid policy initiatives have been implemented often without clear evidence to justify decisions that are made.

As discussed throughout this book, early years policy is central to all political agendas, whether it be to create 'school-ready' children or to tackle more perceived systemic problems with society. This chapter seeks to debate where the direction of policy discourse is taking early years services in the future.

Values versus performativity

With increasing policy attention the early years sector has seen an increasing amount of challenge, responsibility and accountability. This is now clearly highlighted in the new proposed standards for early years teachers (DfE 2013b). One of the proposed standards is '2.1 Be accountable for children's attainment, progress and outcomes.'

Performativity, once an alien concept, is now the domain of the early years. Given that the main driver for the expansion of children's services is economic, Urban (2008) questions whether it is actually legitimate to talk about children's services being for the benefit of children as the services are actually provided for the benefit of economic prosperity.

Individual practitioners find themselves accountable to parents, local authority officers (although this role is to be lessened), government through the legislative framework that is Ofsted, and society as a whole. They are challenged to provide a nurturing environment that they believe in and can be ethically comfortable with, while having to be beholden to government edicts that might not sit peacefully with their values and beliefs about early years pedagogy.

Indeed, as Powell (2010) points out, there is little indication within policy as to the personal values and dispositions that an Early Years Professional (EYP) should have. She states that the Children's Workforce Development Council (CWDC) has a checklist that suggests the necessary aptitudes to be:

- A genuine liking for and interest in children and their development.
- Good communication skills with children and Mums, Dads and other carers.
- Confidence.
- Patience and professionalism.
- A helpful, caring and understanding nature.
- An ability to work with parents and carers as well as with children.
- A commitment to social inclusion.
- The ability to work effectively as part of a team.
- A commitment to undertake training.
- A sense of fun.

(CWDC 2009: 1, cited in Powell 2010)

In reality the only check on this comes from a Criminal Records Bureau (CRB (now Disclosure and Barring Service (DBS)) clearance, which simply requires that the prospective employee has not been found guilty of any specific crimes against children.

- Changes to early years policy have been rapid and continue to develop.
- Early Years Professionals are becoming increasingly scrutinised by society as a whole.

The drive to up-skill the workforce

The need to consider the professional development of staff working in the early years was noted by the developers of the HighScope approach in the 1960s. It was acknowledged then that having staff who could interact appropriately with children to extend their thinking was a necessity in order to maximise children's cognitive development (EPPE project – Sylva *et al.* 2004). The Plowden report of 1967 discussed the advantages of early years children being taught by teachers, and teaching was starting to be a graduate profession at this stage with the first Bachelor of Education degrees offered in 1968.

The rapid expansion of early years settings in the 1990s and early 2000s called for a rapid increase in the workforce and vacancies were hard to fill.

There has however been a drive to up-skill the workforce. This drive has come partially from research, particularly the above-mentioned EPPE project (2004), but has also been promoted through international influence. The desire for graduate leadership in early years settings has been a challenge and the universal aspiration across provision has altered the childcare offers available to parents with many childminders deciding to leave the market (Richardson 2008).

With up-skilling has come a new burden for many EYPs, of reconciling a value-laden reflective pedagogy with the legislative notion of performativity. The challenge then for EYPs is two-fold – managing ethical practice while fulfilling legislative frameworks – and this for a profession that is still largely without voice, status or pay. Adding accountability to the mix creates a new tension for the workforce.

Accountability to the market (parents)

The challenge of being accountable to the market has been well documented by Osgood (2012), who suggests that it is still largely the middle classes who dominate the consumers of the sector. As McGillivray (2008: 251) found in her research with EYPs, they 'talk of being *under siege* and *under-valued*: a language of inferiority and conflict'.

The participants in her research suggest that they felt under-valued by parents. This is profoundly apparent in the work of Osgood (2012), who analyses the issue in terms of wave 2 feminism, which she suggests has largely passed by working-class women and once again has been dominated by the middle classes. She suggests that discourses about work–life balance, for instance, relate only to middle-class women balancing childcare and careers in traditional professional occupations and do not appear dominant in the discourse about working-class women's lives, many of whom are also balancing work in settings that have inferior working conditions, particularly in terms of family-friendly working practices, and who also have childcare responsibilities. There is also a tension in the types of services that are provided. The better quality State provision is targeted at those who have significant disadvantage in terms of economic viability. A stated aim of provision is to redress economic disadvantage. This in turn means that those women from the traditional middle class, the professional women wishing to return to careers, are forced to seek childcare in the private sector that can offer the hours needed and for the majority of the week. This creates a tension in that the more qualified and confident EYPs tend to work in state provision, where terms and conditions are better, while the least qualified staff find themselves in the private sector with a parent population that consists of the more outwardly competent and demanding professional women. This is of course a generalisation, but the tension is a very real one.

This triangle of care relationship between parent, key worker and child (Brooker 2010) is central to the flourishing of the child and family and also it could be argued to the well-being of the practitioner. Brooker (2010: 184) suggests that 'parents who view themselves as "professionals" may exercise power over practitioners whose professional qualifications they hold to be of little value'. Indeed, Nutbrown (2012) comments on the confusion caused by the multiplicity of professional qualifications that early years workers hold. While she acknowledges the positive impact that EYPs have on their settings, she concludes, 'however hard we try, I do not believe a status that is not the same as QTS will ever be seen as equal to QTS' (ibid.: 5.12). Nutbrown (2012) seems to suggest that the title of teacher is understood by everyone and that the title affords the holder greater status and respect than does the status Early Years Professional (EYP). This is of course in contrast to the Nordic cultures, where the early years pedagogue is afforded high status, but does mirror the pattern of up-skilling noted in Chapter 3 in New Zealand, whereby a single-status early years teacher has been the solution to the issue of parity and professional standing. The union, Aspect, noted the disparity in its 2009 report and commented on the split-status model of EYPS and QTS and it has actively tried to seek answers on the future commitment of the political parties to the status.

It is only recently that early years workers seriously considered being members of unions to represent their rights. Aspect, the union for professionals in childcare services, began a dedicated area for EYPs on its website (www.aspect.org.uk/eyp/tag/eyps) and promoted itself as the union to represent the interests of EYPs. In 2009 it analysed the findings of the first EYP survey and published the first agenda for promoting EYP issues. In terms of professionals having a voice and agency this was a significant development.

The recent publication of *More Great Childcare* (DfE 2013a) acknowledges the confusion over terminology and is changing the title of the current EYP to EYT (Early Years Teacher). This title will not, however, give the holders QTS, so therefore there is not parity across the sector. Nutbrown (2013) indeed argues that it will only increase parental and societal confusion by using the term 'teacher' when it means different things depending on the course that the practitioner has followed. She says:

> Are Early Years Professionals simply being renamed? If so is this not insulting? . . . Will this name change without any other apparent change, mislead parents? And is this not insulting and misleading to those who undertake Early Years Teacher courses? How would it be if the reverse was the case and it was decided, at relatively short notice, with no justification, to rename teachers in secondary schools 'Secondary Years Professionals'? It would not work and I sincerely believe it would similarly fail in the Early Years.
>
> (ibid.: 7)

She then goes on to point out that it is only those who work with the youngest children who will not have QTS status, with current early years QTS programmes concentrating on the 3–7 age range and the new EYT (non-QTS) being for the 0–5 age range:

> Yet again, those who work with young children are offered a lesser status (and we should realistically anticipate, poorer pay and conditions than those who work with older children) but a title that makes them appear to have the same role and status.
>
> (ibid.)

- A new Early Years Teacher status is to be introduced from September 2013. The status does not confer QTS as recommended in the Nutbrown report (2012).
- EYPs often feel under-valued by society as a whole and the new title Early Years Teacher seeks to alter public perceptions of the workforce.

Changing professional perceptions

Brooker (2010) also looks at Levinas's (1989) ethics of encounters, whereby she suggests that the role of professionals is to respect the other – the parent or child with whom they work. This again redefines the role of practitioners and requires them to be able to recognise and actively realise their own prejudices and to disengage these. This level of engagement, I would suggest, requires education in critical reflective practice, and a growing maturity and open-mindedness to achieve competently (MacNaughton 2005). Many students on our early years courses comment upon how their views of, and how they engage with, parents have changed dramatically throughout their degrees. Indeed, this disruption to their known practice and recognising their own and others' prejudices is seen by them as being one of the greatest benefits of their degree-level education.

Brooker (2010: 190), in researching the views of professional parents, found that despite this:

> In these instances both parents and practitioners seem unable to take the perspective of others, to imagine how it might feel to be the other caregiver. Their responsiveness, and attentiveness, is exercised within the limits of their own point of view, and the 'care' which is provided represents professional rather than emotional labour.

The narrative of learning outcomes is now also the domain of the EYP. The EYFS (DfE 2012) suggests the value of play but this in itself raises a product versus process tension in accountability to parents. If play is very much seen as process by the EYP, there are no hard data to justify parental expenditure on the provision. In an educational market that is driven by targets and outcomes in terms of SAT results, GCSEs, A-levels and UCAS tariffs, there may be seen to be an undervaluing of process by the market. Certainly the desirable outcomes and EYFS profile scores have added quantifiable data to the early years market. The new two-year-old 'tests' could be seen as a further political attempt to justify more expenditure at a time of economic restraint. The funding for these children is being distributed on the same basis as free school meals. The ability to administer and report on these tests is now explicitly documented in the proposed Early Years Teachers' Standards (DfE 2013b: 6.2).

Accountability to society

The Labour and Coalition governments have both positioned early years provision as a pivotal force in addressing both social disadvantage and the creation of chances for children through their life course, enabling the disadvantaged to escape from poverty. This policy is clearly linked to the longitudinal work of the American Head Start programme. An awareness of the importance of the early years through research in the field of neuroscience has shown that experiences within the first five years of life can be determinants of future success of the individual (Goswami 2007). Secure relationships and stimulating environments have a particular influence on future well-being (Gammage 2006). This then places a great burden on the early years workforce. Vaughan and Estola (2007) urge us to look at the 'gift paradigm' in early childhood education, suggesting that there are two competing voices: the gift paradigm and the exchange paradigm. The gift paradigm, they argue, is feminine and helps both giver and receiver to flourish. They explain it thus:

> The logic of the exchange paradigm requires an equal payment for each need satisfying good, while the gift paradigm contains a transitive logic by which a giver unilaterally satisfies the need of a receiver and thereby establishes bonds of mutuality and trust. The exchange logic is ego-oriented while the gift logic is other-oriented. The return payment, in fact, cancels the gift and turns the value-attributing mechanism back from the receiver towards the giver. The exchange paradigm and the values of ego-orientation that are associated with it are widespread today as the principle of the market, and they influence all our thinking.
>
> (ibid.: 247)

The gift paradigm is compared to the process of mothering, where gifts in terms of love and care are given in abundance with no measurable returns. This would of course be contested by many mothers who would argue that the love they feel for, and get from, their children more than repays the care activities and emotional labour they provide. Indeed, this fulfilment contributes to the mother's flourishing. This is all very well within the confines of the attachment relationship that hopefully exists between mother and child, but the operation of this paradigm within the early years setting is being squeezed out by the exchange agenda: 'In present times the exchange paradigm often frames education as business' (ibid.). Vaughan and Estola (2007) acknowledge their feminist perspective and suggest that the exchange paradigm is essentially masculine and as such dominates. The gift-giving paradigm is seen as qualitative and other-oriented, while the exchange paradigm is seen as being quantitative and egocentric. The analysis of the two paradigms within contemporary society in the UK also offers a new appraisal of man's nature, the term 'homo-economicus' being suggested.

- ■ Both the Labour and Coalition governments have positioned early years provision as a pivotal force in addressing both social disadvantage and the effects of poverty.
- ■ Research in the field of neuroscience has shown that experiences within the first five years of life can be determinants of future success.

Accountability to legislation

Early years practitioners are now accountable to legislative frameworks – the EYFS (2012) sets the parameters for the content of their work. This, according to Dyer and Taylor (2012), can create a challenge as they suggest:

> Focusing on the detail of curriculum outcomes may well inhibit the promotion of broader principles, and many Early Years professionals would identify an inherent technical limitation as being at the heart of the discussion around quality in Early Years provision.
>
> (ibid.: 553)

Their research, which has been conducted with a number of EYPs, goes on to explain how the practitioners with whom they are working sum up quality in their work. The tension between what they believe to be right and the aspirational educational aims for their work is summed up by participant 5:

> Participant 5 defined good practice in terms of approach to children and enthusiasm for the job: caring about children, caring about their development, not just caring about their educational performance, caring about their personal life as well.
>
> (ibid.: 557)

Often the practitioner experiences some disaffection when personal reflective pedagogy does not sit easily with overly bureaucratic policy.

An example of this would be when practitioners complain that the need to document and provide evidence against profile indicators takes them away from direct interaction with children. This is often true of the more highly qualified staff who find that administrative burdens mean that they spend less and less time in direct contact with the children. While implementing policy on the one hand, this performativity-led policy has undermined one of the aims of graduate pedagogic leadership, where research shows that quality is significantly increased when the graduate spends time in direct contact with the children (Nutbrown 2012: 5.8).

However, the regulation states that the ratio of children to adults can be greater where the degree-level practitioner works in direct contact with the children. This premise is now being debated with the thrust to deregulate ratios (Truss 2012). Grenier (2013), in his blog, comments on this particular announcement by reviewing the literature on group size and concurs that the evidence suggests that another conclusion should be reached. He cites Munton et al. (2002: 59), where the research shows that 'higher staff:child ratios are associated with better quality childcare'. This also links to the fulfilment of the staff (MacNaughton 2005), who generally resist the homo-economicus construction of their identity within institutional childcare (Vaughan and Estola 2007).

- Those who work in early years often find there is a tension and challenge created by the legislative frameworks.
- Performativity can undermine practitioners' own graduate pedagogic leadership and lead to graduates actually spending less time with the children.

Challenge of the EYP/EYT status

Simpson (2010), in trying to unpack concepts of professionalism among EYPs, finds that the inability of government to give EYP the same status as QTS has indeed created a divided early years service. He illustrates the tension with the story of Emma who held EYP and HLTA status. She recounts how, when given responsibility by management to lead change in play practice within the school in which she worked, she found resistance from those who held QTS. Simpson (2010) implies that the Foundation Stage teachers felt that Emma was in some way acting above her status and they:

adopted an approach she described as 'a sort of load of cotton wool, it wasn't a stone wall, it was more subtle than that'. She would, for example, prepare plans each week and they would be 'ignored'. Emma observed the effect this had in regard to her professionalism and sense of value – 'it erodes your self-esteem' – and her enthusiasm waned. Eventually she indicated to the head teacher that 'this isn't working' and she was 'just took out' of having direct involvement in the early years side of the school's work.

(ibid.: 10)

In this case much more credence was attributed to Emma's HLTA status, which was never designed to be equivalent to QTS, than her EYP status. Simpson (2010: 12) goes on to note that the tensions between the two statuses are causing a split workforce and that 'it is something that is potentially threatening to the development of a democratic form of professionalism emerging in the early years characterised by dialogue, openness to others and "border crossing"'.

This tension between those working in early years is one that has historic routes but is a tension that the New Zealand government avoided in their policy implementation for early years up-skilling (Dalli 2008) by creating one qualification for all early years services. This is what the Nutbrown review (2012) suggested as a way forward for England, but which has since been dismissed in the *More Great Childcare* policy document (DfE 2013a), as discussed earlier. It is therefore assumed that EYT status will have the same limitations as EYP status, although the entry requirements for EYT courses will from 2014 be the same as those for QTS courses.

Simpson (2010: 13) concludes by suggesting that EYPs have 'bounded agency' to act as change agents and that indeed some acted as role takers rather than role makers, 'even adopting role distance from their early years professional work'. In the author's experience those on early years foundation degrees, which were supported and to a large extent continue to be supported by local authorities as the stepping stone to EYPS, often question the validity of this trajectory to the status, especially given the short contract periods granted to institutions to deliver the programmes. Students wonder whether the status will continue after the end of current contracts and, if not, whether the status, once achieved, will continue to be recognised.

This lack of long-term commitment by successive governments has led to a feeling of uncertainty about the status itself. The commissioning of various reports (Nutbrown 2012; Tickell 2011) to look at the future development of early years policy and the future of the workforce has

reinforced this unsettlement of a status that was just starting to bed down. Indeed, Nutbrown (2012) acknowledges the difficulty of the two-tier system, which is why she suggested a new QTS for 0–8 and a conversion route for those who have EYPS to gain the new suggested qualification. In reality the issue has been fudged and those who hold EYP will be able to call themselves Early Years Teachers (DfE 2013a) and new candidates in 2013/2014 will work to Early Years Teachers' Standards. This, however, continues the uncertainty as no existing provider has a contract to deliver EYT beyond 2014. Institutions are already finding it difficult to recruit to entry pathways and it is hard to see how, when given the parity of qualification needed to enter EYT courses and QTS courses, recruitment will be maintained. It would seem likely that most candidates would seek the QTS route. Indeed, we are finding in our own

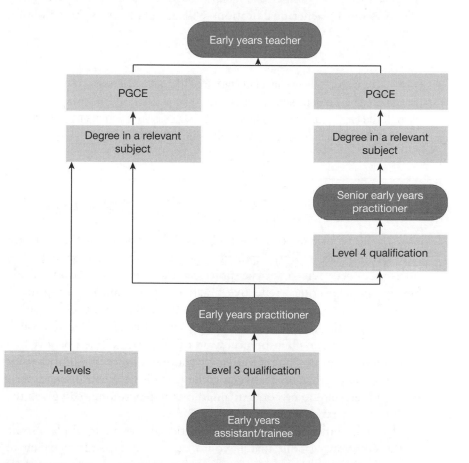

FIGURE 5.1 Some proposed typical routes through a career working in the early years
Source: Nutbrown (2012: 47).

institution that foundation degree students are choosing a traditional 'top-up' to BA Hons level rather than the funded Undergraduate Practitioner Pathway (UPP) traditionally taken to achieve EYP. Practitioner students often lack traditional GCSE qualifications in maths and now the additional requirement for science will stop many applying. The burden of the skills tests will also put even more pressure on the students and if they do overcome all those hurdles why apply for EYT when you could gain QTS? Poor recruitment to EYT courses will I suspect lead to a future rethink.

The proposed routes to a career in early years will not at the present time incorporate PGCE as proposed by Nutbrown (2012), but will have an EYT course 'add-on' after a full degree is achieved or in the last year of an undergraduate course. We have yet to see what the new courses proposed from September 2014 will look like, but it is clear that parity of professional teacher qualifications will not exist across the education service for children from 0–16.

- The inability of government to give EYP the same status as QTS has created a divided early years service.
- The lack of long-term commitment by successive governments has led to a feeling of uncertainty about the status itself.

Reflective practice

One of the requirements of the EYPS and the proposed EYT standards is to demonstrate reflective practice; however, there is a great deal of difference between reflective practice and the recognition of the development of critical reflective practice, the second requiring much emotional labour from the participant. In order to develop critical reflective practice the practitioner needs to have been introduced through education to certain philosophical ways of thinking. While I believe that this thinking can be done intuitively by a practitioner, it is only recognition of this as critical reflective practice that allows the intuitive experience and response to be contextualised by the practitioner and given the validity it deserves (MacNaughton 2005).

Indeed, to me, critical reflective practice allows me to displace some of the emotional labour that I would otherwise expend on trying to reconcile a problem. It gives a framework in which to locate the experience, talk about it and use it to enhance one's own practice and the practice of others. To me the ability to critically reflect is an essential tool of leaders and managers, both for their own well-being and for them to lead sensitively and nurture their staff. Indeed, leaders and managers of flourishing settings have to subscribe to the gift paradigm to fully fulfil the potential development of staff. A graduate entry pathway student of mine came to me to say that she wished to withdraw from the course. When asked why, she described her experience on placement and declared that she was overwhelmed by the requirements of the EYP status. She was in a setting that was part of a business–run chain in an area of deprivation in a large city. She described the setting as being staffed by young girls with little education and training who lacked the ability to act within a reflective practice lens. She saw the difficulties that the degree-level practitioner had in managing this setting, as managing was all that could be aspired to, and decided that she was not comfortable with putting herself in the market for a similar position. The setting was obviously not flourishing and neither could anyone within it. Economic viability and profit were the dominant discourse and the exchange paradigm silenced all others.

Truss (2012) alluded to a growing level of professionalism within the early years sector with graduate practitioners as being one of the major reasons for trusting their professional responsibility for determining ratios. While this can be seen as a positive aspiration, the reality is that for those who operate within the exchange paradigm it opens up an agenda of cost-cutting and exploitation. Indeed, the reflective EYP particularly within some, not all, of the for-profit sector will have to collude with that agenda or to seek work in another type of setting where professional integrity and voice have agency.

- Critical reflective practice may help practitioners cope with the amount of emotional labour they expend in their work.
- Truss (2012) has suggested that the growing level of professionalism within the sector allows for the self-determination of ratios.
- Many of those within the sector express disquiet as to the implications for self-determined ratios.

What we can determine is happening to policy at the moment

From the policy announcements that we can see from the current Coalition government we can see something of the basis of future policy. Certainly, 'narrowing the gap' and trying to create a more equal society seems to be on the agenda of all political parties. The gap between rich and poor is being documented as the biggest outside the USA, Mexico and Israel (OECD 2011). We have taken many of our child deficit reduction policies and intervention programmes and strategies from the USA, but the data would suggest that these policies within the big picture of national change have done nothing to reduce inequality of opportunity in terms of the gap between the richest and poorest in society. Indeed, the reverse seems to be true in that the gap between the richest and poorest within the USA and the UK is growing, while in France, Hungary and Belgium it seems to have shown little change and inequality is actually seen to be decreasing in Turkey and Greece. The position is of course complex and recent global economic events will have impacted on the figures. The point remains that, outside Mexico, the USA has recognised and tried to tackle social inequality through policy interventions within the early years, through successive administrations, but it appears simply to have grown inequality rather than 'closed the gap'. Could it be that the strategy of trying to 'fix' a single aspect of inequality is not going to work. Isolating a perceived deficit group and providing enrichment to level the attainment playing field might not be the answer. Instead, we might need to spend our time and energy creating holistic change based on our knowledge of human fulfilment and flourishing societies where the majority of citizens feel worthy and positive about themselves.

The recent publication, *The Spirit Level* (Wilkinson and Pickett 2010), was initially met with enthusiasm from politicians of all parties. Indeed, Booth (2010) in *The Guardian* claimed: 'Cameron quoted the book in a pre-election address envisioning the "big society", the former Labour foreign secretary Jack Straw took it on holiday and Michael Gove, the education secretary, said it was "a fantastic analysis".'

Booth (2010) then notes how influential government 'think tanks' then went on to deride the big ideas within the book when it became clear that they would not benefit financially the richest within UK society.

So on 7 July, the Taxpayers' Alliance, a campaign group for lower taxes and lower spending, which is also bankrolled by wealthy Conservative donors, branded the book 'flimsy' and issued a damning report.

What this suggests is that elected MPs, when free to read and think their own thoughts, can actually construct ideas for themselves, but that these ideas are often hijacked by the self-interest groups that dominate UK society. Indeed, a similar report criticising the ideas was published in the USA at the same time; however, the authors insist they did not collude.

Significant also was the Coalition sacking in September 2012 of Sarah Teather, a Liberal Democrat minister, and her replacement with Elizabeth Truss, a Conservative MP. This signalled a change in policy as it was well known that Teather was finding some of the ideas on welfare reform difficult to support. Indeed, unburdened from her role of minister, she felt able to speak out and is reported in *The Guardian* as having said:

> Having an incentive in the benefits system to encourage people to work is a good thing . . . It is a good thing because it encourages people to participate in society. But having a system which is so punitive in its regime that it effectively takes people entirely outside society, so they have no chance of participating, crosses a moral line for me.
>
> (Teather, in Helm 2012)

Truss comes from a strong exchange model, having come into politics from an accountancy background. Ben-Galim (2013) comments on the first of Truss's announcements, about childminder ratios, that 'rumours suggest that there is a Yellow–Blue battle raging in government about the new childcare support package'. Ben-Galim goes on to point out that the current looking towards France for our solutions fails to take context into account. She notes that the French have a 'pro-natalist family policy' with very generous leave allowances for parents. This means that the majority of children under three are still cared for in the family home. She concludes on this issue by saying:

> So the comparison with France does shed light on a different system from which the UK can learn, but it is misleading to infer from it that looser ratios for childminders have much if any impact on childcare costs, since the proportion of under 5s for whom they cater is small.
>
> (ibid.)

She then goes on to point out that, in the écoles maternelles, which cater for the majority of those from deprived backgrounds, there is a far better adult to child ratio. The issue of staff qualification and profession-alisation is also pointed out. Ben-Galim (2013) comments that this is a central part of the debate and that in both France and the Nordic countries a greater proportion of staff have higher-level qualifications.

Using ratios as an indicator for costs is therefore limited given the different levels and status of qualifications. The early years workforce has a critical impact on outcomes for children and the challenge of developing a highly trained and well-paid workforce remains urgent and cannot be left to market principles. Truss (2012) is right to focus on quality but it is a real stretch to suggest that slightly looser ratios will lead to lower prices and higher salaries (not least because in many European countries with different ratios to the UK, pay rates are set by national regulation or collective bargaining) (ibid.)

It does appear that there is little agreement across parties as to the future direction of the specific actions of policy, the Coalition not agreeing among themselves and Labour having recently launched a new project for the development of policies for 2015. Reay (2012), in her paper published for the Labour Party think tank known as 'Class', suggests that we need to rethink the education system radically and not tinker at the edges if we are serious about social equity.

Where does this leave the children of the UK in terms of flourishing in their early years and can we see an indication in policy that the pillars of flourishing (happiness, flow, meaning, love, gratitude, accomplishment and growth), as determined by Seligman (2011), are being carefully considered when making policy decisions? Seligman says:

> The time has come for a new prosperity, one that takes flourishing seriously as the goal of education and of parenting. Learning to value and attain flourishing must start early – in the formative years of schooling – and it is this new prosperity, kindled by positive education that the world can now choose.
>
> (2011: 97)

The announcements to date from the current Coalition suggest that flourishing is low on the agenda. There are certainly few if any indications that it features in their construction of quality.

Conclusion

To summarise then, where are the political indicators taking us in terms of future policy? It appears that we can expect politicians to consider:

- introducing a new status degree-level qualification and for that to be named Early Years Teacher for the 0–5 age range (DfE 2013a; Nutbrown 2012; Truss 2012);

- some deregulation, particularly the abandonment of statutory ratios (Truss 2012);

- an intervention agenda whatever the political persuasion of the government (Field 2010);

- performativity of services that will continue to underpin policy (Conservative Party website 2013).

What is not clear is how child well-being will be addressed. This particular issue does not seem to be clearly signposted by any particular party. The Conservatives in their 2010 manifesto did state that 'we will make Britain the most family-friendly country in Europe', a very bold aim considering the term of government is only five years. The Green Party did allude to child well-being by highlighting the needs for childcarers to be recognised but didn't really propose how they would suggest policy initiatives to improve the current situation. The Labour Party placed much of its emphasis for the future on lengthening the amount of paid leave parents can take in a child's first year, emphasising the progress made to date whereby mothers' paid leave entitlement had increased from six to nine months during their last term in office. The Liberal Democrats also concentrated on making suggestions on leave for parents (Aspect 2010). The Green Party, Labour and the Liberal Democrats all emphasised a fairer society in their manifestos; the only two parties who did not emphasise this were the Conservatives and UKIP (ibid.).

It would seem that the flourishing of children will come from the commitment and dedication of the workforce, so the continuation of the professionalisation agenda should be viewed as the greatest contribution policy can make implicitly to the flourishing of children and families. The continuation of the drive to create a degree-level education for those working in early years should be seen as the most significant action that will enable children to flourish and it is to be hoped that, when the economic situation improves, this will once again be seen as necessary rather than continuing to be downgraded to desirable. This is the agenda that we must hope all political parties continue to subscribe to so that there can at least be one long-term policy commitment regardless of political affiliation.

REFLECTIVE QUESTIONS

- How do you think policy decisions could help children and practitioners to flourish?
- How do you employ reflective practice in your day-to-day work with children and families?
- Do you think the new EYT status will be successful?

References

Aspect (2009) *In Their Own Words: EYPs speak out*, Wakefield: Aspect. Available online at www.aspect.org.uk/eyp/wp-content/uploads/2009/04/eyp-p-survey-report.pdf (accessed 5 March 2013).

Aspect (2010) 'Election fever reigns: but where next for early years?', *EYP Zone*, 11 May. Available online at www.aspect.org.uk/eyp/tag/eyps (accessed 5 March 2013).

Ben-Galim, D. (2013) 'The Coalition's mid-term review was surprisingly silent on childcare'. Available online at http://conservativehome.blogs.com/think tankcentral/2013/01/dalia-ben-galim.html (accessed 17 January 2013).

Booth, R. (2010) 'The Spirit Level: how "ideas wreckers" turned book into political punchbag', *The Guardian*, 18 August.

Brooker, L. (2010) 'Constructing the Triangle of Care: power and professionalism in practitioner/parent relationships', *British Journal of Educational Studies*, 58(2): 181-96.

Dalli, C. (2008) 'The new teacher in New Zealand', in Miller, L. and Cable, C. (eds) *Professionalism in the Early Years*, London: Hodder Education.

Department for Education (DfE) (2012) *The Early Years Foundation Stage (EYFS)*, London: DfE.

Department for Education (DfE) (2013a) *More Great Childcare: Raising quality and giving parents more choice*, London: DfE. Available online at www.gov.uk/government/uploads/system/uploads/attachment_data/file/170552/More_20 Great_20Childcare_20v2.pdf.pdf (accessed 11 April 2013).

Department for Education (DfE) (2013b) *Consultation on Teachers' Standards (Early Years)*, London: DfE. Available online at www.education.gov.uk/consultations/index.cfm?action=consultationDetails&consultationId=1886& external=no&menu=1 (accessed 11 April 2013).

Dyer, M.A. and Taylor, S.M. (2012) 'Supporting professional identity in undergraduate Early Years students through reflective practice', *Reflective Practice: International and Multidisciplinary Perspectives*, 13(4): 551–63.

Field, F. (2010) *The Foundation Years: Preventing poor children becoming poor adults: The report of the Independent Review on Poverty and Life Chances*, London: Cabinet Office. Available online at www.nfm.org.uk/component/jdownloads/finish/74/333 (accessed 2 July 2013).

Gammage, P. (2006) 'Early childhood education and care: politics, policies and possibilities', *Early Years: An International Journal of Research and Development*, 26(3): 235–48.

Goswami, U. (2007) *Cognitive Development: The learning brain*, New York: Psychology Press.

Grenier, J. (2013) 'Feeling a bit offended by the Nutbrown review'. Available online at http://juliangrenier.blogspot.co.uk/2012/06/feeling-bit-offended-nutbrown-review.html#more (accessed 10 April 2013).

Helm, T. (2012) 'Demonisation of the poor is taking place . . . horrible things will happen', *The Guardian*, 17 November.

Levinas, E. (1989) 'Ethics as first philosophy', in Hand, S. (ed.) *The Levinas Reader*, Oxford: Blackwell.

McGillivray, G. (2008) 'Nannies, nursery nurses and early years professionals: constructions of professional identity in the early years workforce in England', *European Early Childhood Education Research Journal*, 16(2): 242–54.

MacNaughton, G. (2005) *Doing Foucault in Early Childhood Education: Applying poststructural ideas*, Abingdon: Routledge.

Munton, T., Mooney, A., Moss, P., Petrie, P., Clark, A. and Woolner, J. (2002) *Research on Ratios, Group Size and Staff Qualifications and Training in Early Years and Childcare Settings*, London: Thomas Coram Research Unit, Institute of Education, University of London.

Nutbrown, C. (2012) *Foundations for Quality: The independent review of early education and childcare qualifications. Final report*, London: Department for Education.

Nutbrown, C. (2013) *Shaking the Foundations of Quality? Why 'childcare' policy must not lead to poor-quality early education and care*. Available online at www.shef.ac.uk/polopoly_fs/1.263201!/file/Shakingthefoundationsofquality.pdf (accessed 11 April 2013).

Organisation for Economic Co-operation and Development (OECD) (2011) *Divided We Stand: Why inequality keeps rising*, Paris: OECD.

Osgood, J. (2012) *Narratives from the Nursery*, London: Routledge.

Plowden, Lady B. (1967) *Children and their Primary Schools: A report of the Central Advisory Council for Education (England)*, London: HMSO.

Powell, S. (2010) 'Hide and seek: values in early childhood education and care', *British Journal of Education Studies*, 58(2): 213–29.

Reay, D. (2012) *What Would a Socially Just Education System Look Like?* London: Class. Available online at http://classonline.org.uk/docs/2012_Diane_Reay_-_a_socially_just_education_system.pdf (accessed 17 January 2013).

Richardson, H. (2008) 'Decline in number of childminders', BBC News, 20 August. Available online at http://news.bbc.co.uk/1/hi/education/7570035.stm (accessed 16 January 2013).

Seligman, M. (2011) *Flourish: A visionary new understanding of happiness and well-being*, New York: Free Press.

Simpson, D. (2010) 'Being professional? Conceptualising early years professionalism in England', *European Early Childhood Education Research Journal*, 18(1): 5–14.

Sylva, K., Melhuish, E., Sammons, P., Siraj-Blatchford, I. and Taggart, B. (2004) *The Effective Provision of Pre-school Education (EPPE) Project: Final report*, Nottingham: Department for Education and Skills.

Tickell, Dame C. (2011) *The Early Years: Foundations for life, health and learning*, London: Department for Education. Available online at www.education.gov.uk/tickellreview (accessed 26 January 2013).

Truss, E. (2012) 'Speech to the Daycare Trust conference', 4 December. Available online at www.education.gov.uk/inthenews/speeches/a00218139/daycare-trust-conference (accessed 11 April 2013).

Urban, M. (2008) 'Dealing with uncertainty: challenges and possibilities for the early childhood profession', *European Early Childhood Education Research Journal*, 16(2), special edition.

Vaughan, G. and Estola, E. (2007) 'The gift paradigm in early childhood education', *Educational Philosophy and Theory*, 39: 246–63.

Wilkinson, R. and Pickett, K. (2010) *The Spirit Level: Why equality is better for everyone*, London: Penguin Books.

Policy in practice

6

Up-skilling the workforce

Managing change in practice

Jan Gourd

Introduction

This chapter explores the phenomenon that has engulfed the early years sector throughout the last ten years – up-skilling, a term that implies the acquisition of new skills. The debate for academics and those who research the field is whether skill acquisition is too narrow a term for what is aspired to, the aspiration being that settings are led by someone with a full degree, degrees generally being about a broad educational experience rather than merely a set of skills to be mastered. The up-skilling programme as experienced by a large number of practitioners, as reported in the second EYP survey (Hadfield and Jopling 2012) and as documented in Chapter 7 of this book, goes beyond the development of a new skills set and can often be life-changing for the participants and for the way in which they view their work. Some who engage with the process of up-skilling flourish and generally have a positive impact on their settings, while others find the process exhausting and too demanding to grow and flourish in the way in which we understand flourishing to be.

The impetus for up-skilling

The thrust internationally to develop early years services came with a recognition that quality was better delivered through a well-qualified workforce and that the level of qualification within the UK fell short of the well-documented graduate level thought to enhance quality as shown by the EPPE research (Sylva et al. 2004).

Research carried out by Munton *et al.* (2002) for the Thomas Coram Research Unit found that, internationally, qualifications for early years staff varied but in the main the minimum levels were above those required in the UK. There were also significant variations in the ratios of staff to children. The differences were in part due to how the practitioners' role was understood and in their research they suggested that the early years workforce could be categorised under three distinct groupings dependent on how its members' roles were constructed and viewed. These, they suggested, were the pedagogue, the early childhood teacher and the split-role worker. The pedagogue was seen mainly as being within the welfare system and working with children of 0–6 in a non-school setting. The pedagogue had equal status to the school-based teacher. The early childhood teacher could be seen in both school-based and non-school-based settings but worked as one of a team of professionals, and the split-role worker generally worked with children aged three plus across a vast variety of settings. The role of the pedagogue, they suggest, is more often seen in Nordic cultures where integrated child welfare strategies are most firmly established. They noted that, in New Zealand and in Spain, two countries that were seeking to integrate care and education, the newly developing role was one of early childhood teacher and was based within education.

Pedagogues in the Nordic countries are the core workers, working across a range of services, and they are supported by lesser qualified staff; however, it was noted by Munton *et al.* (2002) that at least 50 per cent of the staff in these countries were qualified to pedagogue level and that the proportion of more highly qualified staff was growing. Sweden, which has more than half its early years workers trained to pedagogue or teacher level, transferred control of early years to education in 1997 and commenced a major programme of reform of the training for early years staff. This programme was to create a single early years training qualification that requires three and a half years of degree-level study and results in teacher status. According to Munton *et al.* (2002: 6.2.2):

> The realignment of early years services is intended, among other things, to open schools and school teachers to influences from early years practice and to encourage and support more team working among pre-school teachers, school teachers and free-time teachers and pedagogues, especially those working with six- to nine-year-olds.

So rather than the 'school-readiness' agenda seen to dominate UK early years policy, the hope within Sweden is that the practice base of pedagogues and early years specialists extends into the six- to nine-year-old phase. This is in opposition to the schoolification agenda promoted by politicians themselves and through government-commissioned reports such as those documented in papers and speeches by Field (2010), Nutbrown (2012), Teather (2011) and Truss (2012).

The 'split system' is currently still dominant within the UK and is defined by Munton *et al.* (2002) as being where childcare services are split between teachers and childcare workers. Each is subject to hierarchical professionalism with varying pay, conditions and status. The roles within the statutory sector are more highly valued by British society. Munton *et al.* (2002) see that England and Brazil have attempted integration but that a true split system operates within France and the USA. In these 'split systems' the levels of qualification are different dependent on the sector within which the individual works. In the USA, while the kindergarten teacher works within the state system, the pre-school teacher does not and does not have the same level of qualification or standing as their kindergarten counterpart. They point out the great variance of qualification that the pre-school teacher might have within this system, varying from no qualification, through competency-based systems to four-year degrees, but these are not consistent or mandatory. England proposes to maintain a two-tier system of Early Years Teachers (EYTs) in non-statutory provision and QTS teachers in the state sector (DfE 2013).

In summary, where there is true integration, levels of qualification and pay are generally similar wherever across that system an individual works. However, where there is a split system this is where the greatest variance in qualification, pay and status occurs, with those working with older children given the higher status. Staff training, both pre-service and in-service, is seen as key to this agenda; however, despite many attempts to create a cohesive system to date it is still viewed as chaotic (Nutbrown 2012). The move to a single system did seem imminent, but the recommendation to give EYPs the same status as QTS teachers was thrown out by the DfE in 2013. The publication of *More Great Childcare* (DfE 2013) caused an angry response from Nutbrown (2013) entitled *Shaking the Foundations of Quality? Why 'childcare' policy must not lead to poor-quality education and care*. The publication of the government policy document and the subsequent response by Nutbrown has led to much debate in the early years sector and has made EYP students question both the validity of their own courses and the validity of the future EYT status.

- The impetus to up-skill came out of recognition of the need for a well-qualified, graduate-led early years workforce.
- The current provision of early years qualifications is seen as problematic.
- It is accepted that EYTs (formerly EYPs) should from 2014 have the same entry qualifications as those aiming for early years QTS.

Staff training and outcomes

A great deal of debate has ensued about the best and most appropriate forms of staff training to 'up-skill' the workforce.

Munton *et al.* (2002) cited evidence that:

- Children scored higher on tests of cognitive and social competence when their caregivers had higher levels of child-related training and formal education (Clarke-Stewart and Gruber 1984).

- Teacher training, both pre-service and in-service, was linked to more positive child outcomes, especially in terms of language and representational skills (Epstein 1993).

- The number of years staff have spent in formal education has a positive impact on outcomes for children (Whitebook et al. 1989; Berk 1985).

- Staff with more training are less authoritarian in their interactions with children (Arnett 1989).

- Experience is no substitute for formal, specialist training (Kontos and Fiene 1987; Howes 1983).

The evidence then suggested the need to up-skill through the achievement of higher levels of qualification with the aspiration that every full daycare setting would be led by a person qualified to degree level by 2015 (Childcare Strategy 2004) (ibid.).

The qualification agenda was already firmly established internationally. Indeed, the HighScope project of the 1960s required a long programme of staff development alongside the implementation of the programme, hence up-skilling was a key priority for the quality agenda of governments even then.

The pace of change to the sector in England came rapidly following the election of the Labour government in 1997. Services that were generally hidden from public discourse suddenly found themselves

Table 6.1 Timeline of government initiatives in the early years sector, 1996–2014

1996–7	Conservative government introduces a nursery voucher scheme in four counties.
1997–8	Voucher scheme is available for all.
1998	Labour party ends the voucher scheme but all four-year-olds are given free part-time nursery education for three terms prior to statutory school entry (term after the child's fifth birthday).
2004	The scheme is extended to all three-year-olds – 12.5 hours of free early education per week for 33 weeks a year.
2005	Children's Workforce Development Council (CWDC) is set up.
2006	Entitlement extends to 36 weeks a year.
	Introduction of EYPS.
2007	An extension of free early years education is offered to disadvantaged two-year-olds in half of the country.
2009	Two-year-old funding is extended to disadvantaged areas across the country.
2010	Entitlement is extended to 15 hours a week.
2011	New EYP contracts are issued with new pathways and, significantly, an entry-level pathway for undergraduates.
2012	The new EYFS is introduced.
	The independent government-commissioned Nutbrown review of early education and childcare qualifications is published, entitled *Foundations for Quality*.
2013	The DfE policy document *More Great Childcare* is published.
	Nutbrown's response document is published, entitled *Shaking the Foundations of Quality? Why 'childcare' policy must not lead to poor-quality early education and care.*
	The first EYT students will start their courses with new EYT standards.
2014	Expected start of new EYT training contracts.

centre-stage and politicians saw that there was political ground to be gained in championing the cause of women (mainly middle class) in pursuing careers. The first actions were taken by a Conservative government, motivated by the need to further boost the labour market by giving women returners an incentive (in the form of vouchers) to return to the labour market. The key dates are shown in Table 6.1.

The ten-year plan (HM Treasury 2004) set out minimum levels of practitioner qualification, staffing ratios and minimum standards as regards health and safety, and sought to have all settings led by someone who was qualified to degree level (Miller and Hevey 2012). A new EYP status was introduced in 2006 and was to be equivalent to QTS but would not allow the bearer to take up a 'teacher' position in the early years. The amalgamation of traditional caring roles with an obligation to educate was always going to be a difficult blend, as McGillivray (2008) acknowledges when discussing the differing employment conditions of each. The reasoning behind this continuation of a split system is unclear, but is likely to have something to do with placating the teaching unions. Also, historically there had been a divide between those who care for children and those who educate them (Sylva and Pugh 2005). The advantage of having an EYP or teacher in an early years setting was set in regulation as only these qualifications could allow a 1:13 ratio of three-year-olds and older and only then if the level 6 holder (or equivalent) was working directly with the children. The less qualified staff were only able to have a 1:8 ratio. Thus, in terms of managing change in practice, the status and up-skilling had some pecuniary advantages to settings that could in theory save on less qualified staff by employing an EYP who was able to count in ratio as being responsible for almost double the number of children but not at double the staffing cost. The financial advantages offered by the government, such as the transformation grant, were also seen as an attractive carrot to business settings that dominated the under-threes' market where the lower ratios were not changed dependent on qualification level.

The English National Childcare Strategy also offered supply-side subsidies in the form of start-up and other business support grants to private childcare businesses. Such start-up grants helped to support the transformation of playgroups into not-for-profit sessional or full daycare businesses and the establishment of out-of-school provision (Miller and Hevey 2012: 114).

The for-profit business sector, particularly involving individual nurseries and small chains, has undergone a period of rapid expansion during the last decade. Miller and Hevey (2012) suggest that they now make up 75 per cent of the private childcare sector. This has, however, squeezed out other providers such as playgroups and childminders. Indeed, Murray (2009), writing in *The Guardian*, suggested that 4,000 childminders had given up childminding since the introduction of the EYFS (DCSF 2008).

The introduction of tax credits to support childcare and to further the economic productivity of the nation by encouraging non-working individuals to return to employment has led to a two-tier system. This system is one of state provision in areas of disadvantage and privately funded care in better off areas. The former is perceived as being of better quality than the latter. Thus it may be that the cycle of disadvantage is altered due to the fact that the better quality provision is going to disadvantaged areas in the main to forward the agenda of equality. However, those who traditionally would have been looked after in the home are being placed in private childcare provision to enable mothers to return to work. Does the flood to institutional childcare lead us to greater problems in the future among those not traditionally at risk from financial disadvantage? Certainly we can see from research that the home environment plays a large part in children's flourishing and that indeed it is those whose mothers have the highest qualification level who seem to do best in our school system (Field 2010). By taking the mothers with those higher-level qualifications back into the workplace are we now creating a lesser childhood experience for those children traditionally seen as advantaged and what are the implications of this in the long term?

It could be argued that children whose parents have higher-level qualifications are spending a large proportion of their time with less qualified adults in a childcare environment that is not the home while their highly qualified parents work. Will this reduce the advantage that these children had been given by birth?

Increasing marketisation of English early years provision has consolidated two parallel childcare markets, one with fully state-funded or subsidised provision for poor children and one for the children of better-off employed parents. Also discernible is a trend towards individual rather than collective responsibility for childcare provision. While sustained by a range of government subsidies, this childcare market does not offer parents and children genuine choice (Miller and Hevey 2012).

It appears that the quality of provision among private providers is seen to be of an inferior quality to state provision due to the fact that the most qualified staff seek the better terms and conditions provided within the state sector. However, the results of the expansion have not been monitored robustly to encourage the development of quality to allow the children to flourish. Indeed, MacNaughton (2005) suggests that, in order to 'bloom', children and practitioners require time to reflect and enter into professional dialogue. The current debate about deregulation and the changes to the child to adult ratio will do little to enhance the conditions for 'blooming'. Truss announced at the Daycare Trust conference in December 2012 that, regarding France's provision, 'the workforce is so highly skilled, that they're trusted to use their expertise to staff their settings as they deem appropriate, with no nationally pre-scribed staff:child ratios in place'.

The message simplistically seems to be that conditions and pro-fessional status will improve if we unburden the system from bureaucracy. The message is sold as 'trusting' the workforce to make the right professional judgements on adult to child ratios rather than imposing them. The idea being that childcare will become more affordable and the pay of practitioners will improve if the adult to child ratio goes up. The same speech does, however, go on to acknowledge that, at the moment, we do not have staff with the same basic qualifications as those in the deregulated international context, so how will the quality of childcare be affected if deregulation precedes qualification enhancement? While most would agree that a highly trained professional workforce should be given professional autonomy and enhanced professional conditions, it is debatable whether an increase in child to adult ratios can compensate for the adult interaction that is seen as key to improving outcomes (Tizzard and Hughes 1984). Also, if this is the case then continuing professional development of practitioners needs to be foregrounded in the policy.

A radical shift needs to take place in the kind of opportunities offered to practitioners to engage in meaningful professional development throughout the course of their careers. It is only with this provision, MacNaughton (2005) argues, that practitioners will continue to bloom and be engaged with their careers rather than 'doing a job'. MacNaughton (2005) illustrates her point with reference to Carla, a practitioner in an Australian Early Years Centre. She interviews Carla about her professional learning. Carla has been working in a research group as well as attending traditional day-course training as part of her specified in-service programme. Carla suggests that it is only the thinking and knowledge that she gains from the research group that actually impacts upon her day-to-day work with the children. It is also that alone that enables her to bloom as a practitioner. She is quoted as saying that, during these one-off days, 'new pedagogical ideas had been poured into her "rut" of normal practices like a heavy burst of rain' (ibid.: 191), but they were soon forgotten after an initial burst of enthusiasm and did not become part of her sustained practice. MacNaughton (2005) suggests that she and the other research group participants were 'starved of the conditions in which critical reflection and pedagogical innovation could grow' (ibid.). The author then goes on to suggest that one of the reasons for this is the fact that the practitioners work with 'untenable staff–child ratios (one adult to five children under two years of age)' (ibid.). The announcement by Truss (2012) of possible deregulation of ratios within England would do little to encourage and advance the possibility of reflective practice for professional development even though it is indeed that professionalism that is suggested as being so important. Thus we have a cyclical argument: the more professional the worker the more children they can cater for and the less time there is for a flourishing of their well-being and for their professionalism to bloom. The stark truth of the matter is that, if we want quality services with highly educated professionals to engage with our youngest children at the highest level, we have to pay for it. The system as a whole has to be financed at a collective welfare level to enable it to flourish and ultimately create the flourishing of society as a whole. Trying to reconstruct the system using the lifetime of a particular parliament is not going to work; there needs to be an all-party' buy-in' to the aims of any investment and it needs to be sustainable in the longer term not just until the next election campaign. Field (2010) argues for a radical reworking of the welfare system and suggests that the period of austerity creates the conditions for that to be possible. Field (2010) recommends that the government consider investment in early years services rather than income transfer as a way of reducing inequality and poverty for children. This suggests a realignment of finances currently available but any real-time cuts to government expenditure (such as the changes to universal child benefit) would need to be reinvested with growth in early years funding. Currently, Australia is reducing the number of children who can be cared for by an individual practitioner, with the under-threes' ratio changing from 1:5 to 1:4 and that for the over-threes changing from 1:15 to 1:12. The requirement in Australia for all staff to be level 3 qualified is being implemented by 2014 with qualified EYTs leading the settings (ACECQA 2013).

- Critical reflective practice needs time to be fully satisfying to the developing professional.
- Through critical reflective practice both the practitioner and the children in their care can be expected to flourish.

Addressing quality

The need to address quality has been a developing discourse. The measurability of that quality has been demonstrated as being central to the minds of politicians keen to show value for money. This discourse has developed further with the findings of Field (2010), showing that educational disadvantage starts before a child reaches five. His subsequent campaign under the auspices of the Foundation Years Action Group is for continued commitment and investment in early years services. His report blatantly states that:

The quality of early education matters. Children who benefited from good quality early education experiences were on average four to six months ahead in terms of cognitive development at school entry than those who did not.

(ibid.: 45)

This quality it seems can be evidenced adequately by Ofsted according to the government:

Quality and professionalism is improving in the sector, with Ofsted's inspection regime one of our system's great strengths. As of last week, parents and providers will be able to see how many good and outstanding providers there are in each local area through a new online tool on Ofsted's website.

(Truss 2012)

The quality debate is viewed simplistically by politicians and the complexity of the concept is sadly diminished and with it maybe the more important flourishing of the practitioner and the child. The report by Mathers *et al.* (2012) on behalf of the Daycare Trust suggests that quality is much more complex and that actually it is viewed differently by different stakeholder groups, but with all agreeing that quality staff were the most important feature of quality provision. Parents viewed quality staff as being friendly, warm and nurturing, whereas the key terms used by local authority staff and providers mentioned qualification level, knowledge and experience.

The rapid expansion in provision and the evidence from research drew attention to the need to increase and develop the workforce. The thrust to up-skill the workforce really came out of the desire to start addressing social disadvantage and out of research such as HighScope, one of the Head Start programmes in the USA, and the EPPE project (2004). Both of these projects alluded to the fact that the quality of the practice was commensurate with increasing outcomes in terms of children's attainment. Findings from HighScope cited by Pound (2005, in Pound 2011: 169) were that:

■ Those who had been involved in HighScope were significantly more likely to be employed.

■ By the age of 27 HighScope graduates earned significantly more than others.

■ Those who had been part of the HighScope experience were less likely to have been involved in crime or to have needed costly support such as for special educational needs, teenage pregnancy or drug abuse.

■   Men who were involved with HighScope were twice as likely as others to have raised their own children.

HighScope claimed that for every dollar invested seven dollars were saved by the State in the longer lifetime course. This would of course be of significant interest to policy makers. The ensuing EPPE report (2004) noted the significant impact of the influence of qualified teachers on a setting in terms of raising the attainment level of the children. It seemed that the influence of the teacher impacted on others working within the setting and so the teacher did not have to be working directly with an individual child for the impact to be felt.

The rapid expansion of the sector following the introduction of free provision for those aged three plus led to the government asking the Children's Workforce Development Council (CWDC), a non-governmental body, to oversee the childcare workforce. This in turn led to local authorities setting up workforce development teams to act as coordinators at the local level.

■   Quality means different things to different stakeholders.
■   Initially the CWDC was asked to oversee the childcare workforce.

Research-informed policy

From the outset the Labour governments had a mantra of 'research-informed policy' to form rationale for policy initiatives (Sylva and Pugh 2005). Government had seen from both from HighScope and the EPPE project (2004) and from international research that we had low investment in terms of gross domestic product (GDP) at 0.4 per cent in early years education (Plantenga and Remery 2009). Also, there appeared to be little coherence in the training of practitioners in early years education and findings of the studies showed that, where provision was led by those with degree-level qualifications, the potential gains in children's attainment were greater. Thus CWDC was tasked with creating a professional degree-level qualification for the sector, taking evidence from EPPE (2004) of degree-holding teachers' impact on practice. Those who attained the new status were to be key change agents in their settings (Simpson 2010), again echoing the EPPE (2004) findings.

CWDC set out its plans for Early Years Professional Status (EYPS), a degree-level qualification equivalent to but not the same as QTS, thus a two-tier system was to be continued despite noises about parity of the two labels. The pathway to EYPS was open to any practitioner who held the minimum of a level 3 NVQ (National Vocational Qualification). Those who held NVQ level 3 as their highest qualification were encouraged to gain early years foundation degrees and then to 'top up' with a third-year BA programme. Achievement at ordinary degree level would allow the applicant entry to the EYPS. This already shows the differential in qualification between teachers and EYPs, as teachers are required to hold an honours degree. In reality most of those who completed a foundation degree and then went on to 'top up' did pursue and gain the full honours; however, in a twist to the 2011 EYP contract, entry from that date onwards only funded the 60 credits needed to allow the award of an ordinary degree, so government itself was limiting the award to a lesser qualification than QTS thereby reinforcing the two-tier system. For those who wished to gain EYPS and were already graduates a shorter graduate pathway to EYPS was introduced. This was originally called the short pathway, renamed in 2011 as the Graduate Practitioner Pathway (GPP). Again, in terms of parity with QTS, the GPP is completed in six months while a PGCE takes a year. The GPP programme does not generally carry postgraduate credits, although some providers incentivise applicants by providing them, while a PGCE will carry them. The route for new graduates without experience, the post-2011 Graduate Entry Pathway (GEP), originally known as the Full Pathway, although commensurate with PGCE in length, again does not generally carry postgraduate degree credits unless an individual provider uses these to incentivise a course. Table 6.2 shows the routes

Table 6.2 Routes to Early Years Professional Status (EYPS)

Highest level of qualification	Pre-2011	2011–15
Foundation degree holder	Long top-up route	Undergraduate Practitioner Pathway (UPP)
Full degree holder	Short route	Graduate Practitioner Pathway (GPP) if degree in relevant subject
		UPP (2) if degree in non-relevant subject
Undergraduate in relevant subject, e.g. Early Childhood Studies	Not available previously	Undergraduate Entry Pathway (UEP) taken in third year of degree
Graduate in relevant field (not working in the sector)	Full route	Graduate Entry Pathway (GEP)

to EYPS. These routes will be retained in 2013 and 2014, although entrants from September 2013 become trainees and the award becomes that of Early Years Teacher (EYT).

Fully funded degrees were seen by some practitioners as a way of gaining a degree without significant financial investment themselves. This allowed some to go on and achieve lifelong ambitions of becoming teachers by following their EYPS with PGCE courses, thus an unintended advantage of government finance was to allow a group of initially underqualified, often low-paid, aspirant teachers the chance to fulfil their career aspirations. In some ways this has allowed some to break a cycle of deprivation for their own particular families as they have been able to access higher-paid employment. Had the status allowed EYPs to teach in the Foundation Stage of schools, maybe many more would have stayed in their current settings knowing that they could move at any time, but many saw the post-EYP period as a window of opportunity and, as they had made a return to study, they decided to continue their journey into teaching at that stage. Many settings therefore, having encouraged staff to achieve EYPS as part of their business plan, soon found their newly qualified staff leaving and were back to square one in terms of graduate leadership, the EYP salary still being much less attractive than that of a teacher (Miller and Cable 2008). Moves in the second Teaching Agency (TA) EYP contract to limit the funded credits to 60 at H level, the equivalent of an ordinary degree, making such candidates not eligible for PGCE, have deterred practitioners from taking the UPP funding, instead preferring to complete a full self-funded honours degree and then taking the GPP to achieve EYPS. The limit of the funding to 60 credits has also made it clear to EYPs that they are viewed as having less status than Qualified Teachers, as they can achieve the status with an ordinary degree whereas QTS requires an honours degree. The new requirement is not clear but certainly initially it seems that in 2013 trainees can be accepted with an ordinary degree. The two-tier system has therefore been reinforced and equivalent status is seen as rhetoric and not reality. The Tickell review (2011) further questioned the value of the status and tended towards a teacher qualification, again underlining that EYPS was not the same as QTS and one was considered superior to the other. In New Zealand it seems that true professionalism was only really gained when one benchmark qualification path was established for all educators and parity of pay with Qualified Teachers was achieved. This process took some 20 years (Miller and Cable 2008). We are not yet on a path-way to achieve that parity and the rejection by the government of the Nutbrown (2012) recommendation to allow EYPs to access QTS routes reinforces that it is not a policy direction that the Coalition aspires to.

- Children in graduate-led settings were seen to achieve more highly than those in other settings.
- EYPS has never had parity with QTS; entry requirements are not the same and the length of time to gain the status also differs.
- Following the Nutbrown review (2012) the Coalition has chosen to continue a two-tier system of qualifications.

Change to self

Many who have been through the up-skilling process talk about how the requirement to engage with education at a higher level than their previous qualification has left them at times confused about who they are. The author's experience of students on Foundation degree Arts (FdA) courses is that, at around the beginning of year two, they begin to notice profound changes in the way they think. Some find this liberating, others disempowering – disempowering because, although they know what it is they want to do, they are not the only ones affected by their new knowledge and they don't necessarily have the authority to be agents of their own destiny. Urban (2008: 136) says:

> The dilemma unfolds between the day to day experience of having to act concretely, spontaneously and autonomously in ever changing uncertain situations which, to a large extent, are determined by factors beyond the practitioner's control, and the pressure that arises from increasing socio-cultural and socio-economic expectations to produces pre-determined outcomes on this complex work context.

It is not surprising, therefore, that individuals who have embarked on 'being' up-skilled find themselves in an uneasy place personally. Often the courses that they have attended have challenged their existing ideas and values and they see those around them through a new lens, both colleagues and sometimes family.

Change to organisations

Organisations quickly found themselves in a position of needing to have a member of staff with a degree. The original target of an EYP in every full daycare setting by 2015 put pressure on those responsible for the settings to encourage their workforce to up-skill. The availability of funding to allow staff to do this with generous backfill was an opportunity many found too good to miss. Indeed, initially the foundation degrees run by my own institution found the participants to have been coerced by their organisations to attend, whereas latterly the students have been self-motivated to apply as they have seen both the benefits to colleagues' self-confidence and also the ability of those colleagues to move into teaching, a much better paid and seen to be more respected profession.

The other major change in organisations has been the influence of the EYP on colleagues. Often EYPs are the younger members of staff who have embraced degree-level study and EYPS as a way of career progression. In order to achieve the standards, prospective EYPs have to demonstrate substantial leadership and management of other staff. This has often caused resentment and disaffection among older and more experienced practitioners who found themselves being told what to do by colleagues for whom they might not have had the greatest respect. This is especially true of Entry Pathway EYPs who have a degree but little or no relevant experience. These full-pathway, now GEP, practitioners often found those within settings viewing them with suspicion and disrespect. Six years on from the first EYPs, most:

> Early Years Professionals were most likely to be senior leaders in private and voluntary/community settings. They were more likely to be middle leaders in children's centres and tended to be practitioners with limited leadership roles in other Local Authority settings.
>
> (Hadfield and Jopling 2012)

This shows a rather two-tier system again with the better qualified staff working in local authority maintained settings and the private sector having the lesser qualified staff with the most qualified leading. It is the private and voluntary sectors then where EYPs are likely to have most agency to change practice, but the higher salaries of the maintained settings often attract the career-minded EYPs as they feel the need for and right to a higher salary (Simpson 2010). They then move to these positions where they are less likely to have the ability to lead and so, in some ways, disaffection has been unwittingly inbuilt into the qualification professionalisation agenda.

Conclusion

The results of the two-year EYP longitudinal study (Hadfield and Jopling 2012) do suggest that ground has been gained in determining a professional status for EYPs, both within the EYPs themselves, in their confidence in their own ability, and in acknowledgement from fellow professionals. The awareness of the status among parents and the wider public is still reported as low.

Equally persistent though was the belief among practitioners that parents (82 per cent), other professionals (68 per cent) and people outside the early years sector (91 per cent) did not understand what EYPS meant (ibid.: 24).

In the second EYP study EYPs showed an increasing confidence in leading colleagues and colleagues' willingness to accept their ideas and suggestions. The positive response rate went from 49 per cent in the 2011 survey to 67 per cent in the 2012 one.

Maybe, as these practitioners reflect on their recent education, they begin to flourish and increasingly find their voice and recognise their agency in being able to bring about change that fits with their own personal philosophy of early years. This view, although in the differing context of social care, is supported by Boddy (2011). Boddy suggests that lower-qualified workers, meaning below degree level, do not have 'a resource of professional reflection' and rely very much on intuition (ibid.: 114) . It is this resource of professional reflection that is key in the work of EYPs. Boddy (2011) also suggests that the social pedagogues in her study developed the terminology 'professional heart' to explain the complex dynamic between professionalism on the one hand and a genuine caring relationship between them and the children in their care on the other. She expands this notion by describing the work of the pedagogue as 'heads, hands and heart . . . Hands and heart being practical engagement and empathy . . . The heart also needs the head – the balance brought by professional knowledge and reflection on a relationship' (ibid.). So maybe the up-skilling process is the change from intuition to professional reflection. It can be an uncomfortable process for those on the journey but maybe, once the destination is reached and settling in to the new metaphorical location has happened, the true flourishing of the professional, the children and the setting can take place.

REFLECTIVE QUESTIONS

- Who do you think has benefited most from the up-skilling agenda?
- How has the up-skilling policy influenced practice in your setting or placement?
- Has the up-skilling agenda helped the government to achieve its aims?

References

Australian Children's Education & Care Quality Authority (ACECQA) (2013) 'Key changes'. Available online at www.acecqa.gov.au/key-changes (accessed 14 April 2013).

Boddy, J. (2011) 'The supportive relationship in "public care": the relevance of social pedagogy', in Cameron, C. and Moss, P. (eds) *Social Pedagogy and Working with Children and Young People*, London: Jessica Kingsley, pp. 105–24.

Department for Children, Schools and Families (DCSF) (2008) *Statutory Framework for the Early Years Foundation Stage*, London: DCSF.

Department for Education (DfE) (2012) *The Early Years Foundation Stage (EYFS)*, London: DfE.

Department for Education (DfE) (2013) *More Great Childcare: Raising quality and giving parents more choice*. London: DfE. Available online at www.education.gov.uk/publications/standard/publicationDetail/Page1/DFE-00002–2013 (accessed 11 April 2013).

Field, F. (2010) *The Foundation Years: Preventing poor children becoming poor adults: The report of the Independent Review on Poverty and Life Chances*, London: Cabinet Office. Available online at www.nfm.org.uk/component/jdownloads/finish/74/333 (accessed 2 July 2013).

Hadfield, M. and Jopling, M. (2012) *Second National Survey of Practitioners with Early Years Professional Status: Part of the longitudinal study of early years professional status*, London: DfE.

HM Treasury (2004) *Choice for Parents, the Best Start for Children: A ten year strategy for childcare*, London: HMSO.

McGillivray, G. (2008) 'Nannies, nursery nurses and early years professionals: constructions of professional identity in the early years workforce in England', *European Early Childhood Education Research Journal*, 16(2): 242–54.

MacNaughton, G. (2005) *Doing Foucault in Early Childhood Studies: Applying poststructural ideas*, Abingdon: Routledge.

Mathers, S., Singler, R. and Karemaker, A. (2012) *Improving Quality in the Early Years: A comparison of perspectives and measures*, Oxford: The Daycare Trust.

Miller, L. and Cable, C. (2008) *Professionalism in the Early Years*, Abingdon: Hodder Education.

Miller, L. and Hevey, D. (2012) *Policy Issues in the Early Years*, London: Sage.

Munton, T., Mooney, A., Moss, P., Petrie, P., Clark, A. and Woolner, J. (2002) *Research on Ratios, Group Size and Staff Qualifications and Training in Early Years and Childcare Settings*, London: Thomas Coram Research Unit, Institute of Education, University of London.

Murray, J. (2009) '"They're trying to make us all into academics." Why have 4,000 childminders given up the job in 12 months, and will some go "undergound"?', *The Guardian*, 16 June.

Nutbrown, C. (2012) *Foundations For Quality: The independent review of early education and childcare qualifications. Final report*, London: Department for Education

Nutbrown, C. (2013) *Shaking the Foundations of Quality? Why 'childcare' policy must not lead to poor-quality early education and care*. Available online at www.shef.ac.uk/polopoly_fs/1.263201!/file/Shakingthefoundationsofquality.pdf (accessed 11 April 2013).

Plantenga, J. and Remery, C. (2009) *The Provision of Childcare Services: A comparative review of 30 European countries*, Luxembourg: Office for Official Publications of the European Communities.

Pound, L. (2011) *Influencing Early Childhood Education*, Maidenhead: McGraw-Hill.

Simpson, D. (2010) 'Being professional? Conceptualising early years professionalism in England', *European Early Childhood Education Research Journal*, 18(1): 5–14.

Sylva, K. and Pugh, G. (2005) 'Transforming the early years in England', *Oxford Review of Education*, 31(1): 11–27.

Sylva, K., Melhuish, E., Sammons, P., Siraj-Blatchford, I. and Taggart, B. (2004) *The Effective Provision of Pre-school Education (EPPE) Project: Final report*, Nottingham: Department for Education and Skills.

Teather, S. (2011) 'Sarah Teather on reforming Early Years: written statement to Parliament'. Available online at www.gov.uk/government/speeches/sarah-teather-on-reforming-early-years (accessed 3 July 2013).

Tickell, Dame C. (2011) *The Early Years: Foundations for life, health and learning*, London: Department for Education. Available online at www.education.gov.uk/tickellreview (accessed 26 January 2013).

Tizzard, B. and Hughes, M. (1984) *Young Children Learning: Talking and thinking*, Oxford: Blackwell.

Truss, E. (2012) 'Speech to the Daycare Trust conference', 4 December. Available online at www.education.gov.uk/inthenews/speeches/a00218139/daycare-trust-conference (accessed 11 April 2013).

Urban, M. (2008) 'Dealing with uncertainty: challenges and possibilities for the early childhood profession', *European Early Childhood Education Research Journal*, 16(2): 135–52.

7 | The impact of foundation degrees on practitioners

Zenna Kingdon

Introduction

This chapter will look at the impact of a specific foundation degree on a group of practitioners. In order to contextualise this it is essential to explore the policy drivers and initiatives that have impacted on the early years sector, particularly from 1997 and the election of New Labour onwards. Foundation degrees for early years practitioners sat within a policy context in which there were drivers to up-skill and professionalise the workforce. Within this chapter those particular drivers are explored with reference to the Laming report (2003) and the EPPE (Effective Provision of Pre-school Education) report (Sylva *et al.* 2004), both of which can be seen to have had significant impact within the sector and to have added gravitas to the government's concerns and drivers.

This chapter will also look at the role of higher education with particular emphasis on widening participation. Widening participation has been concerned with the massification of higher education and the inclusion of non-traditional students (Schuetze and Slowey 2002). Practitioners working in the early years sector would usually be considered non-traditional. Issues that concern women as returning learners will also be explored.

Practitioners' experiences of completing the foundation degree will be reflected. From discussions with the practitioners a number of recurring themes have emerged. These included personal development, professional development and the quality of the experience for children and their families. Throughout their discussions notions of what it is to be a critically reflective practitioner are heard along with debates about ethics, values and what it means to be a professional in the early years workforce. These themes can be seen to be linked to the notion of 'flourishing', which is a theme that we explore throughout this book.

The policy context

The introduction of foundation degrees within the early years sector sits within a particular policy context in which the New Labour government of 1997–2010 focused on education and its manifesto commitments to reduce poverty and social exclusion (Taggart 2004). While early years education had not been significantly the focus of governments historically, there had been recurring calls for improved education and training of the workforce from Plowden (1967) to Osborn and Milbank (1987), Ball (1994) and the Audit Commission (1996). The interest in early years education escalated through the 1990s prior to the election of New Labour in 1997. The Rumbold report (1990), *Starting with Quality*, began to identify that young children had needs that were different from those of older children. Recommendations from the report included a suggestion that under-fives should have a curriculum that was appropriate for them and that parents should not be seen as being an enhancement but as essential if children were to gain fully from the experience (Rumbold 1990). To that end, the curriculum known as the desirable learning outcomes (DLOs) (SCAA 1996) was the first that was intended for children under the age of five. It was delivered in all pre-schools that were able to accept the newly introduced nursery education vouchers. Over the next decade the early years sector was subject to three further curricular changes. In 2000, *Curriculum Guidance for the Foundation Stage* (DfES) was published and intended for use with children from the age of three until the end of their Reception year. Next came the introduction of *Birth to Three Matters* (DfE 2003). This document was intended for practitioners who were working with the youngest children. In September 2008 the EYFS (DCSF 2008) was introduced. This combined the two previous documents along with the welfare standards that settings were expected to meet. In 2001, responsibility for childcare services moved from the Department of Health to the Department for Education and Employment (DfEE). This was a significant policy development in that it signalled a different view of the role of early childhood education and care (ECEC) services in England and Wales. Set against this backdrop of fast-paced change a raft of policy initiatives ensued as did the focus on the workforce itself.

After the re-election of New Labour for a second term in 2003, there appeared to be an escalation in the interest in early years. According to

Sylva and Pugh (2005: 11) not only did the government intend to focus on early years provision and provide greater funding, they also intended to 'alter its nature and the way services were delivered'. Also significant in 2003 was the publication of the first phase of the EPPE project (2004) and of Lord Laming's report into the death of Victoria Climbié. The Laming report (2003) could be seen as a watershed moment in the ways in which children's services were delivered in England. While there had been a desire in the 1989 Children Act for closer cooperation between children's services, it had not occurred. The Laming report (2003) was published at a time when the government of the day was wishing to focus on education and social exclusion. The recommendations of the report underpinned those key concerns and demonstrated ways in which the government could be seen to be making positive inroads into their areas of concern. After Laming (2003) the ways in which children's services were delivered became more than simply an ideal. Children's Trusts and Safeguarding Boards were introduced alongside the Common Assessment Framework (CAF) (Waterman 2009).

The events of 2003 were followed by a raft of policy initiatives, many of which focused on the early years sector: the 2004 Children Act, the document, *Choice for Parents, the Best Start for Children: A ten year strategy for childcare* (HM Treasury 2004), and the 2006 Childcare Act. The 1989, 2004 and 2006 Acts were key in demonstrating the government's commitment to the improvement of the experiences of children and their families, particularly in the early years sector. The 2004 Children Act provided the legal underpinning of the *Every Child Matters* agenda (2004), further strengthening the rights of children that had been laid out in the 1989 Act and making clearer its surrounding child protection. The *Choice for Parents* ten-year strategy (HM Treasury 2004) laid out how the government intended to radically "reform the workforce" (ibid.: 6). It suggested that there was general agreement that raising the level of qualifications in the workforce would raise the quality of childcare. Evidence from EPPE (2004) suggested that settings that were supported by qualified teachers, who provided support for less qualified staff, demonstrated significantly better outcomes for children. This was very significant in that all settings in England could be registered and led by someone with a level 3 qualification. A graduate-led setting was in the minority, as there were few staff with level 6 qualifications within the workforce. It became politically expedient to rely on the evidence of EPPE (2004) in order to justify the changes that were to follow. The 2006 Childcare Act formalised the arrangements for the registration and inspection of childcare services and also emphasised the legal duties of local authorities: in securing sufficient childcare for working parents, in providing a parental information service, and in providing information, advice and training for childcare providers. This third Act could be seen to focus on providing care in order to support people, particularly women in returning to the workforce.

While for many this new interest in the early years, and the Acts that supported it, suggested that the early years sector was suddenly being afforded the significance that it had long deserved. However, others were left feeling that what they had to offer was no longer of value. The rhetoric was about up-skilling and professionalising the workforce. The implication from the language was that what went before was in some way deficient (McGillivray 2008). Osgood (2009: 735) argues that the workforce had been constructed in two opposing ways, as the 'salvation of society *and* as shambolic/disordered'. This latter construction led to notions of the need for professionalisation. She further argues (Osgood 2012) that the government had a vested interest in constructing the workforce in deficit terms. This then ensured that there was a need for radical reform. McGillivray (2008) also suggested that the new policy focus on those working with young children raised questions about the practitioners' own response to the debates about education and suitable qualifications. The voice of the practitioner was often overlooked in political discussions. Historically there was a divide between those who provided care for young children and those who educated them. The bringing together of these two into ECEC had a number of implications for the workforce that was to work with these children.

The terminology that described the workforce was disparate and gave no clear indication of the role or level of qualifications of the staff. Between the 1940s and 1960s they were variously referred to as teachers or nannies, emphasising the divide between those in a caring role and those in an educational one (McGillivray 2008). The first of these roles was seen as low-status work while the latter was given value. By the early part of the twenty-first century the titles multiplied – nursery nurse, practitioner, nursery worker, nanny, childminder – and this led to further confusion as to both the role of the worker and his or her level of qualification.

- Successive government reports led to the introduction of a curriculum that is delivered nationally in early years settings.
- Laming (2003) provided a watershed moment in the ways in which early years services were delivered in England.

■ It was politically expedient for the government to describe the early years workforce in disparate terms.

■ The voice of the practitioner was often overlooked in political discussions.

Up-skilling and professionalising the workforce

From the election of New Labour in 1997 there had been an unprecedented interest in the early years workforce. Taggart (2004) argues that early years became politicised as its role in the manifesto's commitment to reduce poverty and social exclusion was recognised. The government felt that by focusing its efforts in the early years not only were there likely to be long-term benefits, but it could also be seen to be doing something that had a positive impact on the lives of many families with young children. Sylva and Pugh (2005) state that New Labour not only intended to increase spending on early years, but intended to change the nature of early years provision and the way in which services were delivered. Research evidence drawn from sources such as EPPE (2004) and the Perry Pre-school Project (1962) demonstrated that money spent on early years education had long-term benefits in that it would save the taxpayer on a ratio of 1:7 (Sylva and Pugh 2005). In order to reap these long-term benefits, the government was aware that it needed a suitably qualified workforce that was able to deliver the desired outcomes.

The Department for Education and Skills (DfES) then appeared to focus on outcomes rather than the workforce itself. The emphasis was on creating a workforce that was able to deliver a particular policy agenda. It was through a 'transformational reform agenda designed to improve life chances for all and reduce inequalities in our society' that reform or up-skilling of the workforce began (DfES 2006: 2). The government invested heavily in this process. The initial round of funding that was used to support the raising of qualifications was known as the Transformation Fund, and £250 million was invested in the first phase of the process. The language and rhetoric throughout was of change, of providing something new, and there was the implication that staff previously were not appropriately skilled or qualified for the new roles that were being defined.

From 2001 there was a new professional role within England, that of Senior Practitioner. In order to attain the status of Senior Practitioner an early years worker needed to have completed an early years sector endorsed foundation degree (EYSEFD). This new qualification was vocational in approach and combined academic study with work-based learning. The new status was largely welcomed by the workforce, as it was recognised as a new level of professionalisation (Miller 2008). The introduction of Early Years Professional Status (EYPS), a graduate-level status that came into existence in 2007, has led to Senior Practitioner Status no longer being clearly recognised. In 2013, EYPS is being replaced by that of Early Years Teacher (EYT).

Early years foundation degrees represent the largest number of foundation degrees in England. By 2007 there were 360 such degrees offered (Miller 2008). Undoubtedly government interest in and funding of qualifications led to the proliferation of such qualifications. The foundation degrees are now often seen as an initial route to EYPS. Students who have completed the foundation degree can take a further 60 credits at level 6 and then be assessed for the status. Recommendations from the EPPE report (2004) were that early years settings should be led by graduates who would lead practice and raise standards. EYPS was initially proposed to be at an equivalent level to that of Qualified Teacher Status (QTS); however, in order to gain QTS students must hold a good honours degree and GCSEs in English, maths and science if they are born after 1979. In order to gain EYPS candidates must hold an ordinary degree and GCSEs in only English and maths; this is changing from September 2013 to include GCSE science. The ongoing differences continue to mark a lack of parity between the two statuses and allow for the lack of commensurate levels of pay. Allen (2011) suggests that there remains a pay gap in the UK between men and women of just over 20 per cent, despite equal pay laws having been in place for over 40 years.

- The role of the early years sector became politicised as its role in reducing poverty and social exclusion was recognised.
- There appeared to be a focusing on outcomes rather than the workforce.
- Early years foundation degrees represent the greatest number of foundation degrees in England.

Women returning to the workforce

The early years workforce is predominantly female at over 90 per cent. In many respects this is to be expected, as historically childcare was seen as the role of women. Early years care and education has been something many women have undertaken, having had children of their own. Often the women have needed to work and earn an income, but they also needed to do something that fitted around caring for their own children, so working in an early years setting has appeared to be the answer. These perceptions of the workforce have often led to a diminishing of the role. Many of the attributes that are valued within the early years workforce, such as caring for and nurturing children, are seen as lacking professional status (Taggart 2011). Osgood (2009) argues that what is considered to be good-quality provision is akin to mothering and specifically a middle-class view of mothering. This has led to the workforce being constructed not merely by gender, but also by class. For women who have been socially constructed in ways that suggest they do not participate in a career that is valued by society or given any real status, to return to higher education has created a number of challenges. Given that the up-skilling of the workforce was predominantly in order that women, mainly middle-class women, could have a choice about whether to return to work, issues surrounding professionalisation have also become problematic. Osgood (2009) further argues that views of what it is to be a professional are determined by a hegemony that is bound by notions of expertise and being learned. These notions are in direct opposition to a workforce that is generally both gendered and working class, and whose members have been told that they are not academic and do not need to be in order to work with young children.

- Attributes that are desired within the early years workforce are often seen as lacking professional status.
- The workforce has been constructed not simply by gender, but also by class.

Widening participation and the role of HE

Traditionally students entering higher education (HE) have chosen to do so and have to compete for their places. The introduction of foundation degrees within HE has had a significant impact on the sector. Edmond *et al.* (2007) commented that foundation degrees were designed to be both vocationally orientated and underpinned by academic rigour. They went on to discuss the fact that the sector was encouraged to develop these routes as the Higher Education Funding Council for England (HEFCE) was not offering additional numbers in other areas. Students accessing foundation degrees were usually considered to be non-traditional. Schuetze and Slowey (2002) noted that throughout almost all developed societies there appeared to be a massification of higher education during the last decade of the twentieth century. This led to a description of non-traditional as 'students, who for a complex range of social, economic, and cultural reasons were traditionally excluded from, or under-represented in, higher education' (ibid.: 313). Within the early years sector graduate-level leadership was a policy decision. This meant that many entering higher education as non-traditional students, without the expected prerequisites of A-levels and GCSEs at A–C, were being coerced into doing so and were being told that it was a condition of them remaining employed. Research by Adnett and Slack (2007) demonstrates that, for many non-traditional students entering higher education, this does not necessarily lead to higher wages. This was a concern of many of the students when entering the foundation degree programme. Despite the range of challenges faced by participants on the programme many of them reported a range of benefits that were not financial, but centred around personal development and increased self-confidence and self-esteem (Dunne *et al.* 2008).

Practitioners' experiences

The remainder of this chapter draws on interviews with practitioners who have completed a foundation degree in early years and child development:

> Our journey in early years began over a decade ago, in a preschool that was on the brink of closure. Our setting has seen radical changes over the last seven years. However with ever changing policy within early years, and as leading staff members, we felt the way forward for our practice would be for us to continue our professional development. With this commitment in mind we embarked on the foundation degree pathway that would ultimately lead to early years professional status (EYPS).
>
> (Carol Savage and Laura Stevens)

It could be suggested that in many ways Carol and Laura could be seen as typical of many foundation degree students. They were mature women who started working in the early years sector because they had children in pre-school. They both left school with few formal qualifications and began their careers within the early years sector as volunteers.

Like many others they were persuaded to take the initial qualifications and soon found themselves running the nursery. As the Labour governments of 1997–2010 began a programme of up-skilling the early years workforce, they decided to participate. While they were engaged in work in a small pre-school they were fully aware of the changes in policy at national level that were having a significant impact on the way in which settings such as their own were to be run. The unprecedented attention that the early years workforce was receiving included recognition that young children need a highly qualified reflexive work-force to meet their needs (Brock 2006; Osgood 2006). Carol and Laura recognised some of these issues when they joined the programme. By the end of the programme they felt that they were familiar with many of the issues that had been raised and were better equipped to address them:

> As reflexive practitioners we feel we have a responsibility to use and share the knowledge that we have obtained from the foundation degree, to shape our pedagogy and that of our staff and colleagues. Our vision for the future is to lead a setting where all staff are trained to the highest standard and share the same commitment to quality and care.
>
> (Carol Savage and Laura Stevens)

Powell (2010: 227) suggests that making sense of policy and values in the current early years workforce 'may become a Herculean task for even the most reflective, analytical and creative of practitioners'. The change that had occurred over a relatively short period of time meant that the practitioners themselves needed not simply to adhere to changing policy but also to question their value basis. Powell (2010) argues that, while there is a huge number of policy drivers shaping the current early years workforce, these policies fail to include values and dispositions. She continues to state that Dahlberg and Moss (2005) have argued for the need to make visible assumptions about these values. Often these values are seen as common sense – something that anyone working within the early years is likely to demonstrate, including being energetic and having a genuine liking for and interest in children and their development. Carol and Laura do appear to be in possession of these common-sense attributes and values. Many of these, it could be demonstrated, they were in possession of long before they joined the foundation degree. It is often these values that continue to be ignored and appear not to be esteemed by policy makers. However, it could be argued that it is precisely these values that many within the early years workforce hold, allowing them to be flexible and responsive in adapting their practice because they have that genuine liking for, and interest in, the positive development of children.

What Carol and Laura would acknowledge that the FdA (Foundation degree Arts) has done for them is to allow them to engage with the new and ever changing policy discourses in meaningful ways. They are able to move beyond simply delivering a curriculum because that is what the government insists they do, to considering not simply what they deliver but how and why they do so. The theoretical knowledge has provided an underpinning to their practice, they now possess are far deeper understanding of child development, and they are able to apply this to their practice.

They have also been enabled to engage in the discussions that surround the early years workforce. This includes recognising, as Osgood (2009) states, that the changes in the early years agenda are politically motivated. Both Carol and Laura said that they had not recognised this prior to undertaking the FdA, but now they were not only able to recognise this, but they were also able to participate in informed debates about the issues that arise.

Entering the debate, whether it be within the learning environment, in their settings or in the wider field, were issues for a number of our students. In her final presentation Tracy Hill discussed how the FdA had enabled her 'to challenge and reflect critically on my practice and . . . enabled me to develop a deeper understanding of theory and knowledge to support not only my practice but the children and staff in my setting'.

It had been in an earlier taught session weeks before the final presentation that the positive impact the foundation degree had had on Tracy became clear. In many respects you would not have known that she was on the programme for the first 18 months. She was quiet, rarely contributing to group discussions. In the last few months of the programme, however, she found her voice. She came in one day and couldn't wait to recount her experience of speaking out at a meeting. Her setting was being threatened by local authority cutbacks. Suddenly she stood up and told the authorities what she thought and how what they were proposing would negatively impact on the children in her care. Brock (2006) discusses the fact that being a professional is not simply about having the appropriate qualifications; it is also about the attitudes and values those professionals hold. It is about practitioners' 'autonomy to interpret the best for children and families' (ibid.: 2). She continues and cites the work of Edgington (2004), Smidt (2003) and Moyles (2002), arguing that the early years workforce needs to be knowledgeable and articulate, and thus able to advocate for its own professionalisation. Tracy would argue that through this programme she has developed these skills and attributes that have empowered her and enabled her to effectively advocate on behalf of the children and families with whom she works. She has developed 'discernible perceived increase in self-confidence, self-esteem' (Dunne *et al.* 2008: 54) and not only the realisation of personal capacity to engage in HE study but also a personal capability in the ways in which she engages within the wider workplace.

The workplace was an issue for other students, particularly for practitioners such as childminders who were working alone. There was no one for them to share their ideas or concerns with on a daily basis. Even where they belonged to a network, professional development continued to be a key issue. Irene Prouse was one such case:

> As a childminder, I can feel isolated from the rest of the Early Years workforce. I am the only registered childminder working with children in the Early Years Foundation Stage in my village. Understanding the need for quality learning experiences, especially for children falling into this age range has given me the drive to raise my understanding of holistic child development.

Irene had a clear drive to become a more formally and professionally qualified early years worker. However, in order to be able to do this she recognised that in her current practice she was isolated and was unable to discuss her understanding and how her knowledge impacted on her practice. Joining the foundation degree programme appealed to her because she would be expected to develop her own ideas, challenge her current position, be supported in developing a personal pedagogy that would further support her understanding of holistic child development, and therefore allow her to better provide for the children in her care. Berthelsen and Brownlee (2005) acknowledge that there has been little research into the relationship between personal pedagogy and the practice of early years educators. Recent interest in this area has meant that workers have needed to develop an understanding of their own epistemology and how this impacts on their practice. The above-mentioned longitudinal EPPE project (1997–2003) (Sylva *et al.* 2004) had a profound effect in England and Wales. There was clear recognition that children who receive high-quality pre-school experiences achieve better outcomes. With this in mind the Labour government set about up-skilling the early years workforce, encouraging many workers to participate in undergraduate programmes that could lead to EYPS. While some members of the workforce were coerced into joining foundation degree programmes, many like Irene, who possessed the values and ideologies (Brock 2006) that were recognised as necessary for members of the early years workforce, chose to seek out programmes that would support them in their professionalisation.

The issue of what it was to be a professional worker was raised time and again. One student discussed her journey from 'just a nursery nurse to a qualified confident early years educator'. The discourse of professionalism within the early years workforce is a recent phenomenon and one that is leading to lengthy debates. Osgood (2012) argues that the current popularity of the promotion of professionalism comes from the drive of the New Labour government to encourage active citizenship through full employment. Until relatively recently the workforce has been described by a variety of indistinct and confusing titles. These descriptions have led to the workforce often seeming to be invisible. McGillivray (2008: 252) suggests that this invisibility 'may also be sustained through lack of voice and presence in policy and discussion'. She argues that there is a danger that workforce reform policy that is simply foisted on the workforce may lead to a conflict in ideologies between policy makers and the workforce. She suggests that a review of the literature would suggest that what it is to be professional is premised on both changing and continuing perceptions, influenced by history, society, ideologies and discourse. What is implicitly written into the current dominant discourse of early years care and education policy includes a problematisation and unsettling of the workforce as change is implemented through workforce reform. Professionalism is usually associated with a high level of knowledge and specific skills and attributes (Osgood 2012, 2006; McGillivray 2008; Brock 2006). What many of the practitioners found through completing the foundation degree was that they were able to recognise the skills and attributes that they already had and articulate them in new ways that demonstrated their professionalism. Liz Bennett discussed how her new sense of professionalism had led to a sense of empowerment:

> As a student working towards EYPS I feel my perception towards Early Years as a profession has changed dramatically and I feel incredibly empowered. It has enabled me to have a voice within inter-professional working and given me the confidence to believe I am a professional worker.

Liz now found herself in a position where she was enabled to hold her own within the wider workforce and would expect that her voice would be heard. Many of the students voiced their confidence to raise questions and to challenge those in perceived positions of authority, including advisory teachers and Ofsted inspectors. Julie Down commented that:

> Through undertaking this degree I critically examine my practice continuously questioning why I am doing things in a particular way and I am able to examine other methods that may be more effective whilst having the knowledge to challenge colleagues beliefs.

The notion of examining practice was another theme that arose through the presentations. For one woman, examining practice in isolation was not enough; there needed to be an in-depth analysis of notions of quality and questions about from whose perspective was quality viewed:

> As Early Years Practitioners we know that every child is important and this is reinforced through the Early Years Foundation Stage ... Having defined this framework of norms should we now be asking *who* are making these judgements about good and bad and *how* are they making them?
>
> (Debbie Long)

Throughout the programme Debbie demonstrated her own development as a critically reflective practitioner. She was particularly concerned with the quality of provision. Debbie explored EPPE (2004), which clearly demonstrates that young children who have high-quality early years experiences have better outcomes in later life. Debbie was clear that each child and family is unique, and it was as a result of this that she found that she began to ask searching questions about the nature of what constitutes quality. What constituted a good experience for one child or family would not necessarily be a good experience for all children and families. Debbie became aware that childcare was only seen as good quality if, as Osgood (2009) says, it could be measured against a middle-class norm. Osgood (2009) further argues that ECEC in England and Wales is conceived of as being like mothering and specifically like middle-class mothering. It was this complex concept that Debbie reflected on as she began to question whose sense of good and bad was taken as being the norm. She began to recognise the gendered and class assumptions that are associated with the early years workforce. Her engagement with the programme allowed her to become critically reflective on these issues and the impact that they have on children and families.

It was clear from the presentations that this particular group of practitioners had developed a level of criticality that they did not have at the beginning of the programme. They not only began to question, but felt that they should be questioning rather than simply accepting policy directives that were delivered as top-down edicts.

Conclusion

This chapter has explored the experience of a group of practitioners on a foundation degree in early years education. The experience of these learners was located within a particular policy context that cannot be seen to affect any other group of learners. Foundation degrees were introduced by HEFCE in 2001. These new two-year qualifications were intended to bridge the gap where there were few suitably qualified people in the workforce (Edmond *et al.* 2007). Foundation degrees were intended to support both the workers and the employers in order that the needs of both could be fulfilled. During the New Labour government of 1997–2010, the early years sector was subject to scrutiny in a way that was unprecedented. Early years was seen as being an area in which political objectives of reducing social inequalities and child poverty could be seen to be delivered. Early years staff were constructed as failing in order that the government could bring about radical change within the sector (Osgood 2012). The results of EPPE (2004) clearly demonstrated that settings that were supported by graduates or teachers produced significantly better outcomes for children. It was against this backdrop that the government set aside funding to support staff in the early years sector in becoming more highly qualified. Initially, the above-mentioned sector endorsed foundation degrees (EYSEFDs) began to appear. These conferred Senior Practitioner Status on graduates. Later, the EYPS came into existence and the concern then became about moving from a foundation degree to a full ordinary or honours degree and gaining the EYP status. These drivers placed a strain on a workforce that historically had been largely unqualified. These policy directives were imposed from the top down on the workforce rather than created in response to a need that was perceived within.

Many practitioners were persuaded into joining programmes where perhaps they did not feel enabled, capable or able to participate. They were entering higher education – something that historically was for the elite – and, for many of them, they would be the first person in their family to gain a graduate-level qualification. Many who entered the process did so with a great sense of trepidation. They would be juggling a degree programme alongside a full-time job. Many also had caring responsibilities that meant that their time was further curtailed. At the end of the process what was clear, however, was that these practitioners would not simply take a qualification away with them. They were enabled to develop their own professional sense of self; they had become critically aware practitioners and had developed self-esteem and self-assurance that they had previously lacked. Osgood (2012) expresses a hope that the workforce may subvert the top-down approach in order that it develops a sense of professionalism that has not been imposed from above. It would appear that the practitioners who participated in this research certainly felt that this was the case. Sally Cowes was able to recognise how being on the programme had supported her both personally and professionally:

> Personally, my gained knowledge has supported my identification of my values and my beliefs. Reflecting on my own ethics and values and appreciating diversity has supported my relationships with all parents and the holistic child.

The practitioners who participated in the foundation degree have been enabled to deliver against the government policy driver of having increased numbers of graduates in the workforce. Probably more importantly, these practitioners have flourished both as individuals and as members of a professionalising workforce. They are able to advocate on behalf of the children and families in their care and to advocate for themselves and their colleagues. For them the foundation degree can be seen to have had a significant positive impact.

REFLECTIVE QUESTIONS

- How do your experiences of professionalisation or becoming a member of the early years workforce resonate with the experiences here?
- How do you perceive that the early years workforce is constructed in terms of professionalisation post New Labour?
- Do you consider that the early years workforce is gendered and is that an issue that you feel needs addressing?
- How do you think a graduate-led workforce impacts on the quality of experience for the children and their families?

References

Adnett, N. and Slack, K. (2007) 'Are there economic incentives for non-traditional students to enter HE? The labour market as a barrier to participation', *Higher Education Quarterly*, 61(1): 23–36.

Allen, G. (2011) *Early Intervention: The next steps*, London: Department of Work and Pensions. Available online at www.dwp.gov.uk/docs/early-intervention-next-steps.pdf (accessed 2 July 2013).

Audit Commission (1996) *Misspent Youth . . .: Young people and crime*, London: Audit Commission.

Ball, C. (1994) *Start Right: The importance of early learning*, London: RSA.

Berthelsen, D. and Brownlee, J. (2005) 'Respecting children's agency for learning and rights to participation in child care programs', *International Journal of Early Childhood*, 37(3): 49–60.

Brock, A. (2006) 'Dimensions of early years professionalism – attitudes versus competences?' Paper from the Association for the Professional Development of Early Years Educators (TACTYC). Available online at www.tactyc.org.uk/pdfs/Reflection-brock.pdf (accessed 4 March 2013).

Dahlberg, G. and Moss, P. (2005) *Ethics and Politics in Early Childhood Education*, London: RoutledgeFalmer.

Department for Children, Schools and Families (DCSF) (2008) *Statutory Framework for the Early Years Foundation Stage*, London: DCSF.

Department for Education (DfE) (2003) *Birth to Three Matters*, London: DfE.

Department for Education and Employment (DfEE) (2000) *Curriculum Guidance for the Foundation Stage*, London: DfEE.

Department for Education and Skills (DfES) (2006) *Children's Workforce Strategy: Building a word-class workforce for children, young people and families: The government's response to the consultation*, Nottingham: DfES.

Dunne, L., Goddard, G. and Woolhouse, C. (2008) 'Mapping the changes: a critical exploration of the career trajectories of teaching assistants who undertake a foundation degree', *Journal of Vocational Education and Training*, 60(1): 49–59.

Edmond, N., Hillier, Y. and Price, M. (2007) 'Between a rock and a hard place: the role of HE and foundation degrees in workforce development', *Education and Training*, 49(3): 170–81.

HM Treasury (2004) *Choice for Parents, the Best Start for Children: A ten year strategy for childcare*, London: HMSO.

Laming, Lord H. (2003) *The Victoria Climbié Inquiry: Report of an inquiry by Lord Laming*, London: Department of Health.

McGillivray, G. (2008) 'Nannies, nursery nurses and early years professionals: constructions of professional identity in the early years workforce in England', *European Early Childhood Research Journal*, 16(2): 242–54.

Miller, L. (2008) 'Developing professionalism within a regulatory framework in England: challenges and possibilities', *European Early Childhood Education Research Journal*, 16(2): 255–68.

Osborn, A. and Milbank, J. (1987) *The Effects of Early Education: A report from the child health and education study*, Oxford: Clarendon Press.

Osgood, J. (2006) 'Editorial: Rethinking "professionalism" in the early years: English perspectives', *Contemporary Issues in Early Childhood*, 7(1): 1–4.

Osgood, J. (2009) 'Childcare workforce reform in England and "the early years professional": a critical discourse analysis', *Journal of Education Policy*, 24(6): 733–51.

Osgood, J. (2012) *Narratives from the Nursery: Negotiating professional identities in early childhood*, London: Routledge.

Plowden, Lady B. (1967) *Children and their Primary Schools: A report of the Central Advisory Council for Education (England)*, London: HMSO.

Powell, S. (2010) 'Hide and seek: values in early childhood education and care', *British Journal of Education Studies*, 58(2): 213–29.

Rumbold, A. (1990) *Starting with Quality*, London: HMSO.

School Curriculum Assessment Authority (SCAA) (1996) *Nursery Education: Desirable outcomes for children's learning on entering compulsory education*, London: SCAA and Department for Education and Employment.

Schuetze, H. and Slowey, M. (2002) 'Participation and exclusion: a comparative analysis of non-traditional students and life-long learners in higher education', *Higher Education*, 44(3/4): 309–27.

Sylva, K. and Pugh, G. (2005) 'Transforming the early years in England', *Oxford Review of Education*, 31(1): 11–27.

Sylva, K., Melhuish, E., Sammons, P., Siraj-Blatchford, I. and Taggart, B. (2004) *The Effective Provision of Pre-school Education (EPPE) Project: Final report*, Nottingham: Department for Education and Skills.

Taggart, B. (2004) 'Editorial: early years education and care: three agendas', *British Education Research Journal*, 30(5): 619–22.

Taggart, G. (2011) 'Don't we care? The ethics and emotional labour of early years professionalism', *Early Years*, 31(1): 85–95.

Waterman, C. (2009) 'Making progress after Laming "Mark II"', *Education Journal*, 116: 25–8.

8 Policy and the change in the early years learning environment

Zenna Kingdon

Introduction

This chapter will critically analyse the development of and changes to the early years learning environment with particular emphasis on play as a pedagogical approach to early learning. The chapter is contextualised in terms of the first considerations of childhood as a phase in its own right, rather than merely as preparation for what the child would become. It is argued that until the work of Rousseau it was not possible to consider how children could be supported in developing and flourishing, considering the rigidity of control that had been exercised over them.

The chapter moves to consider the influence of the Industrial Revolution, Robert Owen, Friedrich Froebel, Susan Isaacs and Rachel and Margaret McMillan. It attempts to make clear links between the work of the last three and the current Early Years Foundation Stage (EYFS) (DfE 2012), looking in detail at the contributions they have made to developments in the understanding of child development. Play and playful pedagogies are critiqued with recognition that, while play is important and valuable in the lives of young children, it is not necessarily the activity from which they gain the most enjoyment (Vygotsky 1978). Play is the dominant discourse of early childhood education, and as such has in many discussions become idealised. The value of play in children's lives is not diminished, however the universal qualities of play are challenged.

Finally, the chapter considers enabling environments and outdoor environments. Clear links are made between enabling environments and flourishing. Children who are included, and whose ideas are valued and enacted, are likely to feel that they are validated in their settings.

The EYFS (2012) focuses on the outdoor environment; however, it does not seem to emphasise in any detail the benefits that are demonstrated by research evidence, so these benefits are discussed here.

A historical perspective on play and cognition in European childhoods

Children and their role in society were described as long ago as the ancient Greeks. Plato, following in the tradition of Socrates, wrote extensively about children and their education. He thoroughly described all aspects that he felt their education should cover. He was particularly concerned with the types of stories that were read to children, suggesting that young children should not be frightened by stories of monsters (Curtis and Boultwood 1966). He explained that play was an important aspect of young children's lives. However, he made it clear that this was necessary for their preparation as future citizens. His concerns were for what they would become in the future, rather than their experiences of childhood.

Aries (1962, cited in Hinitz 2006) suggests that the concept of childhood as a specific phase within a person's life was not conceived until after the medieval period. He drew from images of children within works of art to conclude that children were simply seen as small adults. James and James (2004) suggest that, while there are critiques of and challenges to Aries' view, the concept that childhood was socially constructed from the middle of the fifteenth century onwards remains decisive in early childhood studies. Hendrick (1997) suggests that it is important to distinguish between the cultures that children construct for themselves with their peers and the construction that adults conceive. Corsaro (2005) agrees that societal constructions of childhood are different from children's understanding of the period. For children it is a phase in their lives that they will move through, but for society childhood is a structural form, the components of which are ever changing.

Two discourses of childhood have prevailed – the Puritan and the Romantic. The Puritan tradition suggested that, as a result of concepts of original sin, children were seen as being born evil and only through processes of restitution could they become moral individuals. As a result children had few rights and were often abused (Wood and Attfield 2005). The Romantic notion of children saw them as inherently innocent and naturally good (McDowall Clark 2010). John Locke was the first to argue against original sin. In his work, *An Essay Concerning Human Understanding* (1977), written in 1692, he argues that children are born without innate concepts and ideas. It is from this that he argues against original sin, and that children are shaped by the adults around them. His is the tabula rasa or 'blank slate' approach, suggesting that children develop entirely as a result of their experiences. Locke (1977) began the shift from the Puritan to the Romantic tradition.

It was, however, Jean Jacques Rousseau (1712–78) (Nutbrown *et al.* 2008) who established the notion of childhood as a specific phase rather than simply as a preparation for adulthood and work. He argued against the Christian tradition, suggesting that children should be allowed to respond to nature, particularly during their early years of life. It is from Rousseau onwards that we can begin to identify approaches to early childhood education that support notions of flourishing and supporting the child in developing as an individual.

Johann Pestalozzi (1746–1827) (Nutbrown *et al.* 2008) informed pedagogical thinking of the period. He believed that children should be able to explore and experiment and draw their own conclusions. He and Friedrich Froebel were among the first pioneers who valued childhood as a purposeful phase. They recognised that it was an important and influential period in a child's life. They believed in the child as innocent, and needing care and protection, in contrast to the medieval notion of the child as miniature adult. They also significantly saw children as naturally good (Wood and Attfield 2005). These perceptions of the child further support notions of flourishing, of awareness of self and of self-esteem.

■ Children and childhood were discussed as long ago as the time of the ancient Greeks, but children had few rights and were seen as being in preparation for adulthood.
■ Jean Jacques Rousseau was the first to establish the notion of childhood as a specific phase in its own right.

The Industrial Revolution and the start of universal education

The Industrial Revolution is considered to have begun in England in about 1760. This process of the working classes moving from working on the land to moving into towns and cities and working in factories generated far-reaching alterations in society and impacted on the need for education. Prior to the Industrial Revolution the working classes were largely uneducated. As they moved and undertook new forms of employment, the need for education began to increase. There had been schools in England for hundreds of years, but generally these were not for the children of the working classes and none of these had been for young children. Prior to the Education Act of 1870 there was no universal education. However, the nineteenth century saw both a proliferation of different types of schools and an increase in numbers of children across society who attended them (Gillard 2011). In 1816 Robert Owen opened the first nursery school in England that catered for children as young as three years old (Burger 2011). Owen was a social reformer and experimented both in England and America in creating communities that lived and worked together. As such his nursery school could be argued to be the first employment-related early childcare facility (Staples New and Cochran 2008). Owen had made enormous profits out of the early part of the Industrial Revolution and used New Lanark in Scotland as a blueprint for his ideas for social reform (Donnachie 2000). He owned the cotton mills in New Lanark and created the school to provide education for the children of his workers. He raised the age at which children could start work in the factories from six to ten. Owen's legacy was educational but he was probably more important as a social reformer. Owen is seen as a pioneer of early childhood education. He was influenced by the work of Pestalozzi and had been to Yverdon to visit him and to understand his educational approach (Latham 2002). Pestalozzi's approach was based on supporting children in moving from the 'known to the unknown using developmentally appropriate experiences' (Saracho and Spodek 2009: 299). Owen followed the broadly Romantic tradition of early childhood education. He believed that the early years of a child's life were important and that children should be nurtured. He believed that children should be treated with care; physical punishment was to be avoided. Children were to be given opportunities to; play, go outside and on field-trips. They should learn reading, writing, arithmetic, sewing, music, dance, geography and natural history, as well as modern and ancient history (Pelzman 1998). The breadth of the curriculum was considered to be far greater than any others offered to such young children (Saracho and Spodek 2009). While Owen's approach can be seen to draw parallels with many of the early childhood theorists who influenced current education and practice, it is not his educational approach per se for which he is remembered. Rather, he is associated with the introduction of the infant school.

However, there was a decrease in the numbers of infant schools as attitudes changed and the feeling grew that young children were best cared for in their homes by their families (ibid.). It seems that, as the infant schools disappeared, Froebelian kindergartens began to emerge.

- The Industrial Revolution gave rise to the need for universal education.
- The nineteenth century saw a proliferation of both the numbers and types of schools, as well as of those who attended them.
- The work of Robert Owen will not be remembered so much for its pedagogical approach, but for the introduction of infant schools.

Froebel, Isaacs and the McMillan sisters

Friedrich Froebel was the son of a Lutheran pastor. His mother died before he was a year old, and later his father took the decision to send him to a girls' school. All of these factors were to have a profound influence on his life and work. Originally he intended to practise as an architect, but on meeting with Pestalozzi he became interested in education and decided to train with him. Of the two he was to become arguably the more influential. Froebel founded his own school in order that he could test his own ideas, but this did not occur until he was in his fifties. His kindergarten pedagogy suggested that children should spend time in a kindergarten, or children's garden, in which they were encouraged to participate in structured play and guided play activities that allowed them to explore the world around them. Froebel was resolute that children should engage in play because he saw it as 'the purest, most spiritual activity of man at this stage'. He also suggested that it was important throughout life, being that it was associated with 'the inner hidden natural life in man and all things . . . It holds the sources of all that is good' (1887/1974: 54–5, cited in Manning 2005). Froebel was a deeply religious man. This naturally impacted on the way in which he perceived that children should be educated. He believed that the purpose of education was 'to encourage and guide man as a conscious, thinking and perceiving being in such a way that he becomes a pure and perfect representation of that divine inner law through his own personal choice' (Froebel 1826: 2). Clearly, his educational approach can be seen to be guided by his religious convictions, which were influenced by German Romanticism and the sense of innocence. Froebel discussed play as the work of children, and he developed educational materials called 'gifts' and 'occupations'; however, the concept is more closely associated with Susan Isaacs.

Isaacs (1885–1948), it could be suggested, was the most influential British child psychologist of her generation (Willan 2009). She worked across a number of disciplines during her life: child psychologist, philosopher, biologist, psychoanalyst, free-thinker and educator of children. October 1924 saw her opening the Malting House School; this was an experimental establishment that survived for four years before the funds ran out (Graham 2008). The majority of the children who attended were the offspring of Cambridge dons. There were between ten and twenty children on roll at any given time. Isaacs and a team of observers set up the experimental school to map what she perceived to be the natural development of children's understandings. Throughout the process she worked closely with observers, whose role was to note in detail the behaviour and actions of the children. Isaacs believed that children learn best when their interests are valued and celebrated and their needs are recognised (Graham 2008). Isaacs also believed that children learnt through their own play. She ensured that they had opportunities to build on a large scale, to work collaboratively and to come back to work that they had previously abandoned. For Isaacs, play was 'the child's work, and the means whereby he [sic] grows and develops. Active play can be looked upon as a sign of mental health: and its absence, either of some inborn defect or mental illness' (Isaacs 1929: 9, cited in Willan 2009: 153). She believed that children should have access to a broad-based curriculum that afforded them opportunities in all aspects of their cognitive and physical development. Later, Isaacs worked at the Institute of Education, University of London, founding the department of Child Development. There her students became well-educated pedagogues not teachers, the emphasis being on understanding children rather than teaching (ibid.). She expected teachers to compile detailed observational notes on each child, demonstrating a breadth of knowledge and understanding of that child. The record-keeping system that she instigated was used in Wiltshire up until the 1950s. Links can be made between Isaacs' recording systems and the systematic observation of children that occurs currently as part of the EYFS (2012). Isaacs placed emphasis on the role of play in children's development. Likewise, the EYFS (2012) calls for a balance between child-initiated and adult-directed play opportunities.

Like Isaacs, the work of the McMillan sisters, Rachel and Margaret, can be seen to have links to the EYFS (2012) in both enabling environments and physical development. Rachel (1859–1917) trained in nursing and as a sanitary inspector, as well as being interested in Christian Socialism. All of these factors influenced and impacted on the work of her sister Margaret (1860–1931). Margaret spent a number of years in Bradford and was involved in the Independent Labour Party. There she was elected to the Education Committee, School Attendance and School Management Committees. She had campaigned vigorously to be elected.

In one lecture she spoke of mothers as 'chief educators' (Bradburn 1989: 46), a concept that would have been unheard of at the time. She worked closely with Dr James Kerr, the School Medical Officer, and became interested in the physiology of growth. She campaigned for improved ventilation in schools, for correct breathing to be taught, for school baths and for the provision of wholesome school dinners. In total Margaret spent nine years in Bradford, eight of them on the school board.

She moved to London to join her sister. In 1912 both sisters travelled to America to attend a conference that was concerned with education and medicine. This conference had a significant impact on Margaret's work for the rest of her life.

It was this recognition of the importance of the early years, along with her concern with health and nutrition that led to the setting up of night camps and nurseries. In 1914, in Stowage in Deptford, she and her sister set up the first night camps (Steedman 1990). The intention was that children spent time outdoors in order to develop immunity to infections. Margaret McMillan was certain that 'much ill-health in children was due to poor breathing, foul air, uncleanliness, insufficient exercise and the severe malnourishment which she felt was related to the low wages of the parents' (Bradburn 1989: 48). The first camp was for girls, and the sisters then decided to set up one for boys. Initially there were eight boys who attended the night camp. The numbers quickly rose to 40 (Steedman 1990). After the death of her sister, Margaret named the nursery in Deptford, the Rachel McMillan Nursery. There she 'encouraged children to grow food in the garden for the kitchen and promoted an education which was framed around the needs of the body as well as the mind' (Albon 2007: 199). From approximately 1919 Margaret McMillan began providing training. It was her belief that those who wished to work with young children needed to be suitably trained. She conceived that her training was to differ from that available in other institutions in three ways: first, she believed that young children needed qualified teachers; second, she was training young women to work with children in the slums, so the women needed to visit the children's homes and live in the streets around the area in which they were to work; and, finally, she believed that practice needed to precede academic work. Her initial thought was to keep the training college small, but later she began to develop a training college that could provide training for people right across the country. The Rachel McMillan Training College opened in 1930 and was later subsumed into Goldsmiths' College, London.

The work of Froebel, Isaacs and the McMillans can all be seen to be reflected in the current EYFS (2012).

- Froebel's approach was influenced by the German Romanticism movement. He will be remembered for the introduction of the kindergarten, or children's garden, and for his 'gifts' and 'occupations'.
- Isaacs saw play as the work of children, she felt that it was important to keep detailed and accurate records of children's activities in order to understand the children.
- The McMillan sisters had a significant impact on the health and well-being of young children, as well as the ways in which those who work with young children are trained.

Problems with play

Play is the current dominant discourse of practitioners and policy makers concerned within early years provision and specifically with the delivery of the EYFS (2012). Goouch (2008) suggests that once anything becomes the concern of governments, necessarily the discourse must become non-specialist in order that it can be successfully shared with the media, politicians and the general public. Sutton–Smith and Kelly–Byrne (1984) argue that play has become idealised and that, as a result of this process, there is no clear scientific theory of play. Pellegrini and Boyd (1993: 105, in Ailwood 2003) support this view, saying that play is an 'almost hallowed concept' for teachers of young children. Ailwood (2003) comments that play appears to provide a central point at which the discourses of childhood, motherhood, education, family psychology and citizenship come together and impact on one another. It is in this space that play becomes idealised.

A number of researchers, including Rogers (2011), Brooker and Edwards (2010), Grieshaber and McArdle (2010), Smith (2010, 1984), Ailwood (2003) and Sutton–Smith and Kelly–Byrne (1984), are all providing challenges to this dominant discourse. They are not suggesting that play is not valuable or important in the lives and development of young children. Smith (2010: 1) recognises that play 'certainly takes up an appreciable portion of many children's time budgets'. He suggests that for many children this is their normal mode of behaviour. However, they all challenge the dominant discourse of play as the panacea for all children. Equally the play/not play or work divide causes difficulties. Sutton–Smith and Kelly–Byrne (1984) discuss Milhay Csikzentmihalyi's work on flow. Csikzentmihalyi does not see a work/play divide, rather he focuses on quality of life, which can be identified in both work and play. He uses anecdotal evidence of the surgeon taken on holiday by his wife, who after a couple of days is so bored that he signs up as a volunteer at the local hospital to undertake surgery. For the surgeon participating in surgery was the most enjoyable aspect of his life; for him it provided flow, something generally associated with play.

Grieshaber and McArdle (2010: 1) suggest that many ideas about play are accepted without challenge, including ideas that play is 'natural, normal, innocent, fun, solely about development and learning, beneficial to all children, and a universal right for children'. Vygotsky (1978) provided challenge to the suggestion that play is fun, suggesting that not all play was fun and there were other things in life that gave children greater pleasure. He continued to suggest that pleasure cannot be seen as a defining characteristic of play, but that its role in fulfilling children's needs should not be intellectualised out of existence (ibid.). Equally, what one child describes as fun another may describe as work or in some instances simply not fun. Sutton-Smith and Kelly-Byrne (1984) emphasise play as negative affect. They investigate some of the research into playground behaviour and bullying behaviour, which includes fights and other activities that demonstrate the dominance of some children over others. They discuss a number of initiation activities in which urine is used, again to demonstrate power. Likewise they recognise that play can have sexual and erotic overtones, which would not be associated with innocence and fun. However, this could be seen as being natural and normal as children mature and gain a sense of their gender and role in society, which is something that they develop through play.

Rogers (2011) declares that linking play and pedagogy can be problematic. The link positions play as the opposite to work. This division may 'prevent the integration of play into pedagogical practice' (ibid.: 5). She suggests that play as work can obscure the notion of play as a social control through which notions of the nature and purpose of childhood are passed on. She draws on research evidence to suggest that children between the ages of two and five develop a form of imaginative play that is exclusive to humans. She suggests that this type of play is crucial in developing later life skills, empathy, problem solving, creativity and innovation. Rogers (2011) continues to suggest that we can draw on a range of texts in order to comprehend the multiple ways in which 'children learn, grow and develop within diverse social and cultural contexts' (ibid.: 9).

It is clear that play is not the same across all cultures; Gosso (2010) states that play and playful behaviour occur in all societies throughout the world, although it will not necessarily be what we would recognise or define as play. She has engaged in research with the Parakanã Indians in Brazil. There the children engage in play that is gendered and concerned with later life roles. This behaviour is recognised by both the children and the adults as play. Brooker (2005) uses field notes to describe the scene when two new boys enter an early years setting in England. The teacher welcomes them warmly, sends off their mothers and takes the children to the sandbox where she enthusiastically encourages them to dig. The boys are polite and do as they are asked. When the teacher moves away they look at each other and stop digging, seeing no purpose in the activity. These boys clearly do not recognise this play construct. It appears that educators, and in particular early years educators, place a high degree of value on play. Brooker's (2005) scenario clearly demonstrates that play is culturally situated and does not necessarily universally carry meaning.

Rogers (2011) suggests that early years practices that are dominated by westernised pedagogies of play are even being imported to the third world. She recognises that this approach is problematic. Bangura (2005) argues for 'ubuntugogy' – a pedagogical approach that relies on an African educational paradigm. He argues that, after a number of decades of relying on westernised approaches to education, African nations have found themselves no further forward on the world stage. Rogers (2011: 5) states that the 'pedagogisation of play' has led to play being adopted in order to teach competencies for later life.

Children's right to play has been enshrined in Article 31 of the UN Convention on the Rights of the Child. The Article states that children are entitled to 'rest and leisure, to engage in play and recreational activities' (UN 1989). The Convention has been adopted by all countries in the world other than the USA and Somalia. Grieshaber and McArdle (2010) argue that it is a westernised approach to children that attempts to treat them as a homogeneous group, rather than being concerned with individuals, making no reference to children's differing social, economic, cultural or political circumstances. Wood (2010) asserts that all children are both socially and culturally situated and that, as such, they are part of differing cultural communities. Therefore Article 31 cannot simply be applied in the same way in all situations – the child's specific understanding of play needs to be applied.

Broadhead (2009, 2006, 2001, 1997) has examined how children learn and develop through play. She claims that, while some have argued that play is the work of children, she believes that it is much more than that. It 'is their self-actualisation, a holistic exploration of who and what they are and know and of who and what they might become' (2004: 89). She argues that the work of Vygotsky demonstrates this. His emphasis on the sociocultural nature of cognitive development and specifically on the use of language as a cultural tool of change supports this premise. She asserts that children need a sense of ownership of their learning and that play allows for the co-construction of cognition, allowing children to have the necessary sense of ownership.

Proving that there is a direct correlation between play and cognitive gains is problematic; according to Bartlett (2011) many of the assertions, while having some scientific basis, are overstated. He draws on a range of studies to suggest that, while demonstrating a relationship is possible, many of the studies are flawed. He cites the psychologist Angeline Lillard, who states that original and relevant research needs to be conducted in order to be more certain about the value of play in cognition. Bartlett (2011) seems accepting of Hirsh-Pasek et al.'s (2009) argument that the universality of play demonstrates its value in child development.

Play is valuable where it provides the basis for children to be able to flourish, to develop their own identities and to engage positively with life.

- Play is the dominant discourse of early childhood education and care and is often assumed to be innocent and fun for all children at all times; however, there is clear evidence to the contrary.
- Children's right to play is enshrined in the UN Convention on the Rights of the Child.
- Many westernised approaches attempt to treat children as a homogeneous group rather than as individuals.

Playful pedagogies

Play-based learning has been the basis for practice within the early years sector for many years. While definitions of play are complex and contested, play appears to have a clear role in developmentally appropriate practice (DAP) (Yelland 2011). Within the UK there has been a growing interest in playful pedagogies, an approach to learning and development that combines a number of factors in ways that can be seen to be developmentally appropriate and meeting the needs of the young child (Rogers 2011; Broadhead et al. 2010; Moyles 2010). Broadhead et al. (2010: 177) say that 'play has particular qualities and characteristics' and that practitioners need to understand 'the playing child as a learner, their own roles in relation to playful learning, and the interconnections across these two dimensions of playful learning and playful pedagogies'.

Broadhead *et al.* (2010) clearly suggest that a direct correlation between play and learning can be made through the use of playful pedagogies. Likewise Wood (2010: 13) suggests that it is 'claimed that play underpins learning and development, and that both can be seen in play'. She continues to suggest that 'play should provide evidence of children's progress and achievements along culturally defined pathways'. It would seem that play provides the scaffolding to support children's learning and development. This occurs in ways that are expected, given the cultural situation in which the child finds him- or herself. Corsaro (2005) argues that children form their own peer cultures as part of the process of playing together. He maintains that as part of this process culture is being created. The play that is observed is not only what would be expected, given their cultural expectations, but is also developing new expectations of a culture. Broadhead *et al.* (2010) support this argument, suggesting that the breadth of experience that is provided by play is because it is subject to so many different influences that begin in the child's home situation and are continued into, and are further developed in, early years settings. Moyles (2010) suggests that there are three clear factors that underpin playful pedagogies: play, playful learning and playful teaching. She argues that when the three are combined it is possible to demonstrate that the child is being supported through a playful pedagogy. The first she calls 'pure' play, which is play that is controlled by the child or children. The play 'is highly creative, open-ended and imaginative. This pure play may only be partially achievable in educational settings' (ibid.: 21–2). The rigour of routines in many settings would mean that it would often be difficult to achieve this higher level of child-initiated play. Playful learning can be adult or child initiated, but it must engage children in playful ways. Moyles (2010) suggests that the child may not perceive the activity as pure play, but will nevertheless engage in a playful manner and is likely to learn while interacting with peers. The third aspect is playful teaching. Moyles (2010) argues that activities that are provided for children should be open-ended in order that children can engage with them actively and imaginatively. The materials and resources provided for such teaching are those that the children would associate with play. She goes on to suggest that the children will not necessarily see the activities as play (ibid.). Moyles (2010) suggests that the adult role is to ensure that the activities are well planned and presented and that there are clear links to the curriculum. She further suggests that playful pedagogies have clear links with sustained shared thinking (SST), which is explored in Chapter 9.

It would appear that while play has been studied from a number of different perspectives – education, sociology, psychology, health, anthropology and history – little research has been carried out in early years settings (Broadhead *et al.* 2010). This must at the least appear strange. Play is more likely to occur in early years settings than in any other formal space in which children could be observed. It could be argued that until very recently there were few methodological tools that supported data collection with young children. The work of researchers such as Harcourt *et al.* (2011), Clark and Moss (2010, 2005, 2001) and Einarsdottir (2005) is having a significant impact on research that investigates the ways in which young children experience their lives. This work includes explorations of the children's experiences of play and is likely to support the further development of playful pedagogies in early years settings. These approaches can be argued to support the flourishing of both the child and the practitioner.

- Play, playful learning and playful teaching, when combined, can be seen to create a playful pedagogy.
- Appropriate methodological tools are now being developed that allow researchers to understand children's experiences and views of their environment.
- Relevant research is likely to further support the development of playful pedagogies and the flourishing of both the child and the practitioner.

Managing the environment

The way in which the setting environment is organised and managed will also support the flourishing of the child. The overarching principle of Enabling Environments within the EYFS (2012) suggests that children learn best when they are in an environment that allows them to make decisions about their own learning and that is planned to meet their individual needs. Yelland (2011: 6) argues that 'quality learning environments support children's learning with a rich variety of materials that enable them to explore and make discoveries'. Therefore, in order for a setting to be perceived as a quality environment there are number of things that practitioners need to provide and to do. Practitioners need to stimulate children's innate curiosity, to provide a range of resources, to model skills and behaviours, and to listen to children and to ask questions. Listening to children has become a fundamental principle in early years pedagogy and practice. The work of Clark and Moss (2005,

2001) provides a framework for this approach to working with young children. However, Brooker (2011) is concerned that we need to ensure that listening is not tokenistic but that responses to the children demonstrate that their views were taken seriously. Nutbrown and Clough (2009) investigated how, through Citizenship education, children could be enabled to feel a sense of belonging within a setting. They concluded that in an enabling environment children were enabled to contribute ideas and see that these ideas mattered. In order to ensure that the whole environment is enabling, it needs to be well managed and the views of the participants – the children – need to be reflected within it.

Pack-away settings

Pack-away settings raise particular challenges in creating enabling environments. It is not simply a case that everything has to be set up and packed away every day; there are challenges around the shared use of space and the ways in which children's interests can be followed through from one day to another, which can impact on sustained shared thinking.

The Department of Education draws on data provided by Ofsted when considering the different types of early years settings that exist in England. Ofsted records whether settings are full daycare or sessional daycare and whether the childcare is provided on domestic or non-domestic premises, or by childminders. Settings are registered as full daycare if they provide more than four hours per day. Clearly the government does not know how many settings operate in pack-away premises, as some local authorities choose to record the information but others do not.

In many respects the key to coping with the issues presented in such settings appears to be organisation (Jones 2010; Wright 2010). The EYFS (2012) demands a combined adult-directed and child-initiated approach to the curriculum. Allowing for child-initiated learning can be more challenging in pack-away settings. It would seem, however, that many practitioners who work in pack-away settings are highly committed and demonstrate how these challenges can be overcome. In my current research in pack-away settings I am amazed by the amount on offer to the children each day. Likewise Jones (2010) reports on the variety of opportunities available to the children in the two pack-away settings he visits. He suggests that the key to being able to do so is having a clear routine and demonstrating an awareness of the interests of the children and following them.

Childminders and the EYFS

The introduction of the EYFS (DCSF 2008) provided a real challenge for childminders. While they clearly demonstrated that they knew their children and were able to follow their interests and meet their needs, they had previously been assessed against the care standards; suddenly they were having to take into consideration children's learning and developmental needs. This has proved a challenge for many childminders who do not hold the requisite level 3 qualification that would be needed to run a nursery, and who are not used to planning and delivering a curriculum. The National Childminding Association (NCMA), now called PACEY (Professional Association for Childcare and Early Years), is however reporting that childminders are becoming more professional with 74 per cent achieving good or outstanding grades in their inspections (Evans 2011). There is also evidence that they are undertaking further qualifications including foundation degrees (ibid.).

During 2008, prior to the introduction of the EYFS (2008), numbers of registered childminders dropped dramatically. At their peak in 2004 there were 72,700 and by March 2008 there were 64,648 – a drop of over 8,000. Those who left at the time reported concerns about rises in registration fees, but more concerning was the fact that they would be required to deliver the new EYFS (2008). The decline continued and by September 2009 there were only 56,190 registered childminders. The recession also had an impact on their numbers, but these are now beginning to grow again. PACEY's Catherine Farrell (cited in Evans 2011) suggests that finance is a factor. The cost of putting a child with a childminder is usually less than with a nursery. Farrell says that during the last recession childminder numbers grew. By September 2012 there were 57,149.

Within the home environment childminders are able to support young children to flourish in an enabling environment.

The EYFS and the outdoor environment

The revised EYFS (DfE 2012) has placed a greater emphasis on the outdoor environment. While the theme of Enabling Environments remains, the use of space outdoors and the flow between indoor and outdoor space have gained prominence. Roskos and Neuman (2011) suggest that the environment is fundamental when considering pedagogical approaches. They suggest that it impacts on the social interactions, learning and friendships that occur within it. Therefore the environment of the classroom 'can work for us or against us, which is why it is first, last and always among pedagogical concerns' (ibid.: 110). The outdoor environment needs to be considered in equal measure to that provided indoors. Maynard and Waters (2007) discuss the resurgence of recognition of the value of the outdoor environment for the cognitive development of young children. They recognise that policy makers in both England and Wales are recognising the value of the outdoor environment and embedding it within the curriculum. Maynard (2007: 321) suggests that while children are outside they are 'able to find out about themselves and the world around them in a way that would not generally be tolerated within the classroom'. Outdoors children are given opportunities to build on a much larger scale and experiment with a range of materials and sounds without any apprehension of being reprimanded for leaving a mess or being too noisy (ibid.). The twenty-first-century child has become more sedentary with three key factors leading to this. Opportunities for outdoor play have decreased due to rises in levels of traffic; the institutionalisation of childhood, in which children spend more time in breakfast and afterschool clubs; and finally parents' concerns of perceived notions of increased risk (Waller 2007).

In a more recent article Waters and Maynard (2010: 476) begin to comment on the 'policy move to see young children using outdoor spaces as learning sites'. There is already a body of evidence that demonstrates many of the positive outcomes for children when they are engaged in activities outdoors. Dowdell *et al.* (2011: 24) suggest that 'nature improves awareness, reasoning, observation skills, creativity, concentration and imagination'. They go on to say that there is evidence that children who spend more time outdoors become ill less often and, when they do, recover more quickly (ibid.). The work of Fjortoft (2001) demonstrates that children engaged in play in natural outdoor environments develop better balance and coordination skills than those who only have access to less challenging traditional playground environments. Outdoor play, while demonstrating that it develops a range of positive skills, also carries an element of risk. Risk taking and the ability to assess risk are essential skills that children need to develop (Dowdell *et al.*, 2011; Little and Wyver 2010; Sandseter 2009). If children are not given these opportunities in early life it will often lead to them taking inappropriate risks later in life (Dowdell *et al.* 2011). It would seem therefore that the discussion of the risks and benefits of challenging outdoor play has been won. Children need to be given these play opportunities regularly and from an early age in order to be enabled to flourish as individuals.

- The revised EYFS (2012) places greater emphasis on the outdoor environment, as policy makers are recognising its importance in the cognitive development of young children.
- Risk taking and the assessment of risk are essential skills that young children need to develop; research evidence suggests that this is done best in the outdoor environment.
- The outdoor environment clearly supports children in flourishing.

Conclusion

This chapter has set out to explore policy against the backdrop of the early childhood play environment, the current EYFS (2012) and the historical and cultural influences on policy and provision, while demonstrating links with flourishing. It is clear that, while childhood has been discussed from the time of the Ancient Greeks, until it became valued as a phase in its own right with the work of Rousseau, there was no possibility of seeing how it could clearly link with notions of flourishing. Children need to be valued in the moment to be validated. The Industrial Revolution had a consequential impact on education, while the work of Robert Owen in New Lanark had a lasting impact on the provision of education for young children. The work of Froebel, Isaacs and the McMillan sisters can be seen to have had an enduring influence on early years provision, and their work can quite clearly be linked with the EYFS (2012). Froebel's kindergarten, or children's garden, can clearly be linked to the current interest in the outdoor environment. Isaacs' discussion of play as the work of children links with current play-based curricula. Likewise, her pedagogical documentation can be seen in the current practice of observations and Learning Journeys. The McMillan sisters were concerned with the health of young children. This again included recognition of the importance of the outdoor environment in nurturing children. Current emphasis on outdoor environments includes notions of risk. Research evidence demonstrates that children need opportunities to engage with risk at an early age in order that they develop appropriate life skills and do not undertake unnecessary risks later. Equally, Margaret McMillan's concern with healthy eating is mirrored in the current EYFS (2012). While she was concerned that without a healthy meal children would not be able to learn, current policy makers are concerned with increased rates of obesity and the negative affects they can have on children's education.

Play is the vehicle that policy makers describe as the way in which early education should be delivered. Grieshaber and McArdle (2010) recognise that, while there is clear discussion of child–initiated and adult–led play, there is no linking of the notion of play with enjoyment and fun. There does appear to be an assumption that play is universally appropriate and beneficial for all. Within the chapter there has been some demonstration that play is a contested concept. What is play and enjoyable to one child is not necessarily viewed in the same way by another. Playful pedagogies provide evidence that not all activities that are provided as play will necessarily be seen as such by the child. What is important is that the intention through a particular pedagogical approach demonstrates that the child is valued and included. Notions of participation and inclusion support the child's ability to flourish. Developmentally appropriate practices (Yelland 2011) in an enabling environment can seek to provide an appropriate environment for a child to flourish.

REFLECTIVE QUESTIONS

- How does a good understanding of child development support you in developing both enabling environments and pedagogically appropriate practices that support children in flourishing?
- How does the work of Froebel, Isaacs and the McMillans influence the EYFS (2012)?
- How do you ensure that the outdoor environment provides children with appropriate cognitive challenges and opportunities to assess and manage risk?

References

Ailwood, J. (2003) 'Governing early childhood education through play', *Contemporary Issues in Early Childhood*, 4(3): 286–99.

Albon, D. (2007) 'Exploring food and eating patterns using food maps', *Nutrition and Food Science*, 37(4): 254–9.

Bangura, A.K. (2005) 'Ubuntugogy: an African educational paradigm that transcends pedagogy, andragogy, ergonagy and heutagogy', *Journal of Third World Studies*, 22(2): 13–54.

Bartlett, T. (2011) 'The case for play', *Chronicle of Higher Education*, 57(25): B6–B9. Available online at http://chronicle.com (accessed 30 November 2012).

Bradburn, E. (1989) *Margaret McMillan: Portrait of a Pioneer*, London: Routledge.

Broadhead, P. (1997) 'Promoting sociability and cooperation in nursery settings', *British Educational Research Journal*, 23(4): 513–31.

Broadhead, P. (2001) 'Investigating sociability and cooperation in four and five year olds in Reception Class settings', *International Journal of Early Years Education*, 9(1): 23–35.

Broadhead, P. (2004) *Early Years Play and Learning: Developing social skills and cooperation*, London: RoutledgeFalmer.

Broadhead, P. (2006) 'Developing an understanding of young children's learning through play: the place of observation, interaction and reflection', *British Educational Research Journal*, 32(2): 191–207.

Broadhead, P. (2009) 'Conflict resolution and children's behaviour: observing and understanding social and cooperative play in early years educational settings', *Early Years*, 29(2): 105–18.

Broadhead, P., Howard, P. and Wood, E. (2010) *Play and Learning in the Early Years*, London: Sage.

Brooker, L. (2005) 'Learning to be a child: cultural diversity and early years ideology', in Yelland, N. (ed.) *Critical Issues in Early Childhood Education*, Maidenhead: Open University Press.

Brooker, L. (2011) 'Taking children seriously: an alternative agenda for research?', *Journal of Early Childhood Research*, 9(2): 137–49.

Brooker, L. and Edwards, S. (2010) *Engaging Play*, Maidenhead: McGraw-Hill.

Burger, K. (2011) 'Robert Owen's legacy across national borders', *Journal of Education Research*, 5(2): 161–75.

Clark, A. and Moss, P. (2001) *Listening to Young Children: The Mosaic approach*, London: National Children's Bureau.

Clark, A. and Moss, P. (2005) *Spaces to Play*, London: National Children's Bureau.

Clark, A. and Moss, P. (2010) *Listening to Young People: The Mosaic approach* (2nd edn), London: National Children's Bureau.

Corsaro, W. (2005) *The Sociology of Childhood* (2nd edn), Thousand Oaks, CA: Pine Forge Press.

Curtis, S.J. and Boultwood, M.E.A. (1966) *History of English Education since 1800* (4th edn), London: University Tutorial Press.

Department for Children, Schools and Families (DCSF) (2008) *Statutory Framework for the Early Years Foundation Stage*, London: DCSF.

Department for Education (DfE) (2012) *The Early Years Foundation Stage (EYFS)*, London: DfE.

Donnachie, I. (2003) *Robert Owen: Social visionary*, Edinburgh: Tuckwell Press.

Dowdell, K., Gray, T. and Malone, K. (2011) 'Nature and its influence on children's outdoor play', *Australian Journal of Outdoor Education*, 15(2): 24–35.

Einarsdottir, J. (2005) 'We can decide what to play! Children's perception of quality in an Icelandic playschool', *Early Education and Development*, 16(4): 469–88.

Evans, M. (2011) 'All about . . . childminding', *Nursery World*, 9–22 August: 15–20.

Fjortoft, I. (2001) 'The natural environment as a playground for children: the impact of outdoor play activities in pre-primary school children', *Early Childhood Education Journal*, 29(2): 111–17.

Froebel, F. (1826) *Die Menschenerziehung* (On the education of man), Keilhau, Leipzig: Wienbrack.

Gillard, D. (2011) *Education in England: A brief history*. Available online at www.educationengland.org.uk/history (accessed 3 January 2013).

Goouch, K. (2008) Understanding playful pedagogies, play narratives and play spaces', *Early Years*, 28(1): 93–102.

Gosso, Y. (2010) ' Play in different cultures', in Smith, P. (2010) *Children and Play*, Oxford: Wiley-Blackwell.

Graham, P. (2008) 'Susan Isaacs and the Malting House School', *Journal of Child Psychotherapy*, 34(1): 5–22.

Grieshaber, S. and McArdle, F. (2010) *The Trouble with Play*, Maidenhead: The Open University Press.

Harcourt, D., Perry, B. and Waller, T. (2011) *Researching Young Children's Perspectives: Debating the ethics and dilemmas of educational research with children*, Abingdon: Routledge.

Hendrick, H. (1997) *Children, Childhood and English Society 1880–1990*, Cambridge: Cambridge University Press.

Hinitz, B. (2006) 'Historical research in early childhood education', in Spodek, B. and Saracho, O. (eds) *Handbook of Research on the Education of Young Children*, Mahwah, NJ: Lawrence Erlbaum Associates.

Hirsh-Pasek, K., Golinkoff, R., Berk, L. and Singer, D. (2009) *A Mandate for Playful Learning in the Preschool: Presenting the evidence*, Oxford: Oxford University Press.

James, A. and James, A.L. (2004) *Constructing Childhood*, Basingstoke: Palgrave-Macmillan.

Jones, M. (2010) 'Pack away the daytime', *Early Years Educator*, 12(3): 28–30.

Latham, J.E.M. (2002) 'Pestalozzi and James Pierrepont Greaves: a shared educational philosophy', *History of Education*, 31(1): 59–70.

Little, H. and Wyver, S. (2010) 'Individual differences in children's risk perceptions and appraisals in outdoor play environments', *International Journal of Early Years Education*, 18(4): 297–313.

Locke, J. (1977) *An Essay Concerning Human Understanding* (an abridgement selected and edited by J.W. Yolton), London: J.M. Dent & Sons.

McDowall Clark, R. (2010) *Reconceptualising Leadership in the Early Years*, Maidenhead: McGraw-Hill.

Manning, P. (2005) 'Rediscovering Froebel: a call to re-examine his life & gifts', *Early Childhood Education Journal*, 32(6): 371–6.

Maynard, T. (2007) 'Forest Schools in Great Britain: an initial exploration', *Contemporary Issues in Early Childhood*, 8(4): 320–31.

Maynard, T. and Waters, J. (2007) 'Learning in the outdoor environment: a missed opportunity?', *Early Years*, 27(3): 255–65.

Moyles, J. (2010) *Thinking about Play: Developing a reflective approach*, Maidenhead: Open University Press.

Nutbrown, C. and Clough, P. (2009) 'Citizenship and inclusion in the early years: understanding and responding to children's perspectives on "belonging"', *International Journal of Early Years Education*, 17(3): 191–206.

Nutbrown, C., Clough, P. and Selbie, P. (2008) *Early Childhood Education History, Philosophy and Experience*, London: Sage.

Pelzman, B. (1998) *Pioneers of Early Childhood Education*, Westport, CT: Greenwood Press.

Rogers, S. (2011) *Rethinking Play and Pedagogy in Early Childhood Education*, Abingdon: Routledge.

Roskos, K. and Neuman, S.B. (2011) 'The classroom environment, first, last and always', *The Reading Teacher*, 65(2): 110–14.

Sandseter, H. (2009) 'Affordances for risky play in the pre-school: the importance of features in the play environment', *Early Childhood Education Journal*, 36: 439–46.

Saracho, O.N. and Spodek, B. (2009) 'Educating the young mathematician: a historical perspective through the nineteenth century', *Early Childhood Education Journal*, 36: 297–303.

Smith, P. (1984) *Play in Animals and Humans*, Oxford: Blackwell.

Smith, P. (2010) *Children and Play*, Oxford: Wiley-Blackwell.

Staples New, P. and Cochran, M. (2008) *Early Childhood Education: An International Encyclopedia*, Westport, CT: Praeger.

Steedman, C. (1990) *Childhood, Culture and Class in Britain: Margaret McMillan 1860–1931*, London: Virago.

Sutton-Smith, B. and Kelly-Byrne, D. (1984) 'The idealization of play', in Smith, P. (ed.) *Play in Animals and Humans*, Oxford: Blackwell.

United Nations (UN) (1989) *Convention on the Rights of the Child*, London: Unicef UK.

Vygotsky, L. (1978) *Mind in Society*, London: Harvard University Press.

Waller, T. (2007) 'The trampoline tree and the swamp monster with 18 heads: outdoor play in the Foundation Stage and Foundation Phase', *Education 3–13: International Journal of Primary, Elementary and Early Years Education*, 35(4): 393–407.

Waters, J. and Maynard, T. (2010) 'What's so interesting outside? A study of child-initiated interaction with teachers in the natural outdoor environment', *European Early Childhood Education Research Journal*, 18(4): 473–83.

Willan, J. (2009) 'Revisiting Susan Isaacs: a modern educator for the twenty-first century', *International Journal of Early Years Education*, 17(2): 151–65.

Wood, E. (2010) 'Developing integrated pedagogical approaches to play and learning', in Broadhead, P., Howard, J. and Wood, E. (eds) *Play and Learning in the Early Years*, London: Sage.

Wood, E. and Attfield, J. (2005) *Play, Learning and the Early Childhood Curriculum*, London: Paul Chapman.

Wright, G. (2010) 'A problem shared', *Nursery World*, 15 April: 14–15.

Yelland, N. (2011) 'Reconceptualising play and learning in the lives of young children', *Australian Journal of Early Childhood*, 36(2): 4–12.

9 Research-informed policy – myth or reality?

Sustained shared thinking

Zenna Kingdon

Introduction

This chapter sets out to examine the rise in prominence of the term sustained shared thinking (SST) within early childhood education. The chapter traces how the term was coined as part of the Effective Provision of Pre-school Education (EPPE – Sylva *et al.* 2004) research that initially occurred between 1997 and 2003. The research team, who also conducted the parallel project Researching Effective Pedagogy in Early Years (REPEY – Siraj-Blatchford *et al.* 2002) identified that where SST occurred there were markedly higher outcomes for children. Equally, Siraj-Blatchford (2010) suggested that the indication between a setting that is deemed to be good and one that is identified as excellent will be the latter's use of SST.

While the phrase 'sustained shared thinking' was coined as part of the EPPE and REPEY research, its roots are embedded in pedagogically appropriate practice that has been developed over many years. This chapter makes clear links between SST and the social constructivist theoretical approaches on which it is predicated. SST focuses on individual children's interests and necessarily will support their flourishing as their views and interests are validated and pursued.

Finally, the chapter makes use of a questionnaire that was given to a number of Early Years Professionals (EYPs) who hold roles in a variety of early years settings, including one as an advisory teacher. The questionnaire is used to identify how they are interpreting the policy in practice and to clarify their shared understanding of the approach. It would appear that, while the practitioners do not hold identical views about what SST looks like in practice, their interpretations share many of the same peda-gogical practices and values. The practitioners were clear that SST is a clear marker of quality and that it should be practised in all settings. It would appear that SST is research-informed policy. However, a recent speech by a government minister concerned with early years advocates some deregulation of early years settings that researchers would argue could negatively impact on quality and the settings' ability to engage children in episodes of SST.

EPPE – Effective Provision of Pre-school Education

The term 'sustained shared thinking' has gained prominence since the publication of the EPPE report (2004). The initial piece of research was a national longitudinal research study that followed the developmental progress of 3,000 children across England from 1998 to 2003 (Siraj-Blatchford *et al.* 2003). Siraj-Blatchford *et al.* (2008: 24) argue that the first phase of the EPPE research 'provided the first robust evidence that the provision of high quality early childhood education made a signifi-cant difference to the learning outcomes of young children'. The initial phase of the research had been funded by the Department for Education and Skills (DfES) in 1997 and was then taken up by New Labour. The outcomes of the initial research were so significant that they led to the extension of the research. It appeared to demonstrate that high-quality early years provision could help mitigate the effects of social disadvantage, which was a particular policy driver of New Labour. The second phase of the research was the known as Effective Pre-school and Primary Education 3–11. This second phase continued to demonstrate signifi-cantly enhanced outcomes for children who had attended high-quality pre-school provision (EPPE 3–11, 2008). The research is currently in its fourth phase, Effective Pre-school, Primary and Secondary Education 16+ (EPPSE 16+). Each phase of the research has followed the same group that was initially recruited in 1998. The initial report demonstrated that significantly improved outcomes for young children occurred in settings where SST took place. Siraj-Blatchford (2010) suggested that the marker between a good setting and an outstanding one was the latter's use of SST. It appears that the use of SST to extend children's thinking and cognitive development was what made the setting outstanding, in fact SST was a 'prerequisite for excellence in early years practice' (ibid.: 157).

Within the EPPE report (2004) it was necessary to define what was considered to constitute SST. Siraj-Blatchford (2010) states that it became defined as a pedagogically appropriate method of interacting with children that could be seen in both qualitative and quantitative observations. SST seemed to occur most frequently in interactions that involved a one-to-one relationship of adult and child working together. The nature of the interactions were such that they could be considered to be intellectual, problem solving, problem clarifying, supportive of evaluating activities and extending narratives. It was agreed that, in order for it to constitute SST, both adult and child needed to be contributing to the activity and that it needed to be seen to be both developing and extending the thinking that was occurring.

- EPPE suggests that SST is the marker between a good setting and an outstanding one.
- EPPE demonstrated that high-quality provision could mitigate for social disadvantage.
- SST usually occurs during one-to-one interactions between an adult and a child.

REPEY – Researching Effective Pedagogy in the Early Years

REPEY (2002) reports on the Effective Pedagogy in the Early Years study, which examined pedagogical practices in 14 settings that had been identified within the EPPE study (1998–2003). These settings were all identified as providing good to excellent outcomes for children. The purpose of the study was 'to identify the most effective pedagogical strategies that are applied . . . to support the development of young children's skills knowledge and attitudes' (Siraj-Blatchford et al. 2002: 10). Four aspects of practice were identified by REPEY (2002) as warranting further analysis: adult–child interactions, differentiation and formative assessment, parental partnership and the home education environment, and discipline and adult support in talking through conflicts. The most effective settings were seen to encourage SST. While it would seem that relatively few incidences of the practice were seen in any setting, there were markedly more instances in excellent rather than good settings. The case studies that were undertaken demonstrated that excellent settings provided children with a balance of adult-directed and child-initiated activities, all of which gave opportunities for the staff to engage the children and extend their thinking.

Siraj-Blatchford *et al.* (2008: 24–5) claimed that the findings of the research 'have had significant impact on Government policy . . . it is now recognised that investment in good quality pre-school provision provides an effective means of reducing social exclusion and may help to break the cycle of disadvantage'. Markers of good and excellent settings included staff qualifications and adult:child ratios. The recent speech by Elizabeth Truss (Parliamentary Under Secretary of State for Education) in December 2012 to the National Daycare Trust conference will have started alarm bells ringing for many in the early years sector. While she appears to endorse the Nutbrown review (2012), which calls for a strengthening of the level 3 qualification, she also calls for deregulation of ratios within settings. While we continue to allow settings to be led by practitioners with a level 3 qualification, any changes in adult:child ratios will undoubtedly be a backward step with quality being negatively affected. The evidence of REPEY (2002) clearly demonstrates that instances of SST are significantly less evident in settings that are led by those with qualifications below level 5. The lead practitioner in each setting is expected to plan and lead the curriculum, considering the ways in which a balance of adult-directed and child-initiated opportunities are offered. This includes opportunities to participate in SST.

The introduction of the EYFS (2008)

Following EPPE, the Early Years Foundation Stage (EYFS) (DCSF 2008) was introduced in England. This curriculum provided a shift in early years practice in that all registered daycare providers were expected to deliver it. Previously, childminders and those working with children under the age of three were not necessarily expected to deliver a curriculum per se. The new curriculum provided for children from birth until the end of the Reception year in school. The EYFS (2008) called for an emphasis on interactions between adults and children and particularly focused on instances of SST. In 2010 Dame Clare Tickell was called upon by the Coalition government to conduct a review of the EYFS (2008). Her review, *The Early Years: Foundations for life, health and learning* (Tickell 2011), looked at the ways in which the EYFS (2008) could become less bureaucratic and more focused on supporting children's learning. The review led to the introduction of the reviewed EYFS (DfE 2012) in September 2012. The revised curriculum moved from the six areas of learning, as had been seen in both the EYFS (2008) and its predecessor, *Curriculum Guidance for the Foundation Stage* (QCA 2000), to three prime areas of learning and four specific areas.

There should now be greater emphasis on three prime areas of development: personal, social and emotional development, communication and language, and physical development.

The emphasis on personal, social and emotional development can be argued to demonstrate clear links with SST. Children are only able to effectively interact with those around them if they have positive self-regard and are able to form effective relationships with those with whom they spend time. The work of Bowlby (1952) has provided a framework for much of current thinking about the relationships necessary for children to develop and flourish. He stated that a child should enjoy a warm, intimate and continuous relationship with his or her mother or main carer that gave pleasure to both parties. The EYFS framework (2008) insists that each child is provided with a key worker, someone who has significant responsibility for the welfare of that child. This draws on Bowlby's attachment framework, ensuring that children are given consistent care and support. Broadhead *et al.* (2010) state that relationships are at the heart of the learning process, supporting and scaffolding learning. They draw extensively on the work of Vygotsky (1986, 1978), saying that learning occurs where children are supported by a more able other. They argue that practitioners need to understand the centrality of these relationships in order for children to learn and to develop. If children are not supported in developing effective relationships with those around them, learning will be hampered and SST is unlikely to occur. Therefore effective personal, social and emotional development supported by sensitive appropriately qualified practitioners is crucial.

- The introduction of the EYFS (2008) meant a shift in early years provision and everyone had to deliver it.
- The key worker system draws on the work of Bowlby (1952) and acknowledges the importance of effective relationships.

Early Years Professionals and the Standards

The EPPE report (2004) identified that the qualification level of practitioners working with children impacted on the quality of SST. Those who had the highest level of qualification, particularly those who were qualified teachers, engaged in both the highest frequencies of direct teaching and the highest frequencies of SST. Those practitioners who had lower-level qualifications, below a level 5, were considered to demonstrate significantly better pedagogical practices when they were supported by qualified teachers (Siraj–Blatchford 2010). This research, which underpins both the previous and current governments' drive towards having EYPs in early years settings, clearly demonstrates that, for children to engage in SST, which supports effective cognitive development, appropriately qualified and experienced practitioners are essential. Tickell (2011) continues to recognise that the level of qualification impacts on the quality of provision and suggests that staff should hold a minimum level 3 qualification, with their being an aspiration towards graduates with EYP status in all settings.

The *Early Years Professional Status Standards* have recently been revised (TA 2012); within the initial standards, standard 16 was 'Engage in sustained shared thinking.' Candidates wanting to gain the status need to be able to demonstrate, both in personal practice and in leading and supporting others, their ability to use both planned and unplanned opportunities to support and develop children's thinking and cognitive skills through SST. While within the new standards it is not a headline standard, it remains as '4.2 Engage in sustained shared thinking with children' (TA 2012). The emphasis of it being embedded within the professional standards clearly demonstrates the value that is placed on SST as part of current policy drivers within England and Wales.

SST and social constructivist approaches

While SST appears to be a new concept, coming out of the EPPE report (2004), it could be argued that, while the phrase does not seem to have been adopted, the concept was established through the work of sociocultural constructivists, including Cole (1998), Goncu (1998), Hoogsteder *et al.* (1998) and Trevarthen (1998), ultimately drawing on Bruner's (1996, 1990, 1987, 1986) theoretical frameworks. Bruner (1986) demonstrated that many of his frameworks were developed using Vygotsky's theoretical perspectives. Further links to SST can be identified in the practices of Reggio Emilia.

Vygotsky and Bruner

Lev Vygotsky was concerned with the ways in which learners make progress, focusing on process as well as product in assessment (Daniels 2001). He put the child at the centre of the learning process, seeing the child as an active constructor of knowledge. Vygotsky posited that it was as a direct result of the child's interactions with more knowledgeable others, and social interactions with members of his or her community, that the child developed the necessary apparatus for thinking and learning (Smith and Hart 2004). Vygotsky stressed that learning took place within the specific culture in which the child existed, clearly demonstrating that cognitive development does not occur in isolation but as an aspect of sociocognitive context. A central tenet of his work concerned the 'zone of proximal development' (ZPD) – the difference between something that a child can do today with support but tomorrow may be able to complete unassisted (Vygotsky 1978). He described it as:

> *the distance between the actual development as determined by independent problem solving and the level of potential development as determined through problem solving under adult guidance or in collaboration with more capable peers.*

(ibid.: 86; italics in original)

Vygotsky moved on to consider psychological systems, arguing that psychological research must focus not on the development of new mental functions but the relationships between them and the development of psychological systems (Minick 2005). These psychological processes were known as higher mental functions and included voluntary attention, voluntary memory, and rational, volitional, goal-directed thought (ibid.). It would appear that for Vygotsky the psychological tool was central to his view of children's development. Language mediated in sociocultural contexts supported children's development of knowledge and understanding. The child, while supported by an adult or more able other in the ZPD, would learn and develop. Societal and collectivist perspectives impacted on the child's cultural knowledge and were provided by sociohistorical contexts and day-to-day experiences. While the ZPD could not be considered as SST, echoes are clearly there within initial social-constructivist approaches.

Jerome Bruner (1986: 122) states that he is a constructivist, that he is long persuaded that it is through a process of 'sharing of human cognitions' that knowledge is both transmitted and created. He draws particularly on the work of Vygotsky to support his position. He also refers to the work of Cole and Mehan (cited in Bruner 1986) as contemporary theorists who are equally concerned with the social co-construction of knowledge and understanding, drawing on what is already known by a culture or group. Social co-construction embedded in cultural psychology can be seen to have clear links with SST.

Bruner suggests that cultural psychology provides for human minds a reflection of both culture and history. He suggests that the realities that people construct are within a cultural world – they are social realities. He draws on the work of Roy Pea and David Perkins to suggest that these realities are constructed through a process by which realities are negotiated with others and distributed between them. In this way Bruner sees that, in order that children can construct knowledge, they must draw on the ideas and knowledge around them thus scaffolding new knowledge. He argues that, if we lose sight of this situated and distributed knowledge, we fail to recognise not simply the cultural nature of knowledge, but also the cultural nature of knowledge acquisition. It is this situated and distributed understanding that he sees as a form of scaffolding, in which different members of a cultural group draw on the knowledge and understanding of others to support themselves through their ZPD in order to construct new understandings and knowledge. This scaffolding can be seen as part of the process of SST, as individuals work collaboratively to move their knowledge and understanding forward.

Bruner (1996) suggests that many of the teaching processes that occur are predicated on folk psychologies and folk pedagogies. He suggests that psychology professionals state that folk psychologies reflect certain human traits and tendencies and include ingrained cultural beliefs about the mind. From these folk psychologies arise concerns about not simply how the mind works, but how a child's mind learns. It is from these concerns that folk pedagogies arise. Bruner (1996) describes observations of parents, other adults and older siblings interacting with young children. He states that these observations demonstrate that all of these people have clear ideas, which appear to have a number of similarities, about what is needed in order for children to learn. He suggests therefore that these individuals hold to a clear folk pedagogy even though they would almost certainly not be able to articulate it. He believes that much teaching is premised on folk beliefs of children as learners. Some of these beliefs have inadvertently supported children's learning, while some have equally worked against it. Bruner claims that it is from these folk pedagogies that four dominant models of children as learners arise: as imitative learners, as learning from didactic exposure, as thinkers and as knowledgeable. While historically there has been a tendency for educators to adopt one stance, Bruner (ibid.: 65) feels that the four should be seen as 'a broader continent, their significance to be understood in the light of their partialness'. In order for effective teaching and learning to occur an approach should be adopted that advocates a balance between the four dominant theoretical perspectives. For Bruner (1986) culture is constantly in process of being recreated; it is not a static form but a forum for negotiating and renegotiating meaning. Education is a key forum for fulfilling this function. He claims to have long argued that it is not enough to simply explain what it is that children do, but that it is essential in order to better understand learning and cognition, and to develop an understanding of what the children think they are doing and the reasons for their behaviour. This can only be achieved through a recognition that 'knowledge about the world and each other gets constructed and negotiated with others'(Bruner 1996: 65). Bruner believes that learning is not about one-way transmission, but that in an effective community of learners there are opportunities to emulate and to 'offer running commentary' (ibid.: 21). This process can clearly be seen to have parallels with SST. Both adults and more knowledgeable peers scaffold learning in order that an agreed new understanding is reached. This process is that which occurs through SST where two or more parties contribute to a negotiated new understanding or perspective.

- Vygotsky sees the child as an active constructor of knowledge.
- Vygotsky suggests that language is an essential tool in learning and the co-construction of knowledge.
- Bruner proposes that there are four dominant models of children as learners: as imitative learners, as learning from didactic exposure, as thinkers and as knowledgeable.

Reggio Emilia

Reggio Emilia is an area in northern Italy where a philosophical and pedagogical approach to pre-school education was developed after the Second World War. The approach was not developed by one theorist, but Loris Malaguzzi and Carlini Rinaldi are generally considered to have been instrumental in the development of the approach. The first school began to be developed six days after the end of the war in the village of Villa Cella. Loris Malaguzzi (Edwards *et al.* 1998) heard that the people were creating a school themselves and cycled to see what was happening. He witnessed women finding and washing bricks, while other members of the community salvaged beams from bombed-out houses and other buildings. The parents declared that they would build the school at night and on Sundays. The only funds they had were what could be raised from the sale of a tank, some trucks and some horses that had been left behind by the retreating Germans. In only eight months the school was complete.

Italian schools were controlled by the Catholic Church. Parents of the Reggio Emilia schools declared that they wanted a different kind of school and a different approach to their children's education. The parents were clear that their children had rights and, as part of these rights, they should have opportunities to develop intellectually and be ready for success.

The Reggio Emilia approach developed an education system that was based on interrelationships. Children, teachers and families were all seen as key and were therefore placed at the centre of the approach. It was felt that there was a need to strengthen the relationships between the three parties. Creativity became central to the Reggio approach. However, Malaguzzi (Gandini 1996, cited in Edwards *et al.* 1998) suggests that the influence actually came from the United States and from Bruner, Piaget, Lewin, Rogers and Maslow, whose impact was felt in Italy in the 1950s. He continues to list nine beliefs about creativity in Reggio, the fourth of which is: 'The most favourable situation for creativity seems to be interpersonal exchange, with negotiation of conflicts and comparison of ideas and actions being the decisive elements (ibid.: 76).

This belief, in which interpersonal exchange is central to the creative approach and outcome, again can be seen to have parallels with SST. The Reggio Emilia approach draws on collective and collaborative methods, where ideas are shared, exchanged and developed. Likewise, practitioners engaging in SST will need to participate in interpersonal exchanges that may necessitate conflict as well as comparison in order for new ideas and positions to be negotiated and developed. Mugny and Doise (1978), citing their previous research (Doise *et al.* 1975), demonstrate that children make better cognitive progress when partnered with someone who holds an alternative cognitive position. Their experiments, which were developed based on sociocultural constructivist theory, were particularly concerned with collective cognitive performance. SST appears to be embedded in this approach to developing cognition in young children.

- The Reggio Emilia approach is based on interrelationships: child, pedagogue and family.
- Creativity is central to the Reggio Emilia approach.

Reggio Emilia-inspired pedagogical practices

The pedagogical praxis of Reggio Emilia is based in sociocultural constructivist theory. Clear links can be made between the work of pedagogues in Reggio Emilia and Vygotsky's zone of proximal development. Children engage in projects that often involve a pedagogue, an *atelierista* or artist, their parents or carers and other children with whom they attend their Reggio Emilia pre-primary school. The projects that children undertake are often complex and long term. These projects are closely supported by the pedagogues in order to support children's cognition and development (New 1998). Vecchi (1998) explains how the *atelier*, the space in which the projects are developed and constructed, allows children to develop a range of skills, such as drawing, painting or working in clay, while their pedagogues or teachers develop an understanding of the ways in which children learn. This is clearly a sociocultural co-construction of understanding that can be seen to have links with SST. Dahlberg and Moss (2005) refer to Reggio Emilia as having a pedagogy of listening to the child. They cite Rinaldi (2005: 97), who describes the role of the teacher or pedagogue as a co-creator, rather than 'a transmitter of knowledge and culture'. The cognitive developmental strategies of Reggio Emilia can clearly be seen to be echoed in the language of SST as espoused in the EYFS (2008).

This pedagogical and philosophical approach is being actively encouraged by a number of local authorities within England. Settings are encouraged to work in ways that allow children to work collaboratively on large-scale projects. One particular project was undertaken in Wales (Maynard and Chicken 2010), where teachers worked on a Reggio project in order to understand the philosophy and to share their experiences with the children with whom they work. It became apparent through the project though that staff were concerned that children were not making sufficient progress towards targets due to the slow nature of the project. It is therefore evident (Maynard and Chicken 2010; Zhang *et al.* 2010; Kim and Darling 2009) that teachers who are using a Reggio approach need to be confident in allowing children to lead. This links closely with the findings of the EPPE report (2004) in that practitioners who were confident in their own abilities, and better qualified, were better able to participate in a range of approaches to engage children in their learning and in particular in episodes of SST.

Laura's story

The following vignette describes Laura's story and demonstrates how she was engaged by a practitioner in an experience that would be considered as a 'joint-involvement episode' (Bruner 1996); however, practitioners were not clear as to whether the experience involved sustained shared thinking.

Laura is three. She has been attending the setting for some months and has been identified by the setting as needing support with language development. She does not verbally communicate with the other children or staff. She rarely makes eye contact with them. The setting has talked to the parents and has referred Laura to the Educational Psychologist. They are waiting to hear about an appointment. The setting staff are keen to engage Laura and look for opportunities to understand her interests and to plan to meet her needs.

One morning Laura had been spending time moving around the setting with a toy monkey. She was observed placing the toy in different places, on surfaces and then getting down beside the toy so that her eyes were level with the toy's eyes. Laura then clearly looked in the same direction as the toy. Laura's key worker, Carol, observed the behaviour and went and joined in. She too got down beside the toy in order that her eyes were at the same level and looking in the same direction as the toy's eyes. As Laura moved the monkey around the room, taking time to look, Carol moved with her following Laura's lead. The activity went on for a sustained period of time. During this time nothing was said by either Laura or Carol.

The entire interaction was observed by both the setting manager, who is a graduate with EYPS, and an early years advisory teacher. The two have very different perspectives on their observations. They discussed their observations with reference to sustained shared thinking. The setting manager was clear that this was an episode of sustained shared thinking, while the advisory teacher was equally assured that it was not.

Discussion

This is a clear example of two well-qualified professionals interpreting SST differently. The manager will know both the member of staff and the child well and will naturally be able to add additional information to the scene that she has observed. She will know how Laura behaves from day to day. She will be aware of the ways in which Carol has attempted to engage her and how successful these attempts have been. Equally, the advisory teacher will be familiar with the EYFS (2012) and be clear about what it says about SST. In many respects it is difficult to analyse this particular vignette. We see Laura and Carol clearly jointly engaged in an activity that continues for an extended period of time. It appears from observation that the two are engaged in an activity that involved clarifying a concept (Siraj-Blatchford et al. 2002). Laura appears to want to understand what the toy can see. What is less clear from the observation is whether this activity in any way developed or extended Laura's understanding. While it can be said that the vignette does not clearly fulfil the definition of SST (ibid.: 8), it does however contain elements and appears to fulfil the criteria for an interaction: 'sustained shared thinking interactions include *scaffolding, extending, discussing, modelling* and *playing*' (ibid.: 144; italics in original).

What Laura's vignette demonstrates is that identifying SST is not always straightforward and that many who are well qualified will hold differing opinions on what constitutes SST. Within the REPEY document, Siraj-Blatchford *et al.* (2002: 10) state that they found 'that the most effective settings encourage "sustained shared thinking" but we also found that this does not happen very frequently'. Over the decade since the completion of the first phase of the EPPE research (2004), SST has become part of the vocabulary of early years practitioners and many are attempting to ensure that they are engaging children regularly in SST. However, this is not necessarily as simple as it would appear. For the purposes of this chapter a number of EYPs agreed to respond to a questionnaire that laid out seven questions regarding SST. The practitioners who responded were all from settings that are considered by Ofsted to be good or outstanding. One advisory teacher with EYP also completed the questionnaire.

How do you define SST?

Practitioners gave a range of responses. Some practitioners were clear that SST could happen between children, while others suggested that it could only occur where they were supported by a practitioner. Some practitioners were sure that spoken language needed to occur for there to be evidence of SST, while others felt that non-verbal communication could be seen as part of the process. Within REPEY (2002) there is direct reference to Bruner's 'joint-involvement episodes'. These joint-involvement episodes do not appear to convey the same level of cognitive transformation that are associated with SST, but it could be argued that some practitioners are viewing them in a similar way to SST.

What do you do with children that you believe to be SST?

The second question appeared to elicit more similar responses, in that the respondents talked clearly about listening to children, encouraging children and giving children opportunities to develop their language. Within the REPEY report it is stated that there was a clear distinction made between 'pedagogical interactions', which were face-to-face encounters, and 'pedagogical framing', which was the 'behind-the-scenes' work, including 'provision of *materials*, *arrangement of space*, and the establishment of *daily routines* to support . . . cooperation and equitable use of resources' (Siraj–Blatchford *et al.* 2002: 23; italics in original).

It would appear that the response of the practitioners does not provide this clear distinction between pedagogical interactions and pedagogical framing. The practitioners seemed to see a seamless flow between the two, arguing that without one there could not be the other. The practitioners seemed to be suggesting that both the pedagogical framing and the pedagogical interactions are part of SST.

How do children behave when they are engaged in SST?

The practitioners all discussed children as individuals and clearly stated that while some behaviours may be identifiable, for example increased levels of concentration, engagement and interaction, for many children the response would be dependent on them and the particular activity. Interestingly all of the practitioners made it clear that it would be necessary to observe and assess what that particular child was doing. One practitioner said that some children may appear to have periods of 'blankness' while they are internalising their thoughts. In other children the thinking can manifest in action that can be observed within a schema or cluster of schemas. This clear recognition of the different experiences for different children appears to link with REPEY, in which it is stated that observations 'suggest an association between curriculum differentiation, formative assessment, and curriculum matching in terms of cognitive challenge, and "sustained shared thinking"' (Siraj–Blatchford *et al.* 2002: 12). The research goes on to suggest that these are good pedagogical practices and that settings that do them well are likely to be providing good opportunities for children to make good cognitive progress (ibid.). The practitioners here were clearly identifying these practices.

What would you expect to see when someone is engaging children in SST?

The respondents generally opened with comments about body language, and the need to mirror, to listen attentively and to question sensitively. Many of the respondents talked about genuine interest in the child and what he or she had to say. They discussed sensitive responses that challenged and developed the child's thinking. The practitioners suggest that it should be clear that the child's lead is being followed. Within the EPPE *Technical Paper 10* (Siraj–Blatchford *et al.* 2003) it was noted that in outstanding settings almost half the child-initiated interactions that could provide cognitive challenge were developed by staff in order to provided extended thinking opportunities for the child.

How would you support someone else to develop their practice of SST?

All of the respondents talked about peer-to-peer observations and modelling good practice. They discussed the ways in which SST has been discussed during their staff meetings. However, they all suggested that the extent to which this provided the necessary support for staff members who were finding SST challenging was questionable. The evidence from REPEY (2002) was that staff who were not qualified to graduate level were less likely to engage in cognitively challenging interactions with the children. While those who were less qualified but were led by a graduate would engage more effectively than those who were working alone, they nonetheless did not engage in the same way as those with higher qualifications. It would therefore seem that both EPPE (2004) and REPEY (2002) provide evidence that it is in fact difficult to support practitioners in developing their use of SST if they do not have the initial qualification level themselves.

Do you believe that SST is a marker of quality; if so how and if not why not?

There appeared to be agreement among the practitioners that SST was a marker of quality within a setting. Respondents discussed the fact that practitioners engaged in SST are likely to have a more holistic picture of the child. They also discussed the relationship with the child, suggesting that this would be crucial in order to engage in SST. The ability to engage effectively, supporting development while allowing the child to lead, was also considered to demonstrate both quality and experience. REPEY (2002) drew on the longitudinal study, *Competent Children* (Wylie 2001; Wylie and Thompson 1998), which had been carried out in New Zealand and which followed children from before they were five through their early years and school careers. One of the issues that they were concerned with was the quality of experience that was offered to the children and the long-term impact of early childhood education on the children (Wylie 2001). Wylie and Thompson (1998) suggested that the experience within early childhood education appeared more marked after the child had spent a year in school, and that children who had attended settings that scored highly on their quality marker scale appeared to be doing better in school. Like EPPE (2004), *Competent Children* (Wylie and Thompson 1998) commented on the qualification levels of staff working in early childhood education centres, recognising that the level of qualification impacted on the quality of experience that children received.

Which pedagogically appropriate practices do you associate with SST?

The practitioners all discussed observation and planning, the role of the key person and other adults responsible for planning and leading practice. Equally they made links to particular approaches and practices within early childhood education. The work of both Vygotsky and Bruner was mentioned with particular reference to the scaffolding of children's learning. Montessori's notion of 'help me to do it myself' (Bagby and Jones 2010) was included by some practitioners. The Reggio Emilia approach was cited as appropriate pedagogical practice, as was Clark and Moss's (2001) Mosaic approach. It appears that all of the practitioners considered that putting the child at the centre was fundamental when considering appropriate pedagogical approaches to support SST. REPEY suggests that 'capable educators draw upon a repertoire of pedagogical techniques that have been in some way tested' (Siraj-Blatchford *et al.* 2002: 29), and it continues to suggest that these approaches have also stood the test of both time and experience. The practitioners interviewed appeared to be drawing on pedagogical approaches that can be said to have met these criteria.

This small questionnaire demonstrates that the respondents hold similar values and views of what constitutes SST; however, as with the experience of Laura's vignette the opinions are not necessarily identical. There are clear notions of what constitutes a quality interaction with young children. The ways in which those interactions are enacted will not necessarily be the same.

Conclusion

'Sustained shared thinking' as a term was coined as part of the EPPE (2004) and REPEY (2002) research. The term demonstrably drew on pedagogically appropriate practice that had been developed over many years from a number of theorists working in the field of pedagogy and early childhood education. It is apparent that the term draws on the work of social constructivists, in particular Vygotsky (1978) and Bruner (1996, 1990, 1986), and can be seen to have clear links with the zone of proximal development, scaffolding, and social pedagogies that are predicated on positive folk pedagogies. SST provides opportunities for children to participate in the reflexive co-construction of knowledge through possibilities that offer cognitive challenge, allowing problem solving, concept clarifying and extension of narrative.

As a result of the EPPE (2004) and REPEY (2002) research the term 'sustained shared thinking' became part of the early years policy agenda in both England and Wales. What this chapter has sought to do is to question whether or not such a policy agenda can be deemed to be research informed and to question the extent to which practitioners who work delivering early childhood education and care are truly conversant with the concept and its aims.

It would seem that SST has clearly become a dominant discourse within policy agendas that address early childhood education and care. SST has become an indicator for quality, and research evidence from the longitudinal EPPE project (2004) and the correlating REPEY project (2002) substantiates SST as a marker of quality in early childhood education. This indicator has clearly been translated into policy and can be found within both the EYFS (2012) and the *Early Years Professional Status Standards* (TA 2012). It would seem, however, that there is some discrepancy in the translation of the policy into practice. The practitioners who responded to the questionnaire are demonstrably committed to providing children with a high-quality experience in their settings with opportunities to engage in SST. It is similarly evident that, even among those who are well qualified and understand the concepts of SST, they do not necessarily agree about what evidences the policy in its practical application.

REPEY (2002) clearly identified that quality and qualifications are inextricably linked. In order that children are given opportunities to flourish, they need to attend settings that are led by well-qualified staff who understand how activities such as SST can support their flourishing. While the Nutbrown review (2012) called for a strengthening of the level 3 qualification, there was no clear call for graduates to lead settings. Without this happening there is a chance that opportunities for children to engage in SST will reduce and that their opportunities to flourish will diminish. It appears that SST is a research-informed policy that has been developed from a rich and diverse history of pedagogically appropriate practice. It is to be hoped that understanding of how to deliver it with veracity will continue and develop.

REFLECTIVE QUESTIONS

- How can you ensure that you are developing the appropriate pedagogical practices that will support SST?
- How does an understanding of how children learn support you in delivering SST?
- What do you believe to be the relationship between social constructivist approaches and SST?

References

Bagby, J. and Jones, N. (2010) 'A review of the literature 2007–2009', *Montessori Life*, 1: 44–8.

Bowlby, J. (1952) *Maternal Care and Mental Health*, Geneva: World Health Organization.

Broadhead, P., Howard, J. and Wood, E. (2010) *Play and Learning in the Early Years*, London: Sage.

Bruner, J. (1986) *Actual Minds: Possible worlds*, London: Harvard University Press.

Bruner, J. (1987) *Making Sense: The child's construction of the world*, London: Routledge.

Bruner, J. (1990) *Acts of Meaning*, London: Harvard University Press.

Bruner, J. (1996) *The Culture of Education*, London: Harvard University Press.

Clark, A. and Moss, P. (2001) *Listening to Young Children: The Mosaic approach*, London: National Children's Bureau.

Cole, M. (1998) *Mind, Culture, and Activity*, Cambridge: Cambridge University Press.

Dahlberg, G. and Moss, P. (2005) *Ethics and Politics in Early Childhood Education*, London: RoutledgeFalmer.

Daniels, H. (2001) *Vygotsky and Pedagogy*, London: Routledge.

Department for Children, Schools and Families (DCSF) (2008) *Statutory Framework for the Early Years Foundation Stage*, London: DCSF.

Department for Education (DfE) (2012) *The Early Years Foundation Stage (EYFS)*, London: DfE.

Doise, W., Mugny, G. and Perret-Clermont, A.N. (1975) 'Social interaction and the development of cognitive operations', *European Journal of Social Psychology*, 5(3): 367–83.

Edwards, C., Gandini, L. and Forman, G. (eds) (1998) *The Hundred Languages of Children: The Reggio Emilia approach*, London: Ablex.

Goncu, A. (1998) 'Development of intersubjectivity in social pretend play', in Woodhead, M., Faulkner, D. and Littleton, K. (eds) *Cultural Worlds of Early Childhood*, London: Routledge.

Hoogsteder, M., Maier, R. and Elbers, E. (1998) 'Adult–child interaction, joint problem solving and the structure of cooperation', in Woodhead, M., Faulkner, D. and Littleton, K. (1998) *Cultural Worlds of Early Childhood*, Abingdon: Routledge.

Kim, B. and Darling, L. (2009) 'Monet, Malaguzzi and the constructive conversations of pre-schoolers in a Reggio-inspired classroom', *Early Childhood Education Journal*, 37(2): 137–45.

Maynard, T. and Chicken, S. (2010) 'Through a different lens: exploring Reggio Emilia in a Welsh context', *Early Years: Journal of International Research and Development*, 30(1): 29–39.

Minick, N. (2005) 'The development of Vygotsky's thought: an introduction to *Thinking and Speech*', in Daniels, H. (ed.) *An Introduction to Vygotstky* (2nd edn), London: Routledge.

Mugny, G. and Doise, W. (1978) 'Socio-cognitive conflict and structure of individual and collective performances', *European Journal of Social Psychology*, 8: 181–92.

New, R. (1998) 'Theory and praxis in Reggio Emilia: they know what they are doing, and why', in Edwards, C., Gandini, L. and Forman, G. (eds) *The Hundred Languages of Children: The Reggio Emilia approach – Advanced reflections* (2nd edn), London: Ablex.

Nutbrown, C. (2012) *Foundations for Quality: The independent review of early education and childcare qualifications. Final report*, London: Department for Education.

Qualifications and Curriculum Agency (QCA) (2000) *Curriculum Guidance for the Foundation Stage*, London: QCA/DfEE.

Siraj-Blatchford, I. (2010) 'Conceptualising progression in the pedagogy of play and sustained shared thinking in early childhood education: a Vygotskian perspective', *Educational & Child Psychology*, 26(2): 77–89.

Siraj-Blatchford, I., Sylva, K., Muttock, S., Gilden, R. and Bell, D. (2002) *Researching Effective Pedagogy in the Early Years* (REPEY), Research Report No. 356, Norwich: Department for Education and Skills.

Siraj-Blatchford, I., Sylva, K., Taggart, B., Sammons, P., Melhuish, E. and Elliot, K. (2003) *Technical Paper 10 – The Effective Provision of Pre-School Education (EPPE) Project: Intensive case studies of practice across the Foundation Stage*, London: Department for Education and Employment/Institute of Education, University of London.

Siraj-Blatchford, I., Taggart, B., Sylva, K., Sammons, P. and Melhuish, E. (2008) 'Towards the transformation of practice in early childhood education: the Effective Provision of Pre-school Education (EPPE) project', *Cambridge Journal of Education*, 38(1): 23–36.

Smith, P. and Hart, C. (2004) *Blackwell Handbook of Child Social Development*, Oxford: Blackwell.

Sylva, K., Melhuish, E., Sammons, P., Siraj-Blatchford, I. and Taggart, B. (2004) *The Effective Provision of Pre-school Education (EPPE) Project: Final report*, Nottingham: Department for Education and Skills.

Teaching Agency (TA) (2012) *Early Years Professional Status Standards*, London: Teaching Agency.

Tickell, Dame C. (2011) *The Early Years: Foundations for life, health and learning*, London: Department for Education. Available online at www.education.gov. uk/tickellreview (accessed 26 January 2013).

Trevarthen, C. (1998) 'The child's need to learn a culture', in Woodhead, M., Faulkner, D. and Littleton, K. (eds) *Cultural Worlds of Early Childhood*, London: Routledge.

Truss, E. (2012) 'Speech to the Daycare Trust conference', 4 December. Available online at www.education.gov.uk/inthenews/speeches/a00218139/daycare-trust-conference (accessed 11 April 2013).

Vecchi, V. (1998) 'The role of the atelierista: an interview with Lella Gandini', in Edwards, C., Gandini, L. and Foreman, G. (eds) *The Hundred Languages of Children: The Reggio Emilia approach*, London: Ablex.

Vygotsky, L. (1978) *Mind in Society*, London: Harvard University Press.

Vygotsky, L. (1986) *Thought and Language*, London: MIT Press.

Wylie, C. (2001) *Ten Years Old and Competent: Fourth stage of the Competent Children Project: A summary of the main findings*, Wellington: New Zealand Council for Educational Research.

Wylie, C. and Thompson, J. (1998) *Competent Children at 6: Families, early education and schools*, Wellington: New Zealand Council for Educational Research.

Zhang, J., Fallon, M. and Kim, E. (2010) 'The Reggio Emilia curricular approach for enhancing play development of young children', *Curriculum & Teaching Dialogue*, 12(1/ 2): 85–99.

10 How policy has impacted on parents

Michael Gasper

Introduction

A significant part of policy for successive governments has been to increase the involvement of parents and 'partnership with parents', which emerged as an important theme during the 1980s and 1990s (Education Acts 1980, 1981, 1986 (No. 2), Education Reform Act 1988, Children Act 1989). With the coming of New Labour in 1997, inclusivity and partnership were embedded in policy that, from 2000 onwards, was based in principled practice focused on supporting and developing the whole person and improving the well-being and confidence of children, families and communities and especially unemployed adults, thus encouraging *flourishing* (see Introduction). *Choice for Parents, the Best Start for Children: A ten year strategy for childcare* (HM Treasury 2004) included diverse, fresh services, targeted and universal, many of which became freely available through Sure Start children's centres, the success and practical value of which was recognised by Parliament in establishing Sure Start children's centres in an Act of Parliament in 2006 (Childcare Act 2006, as amended by the Apprenticeships, Skills, Children and Learning Act 2009).

After a decade of plenty, the downturn in economic climate and change in government has led to austerity measures and the reduction and refocusing of many services previously widely available. There is a danger of losing the ethical and principled practice built over more than a decade and focused on holistic improvements. This chapter considers how policy has worked in practice and the relationships Early Years Professionals (EYPs) have developed and built with parents and carers (the impact on parents and children through partnership), how policy has affected relationships between practitioners, parents and partner agencies (the impact on parents and children through partners), and intended and unintended impacts of policy (the impact on parents and children through policy), finally reflecting on what parents and carers can reasonably expect from early years provision in an era of change.

What does partnership really mean?

Partnership implies sharing, which in turn depends on trust. However, partnership does not automatically mean equality. Baldock *et al.* (2007) quote Epstein and Saunders (2002), who provide four models of partnership: a protective model, a school to home transmission model, a curriculum enrichment model and a partnership model. The first two recognise parent as ceding control and direction to professionals, the third recognises collaboration with parents and with community knowledge enriching the process of partnership, and the fourth involves long-term commitment, mutual respect and widespread involvement of parents at all levels, including decision making. In the context of partnership between professionals, parents and children, any one of these models may apply. This is very close to the descriptions of models of organisation of Early Excellence Centres by Bertram *et al.* (2002), which additionally included recognition of the different perspectives of all involved in the process of partnership, whatever its form, involving independent, voluntary and professional agencies, parents and children. Children's centres since 2004 have attempted to live and work to the fourth model above and most have achieved a 'hybrid' model as described by Bertram *et al.* (2002), where different levels (and models) of partnership operate in different aspects and areas of a centre's organisation and practice.

■ Partnership does not mean equality.
■ Children's centres attempt to use a model that involves long-term commitment, mutual respect and parents at all levels.

Theoretical approaches to parent partnership

The value of parent participation is recognised in practice and is grounded in theory, and in particular by the propositions of Bronfenbrenner and colleagues drawing on and extending the 'nature–nurture' debate (Bronfenbrenner and Ceci 1994). Bourdieu (Bourdieu and Wacquant 1992) recognises the social interaction created by systems and relationships (symbolic power) and the way in which the power inherent in classified social orders is used in practice for the more powerful to control the less. This is linked to the theory of social capital, which recognises the ways in which individuals, groups and organisations interact, creating capital through which power can be exercised. Freire (1972) advocates the value and importance of empowering individuals and groups to lift themselves from dependence and subjugation to independence and freedom. Bronfenbrenner (1994) proposes the principle of 'proximal processes', which help transform innate genetically inherited potential into practical attributes by processes taking account of physical, emotional and cultural contexts. Theory and research show the value and importance of parental engagement in the development and learning of their children within the family and outside in formal contexts including nursery and school. Bronfenbrenner (1994) quotes research from Holland (Riksen-Walraven 1978), which showed that where parents took an active interest in their children's school performance attainment increased significantly, but this was also affected by socio-economic contexts and the quality of parental involvement, with families from poorer circumstances achieving lower performance increase. Bronfenbrenner (1994) acknowledges the limitations of his proposals, recognising the complex web of influences of people, situations, cultures and social contexts on the development of children. If we add the emotional factors that underpin and affect well-being, and attributes such as engagement with tasks and challenges, persistence, ability to focus and concentrate, the value and importance of high-quality parental involvement increases and creates the optimum opportunity for flourishing to occur (Park et al. 2004). The philosophy and practice of Freire (1972) reinforces this in terms of adults and of the shift from disempowerment to empowerment. Schweinhart et al. (2005) sets out the achievements of the HighScope programme, which put these principles into practice. Head Start programmes, co-founded by Urie Bronfenbrenner (Brendtro 2006), embodied these principles in practice. A more recent research report, Nurturing Parenting Capability (Gutman et al. 2009), emphasises the mother's personal attributes as a critical factor in each child's development and advocates supporting and empowering parents to improve parenting.

- It is important that individuals are empowered to lift themselves from dependence to independence (Freire 1972).
- There is a complex web of influence on the development of children – people, situations, cultures and social contexts (Bronfenbrenner 1990a).

Parent partnership in practice

Partnership with parents has figured frequently in literature and dialogue but its translation into practice has varied considerably. Partnership in practice clearly means different things when viewed from single or multiple perspectives. For example, researchers and professionals see parents as the children's first educators who know about their children, their children's areas of confidence and their needs, but in practice researchers and professionals also see parents as knowing less than they do in terms of how children learn, what their capabilities and limitations may be and how to move them forward positively. These contradictory viewpoints, together with associated assumptions about starting points and outcomes, influence the reality of the impact of policy and the effect on parents and children by determining practice. In the 1980s Jane[1], a voluntary helper I knew, became a paid member of staff as a teaching assistant and later could have undertaken formal training to increase skill levels but declined. The assumption of those setting up systems to make this possible and implementing them (including myself) was that everyone would want to, and this was not necessarily so. During the next decade there was more encouragement to convert volunteering into paid employment as National Vocational Qualifications (NVQs) took shape, continuing across the millennium to provide more practical steps to achieve this. These initiatives were more successful in attracting individuals to improve their skills and qualifications, especially as they were grounded in practice, but how real was this as partnership?

The hierarchical order maintained clearly defined boundaries, even where volunteers and assistants were included as fully as possible as members of the adult staff team. How could they be fully included? They were not teachers and did not see themselves as such. I have often wondered if that was part of the reason for Jane's decision in the example above. In schools parents were encouraged to work alongside their children and to be more involved in the governing bodies of schools, yet even here the invisible boundaries persisted. At the time I was a Headteacher and it was not until I was introduced in the 1990s to a Social Services Family Centre that I saw genuine partnership. I observed the Social Service professionals providing guidance and access to systems such as funding, sources of equipment, and networks of voluntary and charitable bodies, but without dominating: they facilitated, the families led. At the same time I was also introduced to a Social Services Day Nursery. It was recognisable as any other nursery, yet the way my colleague shared what was happening – the aims, focus and approaches – was a revelation: the language used was about social and emotional needs, confidence and interaction rather than curriculum. Parents were treated as their child's first carers, the ones who knew the child. These professionals facilitated partnership, whereas we believed we worked in partnership with parents yet retained the hierarchical position of superiority. We did achieve success and worked closely with many parents, but the partnership was not equal. I learnt a great deal from working alongside colleagues from different professional heritages and practice, which informed my own understanding and benefitted families.

Reviewing partnerships

Willingness to engage parents and children is not enough on its own and needs constant review to be true partnership. There has been some headway in child protection but also unforeseen issues have emerged. Developments in child protection and safeguarding after 2000 built on closer partnership with the introduction of the Common Assessment Framework (CAF). This supported early intervention and, as a 'request for services', was grounded in principled partnership with parents or carers that was child centred, putting their needs first. It is a voluntary process that can be requested by parents themselves and they can choose what information they wish to share (DfE 2012a). The process involves four steps: identifying needs early, assessing needs, delivering integrated service, and review. It was aimed at prevention by starting the process sooner at a lower level of concern. The unforeseen consequences were that it opened a 'Pandora's box' of previously hidden needs and, while early intervention worked for many families, the process greatly increased the number of cases referred on to Social Services (now Social Care). This continued, increasing the demands at all levels. All agencies have found themselves dealing with more, since leadership of each case fell to the agency and professional initially raising concern. When introduced, cases above level 3 concern were referred on to Social Services. In some local authorities there was initially concern among Social Services that their role was being undermined. Over time this has shifted to concern about overload and a consequent shift in the level at which Social Care is brought in.

As cases increased, agencies became more circumspect in their referrals, and criteria for levels of concern changed. Currently the four levels of concern are: (1) Children with universal needs (no additional needs), (2) Children with additional needs, (3) Children with complex needs (may include children deemed to be 'in need' (1989 Children Act), and (4) Children in need of protection (Mersey Care NHS Trust 2013). There is anecdotal evidence that children's centre staff in some local authorities are now having to take on cases beyond their professional training and skills, which is concerning, and which is currently under review (Munro review – DfE 2010). Schools and children's centres have had to ensure staff responsible for safeguarding have the skills and time to see through CAFs initiated by them, but many schools find that, after the early years, the support from other agencies disappears and they are left to manage without additional support. While policy has improved practice overall, there is an increasing risk that reductions in funding and therefore staffing will mean compromise in the effectiveness of early identification and intervention. The significant lesson from this particular example is that child protection and safeguarding cannot be effective without adequate resources at all levels and agencies need to face the reality of how best to match reduced resources to increasing need.

Mutual trust and respect – foundations for progress

Bourdieu and Wacquant (1992) draw attention to the ways in which the powerful use their power to dominate. Freire (1972) advocates the empowerment of individuals to take control of their own lives through education that is liberating rather demanding conformity and Bronfenbrenner (1990b) and Seligman (2008) argue strongly for holistic approaches. During the last decade pathways developed in pre-school settings, nurseries, children's centres and schools have encouraged parents to come into rooms and areas, initially to help settle their children but also to begin to share in practice. Examples provided by Scandinavian pre-school and early years settings, by settings in Reggio Emilia and in New Zealand, and by centres such as Pen Green in Corby, Northamptonshire, have inspired a level of parental involvement that has grown into partnership grounded in mutual trust, with the professionals and parents respecting each other's knowledge, skills and influence on the children.

Being welcomed and encouraged has enabled parents to participate in practice in pre-school and early years settings as volunteers and to progress by stages to gain recognised qualifications. Parents are now routinely trained as volunteers, are ambassadors within communities, or are school governors or members of parents' forums or advisory boards in children's centres. Many roles include working alongside a member of staff or in tandem with another volunteer and many also lead into award-bearing programmes to increase skill and qualification levels. Training volunteers has become best practice and is recognised as essential and, in this respect, provides equal recognition with staff in terms of routine in-house staff training and development, for example in safeguarding.

The NVQ focused on personal achievement and fulfilment has proved a significant pathway enabling parent volunteers to work towards employment. I met a parent who had successfully travelled from volunteer to paid teaching assistant over a seven-year period, which required great determination, stamina and commitment. She was intending to build on this and undertake a first degree course.

This seems straightforward and logical but what is harder to understand is the effort of will required by those lacking confidence or positive self-image, to make the transition from isolation and fear to restore confidence. The true measure of flourishing success is self-fulfilment rather than hierarchy or status. The commitment of staff and their skill in working closely with individuals over time underpins success. The key worker system in children's centres and individual relationships and support in schools have been catalysts for many, enabling them to overcome fear and to gradually build self-esteem and self-confidence, encouraging them to become involved as volunteers or in more formal roles as 'ambassadors' within a community. For example, in one setting I visited, a parent volunteer had been encouraged and supported over time, progressing from being too frightened to enter, to being a confident ambassador showing visitors and new families around the centre. In both schools and children's centres parents have been encouraged to participate in informal parents' forums, which are an important part of the two-way communication chain, informing decision making and policy direction. These informal groups have the benefit of being less threatening than more formal representations of parents as school governors or members of children's centre advisory boards. Nevertheless these can also be real opportunities for involvement and enable transition to achieving recognised qualifications.

- The powerful can use their power to dominate, while empowerment can lead to individuals taking control of their own lives.
- The partnership with parents in early years has led to parents becoming involved, educated, empowered and enabled to take more formal roles.

The impact on parents and children through partnerships

Siraj-Blatchford and Clarke (2000: 58) define partnership in a multi-agency context as 'A working relationship . . . characterized by a shared sense of purpose, mutual respect and the willingness to negotiate', while

Whittington (in Weinstein *et al.* 2003: 49) considers partnership as 'a state of relationship, at organizational, group, professional or inter-professional level, to be achieved maintained and reviewed'.

They go on to identify what those involved learn from each other, what their own distinctive contribution is, what may be complementary or potentially conflict and how to work together. Wenger *et al.* (2002) underline the importance of members of 'communities of practice' understanding individually and collectively the benefits of participation in order to confidently invest time and effort into the whole. Personal and professional development is a key part of corporate success. Wenger *et al.* go on to stress the dual roles of practitioners in 'double knit' organisations as 'both community practitioners and operational team members, help[ing] link the capabilities of communities of practice to the knowledge requirements of teams and business units' (ibid.: 17–18). If this is true for staff members and individual corporations, why not combinations of agencies and interested parties, including parents and children too? Family centres, children's centres and schools largely achieve this degree of partnership at grass roots level and as individual settings, but examples of partnerships on a wider scale tend to show a significant difference between children's centres and other types of settings at the pre-school stage (Sylva *et al.* 2003).

The success of partnerships between agencies in empowering parents and children has been most clearly evidenced in children's centres. The most recent report produced by the Local Government Association (LGA) and the National Federation for Educational Research (NFER) aimed at providing 'evidence of how children's centre services are targeting the most disadvantaged families'. The report showed that children's centres were targeting:

- children (e.g. those with additional needs, speech and language delay, challenging behaviour);
- parents (e.g. mental health issues, parenting difficulties);
- families (e.g. issues of worklessness, social isolation, poor housing);
- groups (e.g. teen parents, lone parents, black minority ethnic (BME) groups, dads).

(Lord *et al.* 2011: vi)

The report notes the need for effective sharing of meaningful data between Social Care, healthcare services and children's centres. Interview data and case studies in the report support the degree of success achieved when this happens, recognising the value of effective partnership between centres. Consulting with families is acknowledged as an essential part of establishing effective services.

The increased focus on parent partnership

Genuine partnerships with parents and children have increased significantly during the last 25 years. Initiatives such as Every Child a Talker (ECaT – DCSF 2008a), the Early Learning Partnership Project (ELPP) (Dalzell *et al.* 2009) and Parents Involved in their Children's Learning (PICL) (Pen Green Research 2012) aimed at increasing parental involvement in their children's learning in its broadest sense, even though each had a more specific focus, and the Early Years Foundation Stage (EYFS) (DCSF 2008b; DfE 2012c) aimed at building on pre-school engagement and extending parental involvement in the early years. Where they work well, parents and children are able to contribute to decision making in pre-school and early years. However, reorganisation over the last decade, targeted on supporting greatest need, combined with greater reductions in funding, has seen local authorities shift towards two major changes: 'locality' models involving regrouping settings already grouped in smaller collections to construct larger groups with a single leader, and an increase in commissioned management of settings and commissioned service provision. Some smaller schools and church schools have also moved towards federation to survive. Commissioning may mean existing local providers maintaining provision or new agencies coming in. In itself it can be positive or negative depending on the structure and local circumstances. Schools have already begun commissioning aspects of the curriculum, for example sports coaching, music and creative arts, and the move to encourage and fund the development of academies and free schools extends these possibilities. Creating some academies has also involved merging previously separate settings into a larger individual unit. Children's centres are now run by independent providers and charities as well as by local authorities and in many cases have achieved greater success in working as a group within locality models. Some localities and some local authorities, such as Telford, have restructured teams to work across the whole locality, focusing resources on areas of greatest need. In the case of Telford this has achieved a better match of resources and skills to needs. Stoke has reorganized into localities that also match those of police and health services. The impact of policy changes on parents and children seems to be to provide more narrowly targeted services more effectively, at the expense of wider, universal services. Whether retaining local sites will mean that close contact with communities is maintained successfully remains to be seen. Schools still provide opportunities for consultation and changes proposed would suggest that academies and free schools offer more choice to parents and a less restricted curriculum for children. How far changes will include genuine partnership remains to be seen. The impact of policy in these examples has been real and the degree of success cannot be seen in absolute success or failure terms. Critical unknown factors include how financial constraints and reorganisation will affect the future shape of organisations and provision and how the speed of decision making will include meaningful and inclusive consultation. Affordability may well constrain previous needs-based, inclusive approaches but will certainly mean making better use of remaining resources.

Fear of change embodies danger for all agencies. Falling back on a 'silo' mentality, where each unit is in direct competition with others and partnership is the first casualty, is unhelpful and seems strange at a time when business models show the value of cooperation and partnership between potential rivals in order to achieve success for all involved. Collaboration is an active process of partnership in action and is recognised as being mutually beneficial, enabling individual businesses to achieve together what could not be on their own (Wenger et al. 2002: 17), but focusing inwards can be an instinctive reaction.

Since 2000, agencies have been encouraged to engage in 'joined-up thinking' and to develop working practices enhancing multi-agency cooperation and working. Safeguarding in particular has seen cooperation between all main agencies, and children's centres regularly work with healthcare services, Social Care and others such as Job Centre Plus. Within educare, social and medical care, the ability to see families' needs holistically has made a significant improvement for those parents and children involved and has enabled better prioritisation of need and more effective targeting of resources.

Some evidence suggests that new forms of partnership are being developed, particularly those focused on greatest need. Gutman et al. (2009) recognised the importance of mothers in early childhood, and children's centres have worked closely with colleague agencies to develop support and enabling programmes, achieving success by, for example, combining with midwives to promote breastfeeding and health visitors to develop nurture programmes. Maintaining and developing this in times of change remains challenging. The shift towards targeting greatest need and identifying and untangling complexity requires best use of staff experience and skills and partners from different professions to work closely with each other and with the parent and family concerned. The Coalition government's Troubled Families Programme (Department for

Communities and Local Government 2012a, 2012b) has made funding available for sharply focused projects to provide intensive support for families in complex need and many local authorities are seeking to use this. However, at the same time, all agencies, including local authorities, are reshaping their services to match reductions in funding and developing partnerships is much harder when each partner has to focus on reshaping its internal situation at the same time as revising outreach. The success of this particular initiative may depend on how well the lead agency recognises and understands existing partnership work in similar fields and can build on existing knowledge, skills and relationships. This may be limited by the current reductions in staffing and reorganisation, where such continuity is often lost.

- Genuine partnership with parents has increased over the last 25 years.
- Federation has been part of the process that allows settings to survive.
- Collaboration is an active process of partnership in action that is recognised as being mutually beneficial.

The impact on parents and children through policy

In Part I of this book, colleagues provided perspectives on the theory of policy making, in particular challenge and accountability in partnership working. Perspectives and understandings by definition are unique to the individual, and policy makers are those in positions of power. How far can the dynamics of power and decision making involve partnership? In this third section I want to reflect on policy and its impact on parents and children.

Throughout my life there has been a process of a 'roller coaster' of policy influenced change. I was part of the post-war birthrate boom born in the late 1940s into the emerging welfare state (Beveridge 1942), with a National Health Service replacing private medical care. The structure of education was also changing. Social Services did not exist as such. Succeeding decades witnessed shifts away from the familiar towards new initiatives, including the birth of Social Services in the 1960s. Progress was gradual with successive administrations spending almost as much time undoing what their predecessors had set up as in creating their own innovations. Yet change was far reaching and rapid. By the late 1970s and early 1980s debates over more inclusive policies emerged and desire for change encouraged politicians to create bold and radical agendas and to build steadily in the period of stable government that emerged and ran on into the 1990s. Significant changes affected education, health and welfare. Between 1980 and 1997 there was greater emphasis on individual rather than collective rights. This changed again after 1997 and the next decade saw increased emphasis on collective needs, health and social care, linked with education and 'lifelong learning'. However, by the end of the decade the economic situation, which had been buoyant, slumped. The most recent change has come at a time of economic downturn in the developed world, combined with financial crises in Europe that are threatening the existence of the European Union. The mood is more inward looking and 'separate' than outward and collective.

The current Coalition government policy aims to reduce public expenditure and encourage innovative alternatives. Reductions in funding are forcing local government to reduce staffing and to become less involved in direct provision of services and more involved in acquiring, commissioning and supervising services to be provided by others. An example is the initiative announced in November 2011 to encourage voluntary and community groups, which included the following: 'We want to enable voluntary and community sector organisations to take on a greater role in delivering public services' (DfE 2012b: 83).

The particular focus was centred on children and young people with special educational needs (SEN) and learning disabilities and the paper summarises steps taken and planned by the new administration. There is a stated intention to 'help disabled young people and those with SEN prepare for employment, training and independent living after they leave school' (ibid.: 84).

The intention to work with parents and communities and with partner agencies is clear in an area where partnership is critical for success. The emphasis on 'preparation for employment, training and independent living' (ibid.) is also clear.

Other changes focus on reducing reliance on benefits. However, the short-term and possibly longer-term effects of the changes scheduled for April 2013 will have far-reaching consequences. From April 2013 all benefits of any kind will be significantly reduced and have to be claimed online. The effects of the second simple change will be profound: many individuals on benefits do not own computers and those who are currently just managing or just failing to manage will be in a worse situation. In this example policy change will dramatically affect parents and children: health, social care and statutory and voluntary agencies have deep concerns about the likely effects. One authority has extended an initiative, which initially provided a bus with access to IT for isolated communities, to provide internet 'hubs' in locations accessible to the public. These hubs, to be manned by volunteers, have direct links to local authority offices and partner agencies. This may begin to address the IT deficit but not the shortfall in benefits that is predicted. There has been a distinct shift towards what Edwards (1997: 11) refers to as a 'political perspective': in which a specific agenda is promoted which places the social and economic "problems" of unemployment upon the shoulders of those individuals who "lack" motivation and skills'.

Edwards was problematising the 'discourse of derision' used by successive politicians in the 1970s and 1980s to dominate discourse by steering it. This technique is currently being used to justify austerity measures, which include reducing benefits to those who most need them by presenting the negative view of the minority who abuse the system as the rule rather than the exception. Policies passed on to local authorities based on significant reductions in central funding are imposing rapid and significant change. This can be seen as both positive and negative. Negative, because existing systems of support will have to be reduced or cut; positive, because innovative ideas are beginning to emerge to minimise the worst effects and to access alternative forms of funding or provision.

These changes by the Coalition government appear to have involved consultation in some cases but not in others. The previous sections in this chapter illustrated ways in which parents and children are enabled as partners in contributing to the direction and type of services. The dominant discourse is one of sharing, valuing and respecting parents and children's views and, as far as possible, shaping principled practice to meet their needs, as Wenger *et al.* (2002) show in exploring the value of 'communities of practice', where businesses increasingly share knowledge and practice to increase the benefit to all, which would be impossible individually. The notion of a product or service user being brought into the product or service development and design is one that firms have been quick to utilise, where the 'community of practice' is drawn into a loyalty partnership. Wenger *et al.* (2002) stress that this only really works where there is genuine partnership and the community 'is put before commerce'. However, government priorities are different and are dominated by discourses that are primarily about power and control, rather than genuine partnership. Edwards' 'political perspective' is reflected in the concerns expressed by Hartas (2012: 869) that 'views about a "culture of poverty" are likely to trivialize the challenges that families in poverty face'. There is real concern among care agencies, shared by the LGA, that the changes will work against family well-being and lead to increased debt, despair and danger for children and their parents (House of Commons Education Committee 2012).

This is not to suggest that policy making is simple. An LGA/NFER report that explored targeting children's centre services on the most needy noted:

> The study identified the complexity of the task facing children's centres and local authorities in attempting to respond to national policy and address local needs. The process of identifying the 'most needy' families is not straightforward, and depends on service providers working together, drawing on multiple sources of information and interpreting data intelligently to improve services and outcomes.
>
> (Lord *et al.* 2011: 21)

Unfortunately the speed of change militates against consultation and inclusion in either decision making or its translation into practice. Parents and children will find themselves in changed and challenging circumstances. Resultant ill feeling combining with lack of consultation may well undermine previously inclusive consultation. With any change or innovation there are always consequences, some intended and some unforeseen. Policies involving partnership with parents have been well intended but depend on the perspectives of the policy makers rather than those at the receiving end. Baldock *et al.* (2007) note how policy makers can fail to take account of whether those intended to access the benefits of changes are able to. They raise three key questions:

- ■ Are services available equally in all areas?
- ■ Are services affordable for all families?
- ■ Are services available when families require them?

(ibid.: 95)

They also draw attention to issues arising from siblings attending different providers, physical access to locations and whether all services are available at all locations. Given the proposed changes, affordability is likely to be a critical factor. Combine this with whatever reshaping of services comes with the next round of reduced funding and availability may also be threatened. Choice is likely to reduce at best. Working relationships with parents are likely to be at least harder, and may become compromised: partnership may well be much harder to achieve.

■   Innovative alternatives are suggested as ways in which public
    expenditure can be reduced.
■   Centrally imposed policies are resulting in rapid and significant change.
■   The speed of change often militates against consultation and inclusion in
    either decision making or its translation into practice.

Changing contexts

In the last two decades there have been considerable change and real
progress in attitudes towards partnership with parents and inclusion of
children. At its best partnership has moved beyond first point of contact
and parents' forums have provided valuable indications of communities'
needs and desires. Participation has been encouraged in groups involved
with monitoring, planning and decision making and individuals have
been trained as accredited volunteers, ambassadors and assistants. The shift
and progress towards partnership can be demonstrated.

Alongside this, less attention is given to the time and effort required
by individuals to succeed and flourish. This is often obscured because
the time factor in the process is not given sufficient credit. It is too easy
to assume automatic, linear transition and progression. Parents need
support to move from isolation to participation and from dependency
to self-confidence and greater independence. There are no magic wands
or quick fixes and even supported progress will have moments of
regression. The Effective Provision of Pre-School Education (EPPE)
project report (Sylva *et al.* 2004: viii) included the value of parental
involvement and its influence on pre-school and early years achievement
noting, 'the research points to the separate and significant influence of
the home learning environment'.

Lord *et al.* (2011: 22) highlighted a number of key areas in relation
to children's centres that need to be developed:

■   continue to recognise the value of 'universal' services as an
    opportunity for children's centres to engage with parents;

■   take account of the potential stigma attached to the term
    'targeting the most needy families' and consider using the terms
    'supporting families' or 'targeting support' instead;

■   encourage children's centre staff to make professional judgements
    in addressing the needs of individual children and families;

- consider what more could be done to encourage services to share essential data;

- encourage national organisations to recognise and share best practice among local authorities and children's centres in improving outcomes for children and families;

- consider the implications for workforce development of the skills associated with identifying and evidencing impact on the most disadvantaged families.

There is also an emphasis on clarifying CAF level 2 descriptors to avoid confusion between 'families in the greatest need' and 'targeted families'.

All this indicates that more needs to be done and also assumes the current system will continue broadly as it is. Sharing data has been a bone of contention during the last two decades and remains a difficult issue, even within local authorities and the services they run. Avoiding stigma is more problematic: the change in tone that seems to be emerging from government, and that seems to suggest blame, is unhelpful and diverts attention from the reality of addressing need. It is also too easy to accuse those in straitened circumstances of being lazy: political rhetoric can soon shift from describing those in need and needing to *use* the system, to describing those who *ab-use* it. The seductive call for individuals to take charge of their own lives, get off their seats and get going is simplistic in its assumptions about the reality of what this means in practice and flies in the face of ethical, principled practice. As a Headteacher in the 1990s, and later as a researcher, I witnessed first hand the gradual shift made by isolated and disempowered parents towards greater confidence and eventually to independence. The process took time and was not linear or smooth, but gradually crises reduced in frequency and severity. This is still the case with early intervention, whether targeted on greatest need or addressing more universal issues. In their overview of children's needs and parenting capacity, Cleaver et al. (2011) provide a detailed review of issues affecting children whose parents have mental health issues, drug or alcohol dependency or who experience domestic violence, which provides summaries of normal development and known negative effects. They also explore issues around focused intervention, which includes consideration of timescales and recognises a range of timescales to meet specific needs (ibid.).

There are some assumptions around the 'back to work' agenda that are also problematic. The previous government made no secret of the fact that it wanted mothers to return to work and contribute once more to GNP (gross national product). Yet the dangers of returning to work too soon are well documented in terms of the detrimental effects to parent and child bonding and well-being (Ainsworth *et al.* 1978; Bowlby 1953, 1951), and the long-term negative effects for both that can follow (Jakobsen *et al.* 2012), and which in turn involve increased government expenditure. The downturn in the economy has prompted the new administration to find ways of generating job creation and to at least maintain or at best increase levels of employment, but with reduced and more tightly focused support agencies and with reduced salaries and wages. Children's centres, with their principled approaches that have needed a high staff to user ratio to develop the one-to-one support necessary to help raise confidence and well-being, are faced with reductions in funding (and therefore staffing) and refocusing of targets that are shifting away from the contacts with those who can be helped back to work. Some local authorities have relocated children's centres with Social Care and are using them as initial contacts at levels below level 3; others have closed off sections of purpose-built centres to save money. Schools too are changing and it remains to be seen how far parental inclusion will be part of the change agenda for academies and free schools and whatever remains of the former system.

Conclusion

Policy to date has impacted significantly on parents and children in different ways: it has created opportunities for genuine partnership and at best enabled parents to contribute as equals to planning, monitoring and development. Policy has also encouraged partnership working and interagency cooperation, helping identify and prioritise needs of parents and children within local areas. Partnership working has developed and has impacted on parents and children by focusing and making best use of resources and skills. Parents have been enabled to access support and to move from dependence to independence, from isolation to inclusion. Many parents have been encouraged to become volunteers or ambassadors, a first step towards possibly returning to employment. Government policy has supported the development of effective early intervention and integrated working, utilising parents as equal members of school governing bodies and children's centre advisory boards. Increasingly, parents with specific skills have been encouraged to share them. These successes have been based around ethical and principled practice aimed at encouraging children and parents to flourish.

However, the economic downturn has precipitated a significant shift in emphasis. Reductions in funding are forcing a rapid reshaping of local authority function and outsourcing of services. The Coalition government policy is reshaping inherited structures irrespective of their success as well as encouraging greater independence of schools, which may or may not increase parent partnership. Children's centres are attempting to balance the false distinction of 'universal' and 'targeted' services and to work with partner agencies, which are also restructuring while themselves adjusting to reduced funding and outsourced management. Despite the moderating influence that comes with coalition, changes are approaching that will reduce access to state benefits and the amounts available to those in need. The impact of all this on parents and children will be significant: whether it will be positive or negative hangs in the balance and may depend on innovation and creativity by those already committed to supporting their cause.

REFLECTIVE QUESTIONS

- How can we ensure that children and families are kept at the heart of policy decision making at all levels?
- How can we approach maintaining the balance between policies that allow for constant adjustment to meet changing needs and consistency of provision?
- All policies carry unforeseen consequences that may have a positive or negative impact on children and families: how might this be minimised?

Note

1   All names have been changed.

References

Ainsworth, M.D.S., Blehar, M.C., Wakes, E. and Stayton, D. (1978) 'Patterns of attachment: a psychological study of the strange situation', in Bruce, T. (ed.) (2010) *Early Childhood: A guide for students*, London: Sage.

Baldock, P., Fitzgerald, D. and Kay, J. (2007) *Understanding Early Years Policy*, London: Paul Chapman.

Bertram, T., Pascal, C., Bokhari, S., Gasper, M. and Holterman, S. (2002) *Early Excellence Centre Pilot Programme Second Evaluation Report 2000–2001*, DfES Research Report No. 361, Norwich: HMSO.

Beveridge, W. (1942) *Social Insurance and Allied Services* (Beveridge report) (Cmd 6404), London: HMSO. See also: www.open.edu/openlearn/history-the-arts/history/history-science-technology-and-medicine/history-medicine/birth-the-welfare-state) (accessed 14 January 2013).

Bourdieu, P. and Wacquant, Loïc J.D. (1992) *An Invitation to Reflexive Sociology*, Chicago, IL: University of Chicago Press.

Bowlby, J. (1951) *Maternal Care and Mental Health*, Geneva: World Health Organization, in Bruce, T. (ed.) (2010) *Early Childhood: A guide for students*, London: Sage.

Bowlby, J. (1953) 'Childcare and the growth of love', in Bruce, T. (ed.) (2010) *Early Childhood: A guide for students*, London: Sage.

Brendtro, L. (2006) 'The vision of Urie Bronfenbrenner: adults who are crazy about kids', *Reclaiming Children and Youth*, 15(3): 162–6.

Bronfenbrenner, U. (1990a) 'Five critical processes for positive development', in *Rebuilding the Nest: A new commitment to the American family*, Milwaukee, WI: Family Service America. Available online at www.montana.edu/www4h/process.html (accessed 13 January 2012).

Bronfenbrenner, U. (1990b) *The Ecology of Human Development*, London: Harvard University Press.

Bronfenbrenner, U. (1994) 'Ecological models of human development', in *International Encyclopaedia of Education, Vol. 3* (2nd edn), Oxford: Elsevier. Available online at www.psy.cmu.edu/~siegler/35bronfenbrenner94.pdf (accessed 10 July 2013).

Bronfenbrenner, U. and Ceci, S.J. (1994) 'Nature–nurture reconceptualized in developmental perspective: a bioecological model', *Psychological Review*, 101(4): 568–86.

Cleaver, H., Unell, I. and Aldgate, J. (2011) *Children's Needs – Parenting Capacity: Child abuse, mental illness, learning disability, substance misuse and domestic violence* (2nd edition), London: TSO.

Dalzell, R., Watson, A. and Massey, K. (2009) *A Report on the Early Learning Partnership Project*, London: Family and Parenting Institute.

Department for Children, Schools and Families (DCSF) (2008a) *Every Child a Talker (ECaT)*. Available online at http://webarchive.nationalarchives.gov.uk/20110809091832/http://teachingandlearningresources.org.uk/node/6824 (accessed 7 November 2012).

Department for Children, Schools and Families (DCSF) (2008b) *Statutory Framework for the Early Years Foundation Stage*, London: DCSF.

Department for Communities and Local Government (2012a) *Troubled Families Programme: Financial framework for the Troubled Families programme's payment-by-results scheme for local authorities*. Available online at www.gov.uk/government/uploads/system/uploads/attachment_data/file/11469/2117840.pdf (accessed 14 January 2013).

Department for Communities and Local Government (2012b) *Troubled Families Programme*. Available online at www.gov.uk/government/policies/helping-troubled-families-turn-their-lives-around (accessed 14 January 2013)

Department for Education (DfE) (2010) *The Munro Review of Child Protection 1st Report – Child Protection: A systems analysis*, DFE-00548–2010. Available online at http://webarchive.nationalarchives.gov.uk (accessed 14 January 2013).

Department for Education (DfE) (2012a) *Common Assessment Framework (CAF)*. Available online at www.education.gov.uk/childrenandyoungpeople/strategy/integratedworking/caf (accessed January 2013).

Department for Education (DfE) (2012b) *Support and Aspiration: A new approach to special educational needs and disability: progress and next steps*, London: HMSO.

Department for Education (DfE) (2012c) *The Early Years Foundation Stage (EYFS)*, London: HMSO.

Edwards, R. (1997) *Changing Places? Flexibility, lifelong learning, and a learning society*, London: Routledge.

Epstein, J.L. and Saunders, M.G. (2002) 'Family, school and community partnerships', in Baldock, P., Fitzgerald, D. and Kay, J. (2007) *Understanding Early Years Policy*, London: Paul Chapman.

Freire, P. (1972) *Pedagogy of the Oppressed*, London: Penguin.

Gutman, L.M., Brown, J. and Akerman, R. (2009) *Nurturing Parenting Capability: The early years*, Research Report No. 30, London: Centre for Research on the Wider Benefits of Learning, Institute of Education, University of London.

Hartas, D. (2012) 'Inequality and the home learning environment: predictions about seven-year-olds' language and literacy', *British Education Research Journal*, 38(5): 859–79.

HM Treasury (2004) *Choice for Parents, the Best Start for Children: A ten year strategy for childcare*, London: HMSO.

House of Commons Education Committee (2012) *Foundation Years – Sure Start Children's Centres*. Written evidence submitted by the Local Government Association, December. Available online at www.publications.parliament.uk/pa/cm201213/cmselect/cmeduc/writev/surestart/contents.htm (accessed 14 January 2013).

Jakobsen, I., Horwood, L. and Fergusson, D. (2012) 'Childhood anxiety/withdrawal, adolescent parent–child attachment and later risk of depression and anxiety disorder', *Journal of Child and Family Studies*, 21(2): 303–10.

Lord, P., Southcott, C. and Sharp, C. (2011) *Targeting Children's Centre Services on the Most Needy Families* (LGA Research Report), Slough: NFER. Available online at www.nfer.ac.uk/publications/LGTC01 (accessed 12 July 2013).

Mersey Care NHS Trust (2013) *Specialist Management Service: Safeguarding children*. Available online at www.merseycare.nhs.uk/What_we_do/CBUs/Specialist_Management_Services/Safeguarding/Safeguarding_Children.aspx#Child assessment (accessed 10 January 2013).

Park, N., Peterson, C. and Seligman, M.E.P. (2004) 'Strengths of character and well-being', *Journal of Social and Clinical Psychology*, 23(5): 603–19.

Pen Green Research (2012) *Parents Involved in Children's Learning (PICL)*, Corby: Pen Green Research Base.

Riksen-Walraven, J.M. (1978) 'Effects of caregiver behavior on habituation rate and self-efficacy in infants', *International Journal of Behavioral Development*, 1: 105–30.

Schweinhart, L.J., Montie, J., Xiang, Z., Barnett, W.S., Belfield, C.R. and Nores, M. (2005) *Lifetime Effects: The HighScope Perry Preschool Study through age 40*, Ypsilanti, MI: HighScope Press. Available online at www.highscope.org/file/Research/PerryProject/specialsummary_rev2011_02_2.pdf (accessed 15 January 2013).

Seligman, M.E.P. (2008) 'Positive health', *Applied Psychology: An International Review*, 57: 3–18.

Siraj-Blatchford, I. and Clarke, K. (2000) *Supporting Identity, Diversity and Language in the Early Years*, Buckingham: Open University Press.

Sylva, K., Melhuish, E., Sammons, P., Siraj-Blatchford, I., Taggart, B. and Elliot, K. (2003) *The Effective Provision of Pre-School Education (EPPE) Project. Findings from the Pre-School Period.* Available online at www.ioe.ac.uk/projects/eppe (accessed 13 January 2013).

Sylva, K., Melhuish, E., Sammons, P., Siraj-Blatchford, I. and Taggart, B. (2004) *The Effective Provision of Pre-school Education (EPPE) Project: Final report*, Nottingham: DfES.

Weinstein, J., Whittington, C. and Leiba, T. (eds) (2003) *Collaboration in Social Practice*, London: Jessica Kingsley.

Wenger, E., McDermott, R. and Snyder, W.S. (2002) *Cultivating Communities of Practice: A guide to managing knowledge*, Boston, MA: Harvard University Press.

Conclusion

Jan Gourd and Zenna Kingdon

Although this book has contributions from a number of authors, we came together from a common background in delivering early years education to practitioners and students. Through the writing of the book we have found a number of common themes that include notions of perform-ativity, professionalisation, economic concerns, the apparent tension between pedagogy and policy, political interventions causing incoherent policy agendas, and a concentration on deficit models in policy directives. In examining all of these issues what became apparent to us as authors was the little regard policy makers had for considering the flourishing of the individuals involved and the flow of their lives.

Performativity appears to be a clearly dominant driver across the early childhood education and care (ECEC) sector. We recognise that policy seems to be increasingly formulated within a performativity agenda and fails to address the well-being of those concerned, including practitioners, children and their families. Performativity is quantitative in its approach and is concerned with measurable outcomes against particular norm-referenced targets. The monitoring of these targets and the subsequent allocation of finance creates a competitive market-led approach that impacts on settings, children and parents. The new two-year-old checks have led to parents being concerned about their children's ability to achieve at a much younger age. This agenda has been ongoing since the introduction of SATs (Statutory Assessment Tests) at the end of Key Stage 1 in 1990. Since then we have seen the introduction of a number of curricula and associated targets that have dealt with ever younger children. The introduction of league tables for primary schools in 1992 set the scene for a highly competitive education system, which has now led to Ofsted creating performance tables for daycare provision

(Truss 2012). Performativity leads to challenges within the early years sector because it creates tensions and provides challenges that do not necessarily fit well with an individual's preferred pedagogical stance. Thus working in the early years can have detrimental effects on the practitioner's ability to flourish as defined by Seligman (2011).

Since the economic downturn of 2008, there has been an increasing need to justify expenditure in times of austerity. This has expediated the desire of politicians to show that the decisions they are making are good ones, which can be supported by tangible outcomes in terms of performance data. This has further supported the performativity agenda as well as accelerating the need for each member of society to play a full part in becoming an economically viable individual. The need for women to return to the workplace after having children has never been greater. Research evidence, including that from EPPE (Sylva *et al.* 2004), demonstrates that there are significant long-term gains to be had from high-quality early years experiences. Determining the nature of quality is a highly contested arena. However, it is clear that high-quality experiences have associated economic consequences. While both New Labour and the current Coalition government recognised the need for investment in the quality agenda, the recent change in control of early years services from Teather (Liberal Democrat) to Truss (Conservative) seems to have signalled a new desire to look at perceived value for money rather than undertake a thorough analysis of quality. This agenda is in response to concerns about the cost of childcare in relation to wages, which seems to be impeding the ability of women to return to the workforce. Hence a tension is created for individuals and families in determining whether their prosperity will be greater by returning to the workplace or remaining at home on benefits until children are at least of school age. Children are only likely to flourish in circumstances where the family is financially viable and so the dilemma disrupts the flow. Current economic agendas seek to limit the choice by making returning to the workplace more financially attractive.

Professionalisation has been part of the economic agenda. There has been a drive to create a graduate-led workforce within the early sector that has had associated economic implications. The professionalisation agenda has been about creating a workforce within the early years sector that is comparable with most of the rest of the western world. New Labour was particularly concerned with creating a world-class workforce. This necessarily led to a professionalisation agenda that continues to be subscribed to by the Coalition government. Research-based evidence from EPPE (2004) demonstrated significantly better outcomes for children where settings were led by graduates and, in many cases, specifically teachers. Notions of professionalism vary from having technical competence to being critically reflective practitioners with appropriate academic qualifications. The government agenda tended to focus on the former while research and academics have been concerned with critical reflective practice as a prerequisite for professionalism (MacNaughton 2005). Critical reflective practice is associated with graduate professionals, while technocratic qualifications such as the NVQ level 3 require accomplishment of a specific skill set. The ability for practitioners to flourish is diminished when they are working to a techno-rational agenda. While they are prohibited from flourishing as professionals they will also find it challenging to support the flourishing of the children and families with whom they work, particularly when working to a highly driven, government performativity agenda.

The performativity agenda links directly to the deficit model view in which successive governments have located early years services and intervention agendas as solutions to societal ills. They have continually viewed children and their families as lacking in some way and have sought remedies to enable each to reach a perceived normative state. The introduction of specific early years curricula foregrounds this, providing a structure against which children can be measured. The individual child's right to develop at his or her own pace is ignored and pressure is exerted to remedy deficits whenever they occur. An example of this would be the numerous reading interventions such as Letters and Sounds (2007), which not only provides quantifiable data but severely limits a creative pedagogical approach. Field (2010) argues for the role of compensatory early childhood education, a notion that is predicated on a deficit model of children and childhood. Each stage of childhood appears to be seen as preparation for something else. This seems to advocate a view of childhood that returns us to the work of the pre-Romantic era. A view of childhood in which each phase is merely preparation for the next fails to allow children to flourish in their current state.

A constant issue within all education is that policy is used as a political football. Successive governments have sought to place their unique stamp on all aspects of the curriculum. This includes issues addressing both pedagogy and qualifications of the staff. Pedagogical approaches should be developed by the practitioners; however, certain curricula mean that particular pedagogical discourses dominate. Likewise, different political parties subscribe to different priorities in determining appropriate levels of qualification to support their quality agendas. These agendas are often subject to spin and emotive language that suggest to parents that a political party's particular stance will offer the best opportunities for all children. The language used suggests best outcomes and highest attainment possible for every child are at the heart of that party's specific agenda. The current position with the Coalition government makes the situation subject to greater instability as mid-term each party tries to re-establish its own identity. This is the case in any split-party government and current indicators suggest that this may be an ongoing situation that is new to our political landscape in the UK. This is, however, the dominant position in many European countries. Political agendas are necessarily in a party's self-interest and, while they may subscribe to being in children's interests, they rarely view the child holistically and fail to recognise the security and stability that are necessary to embed a policy and to promote the longer-term flourishing of the system with its associated impact on children and their families.

Increasingly, policy has impinged upon pedagogy, probably not through a specific policy driver that has been considered and researched, but through unintentional specificity of intended curricular outcomes. The training agenda of the techno-rational qualifications such as NVQ level 3 will not have expanded critically the concept of pedagogy and will have immersed the participants in a narrow definition of the term, suggesting this is how the curriculum should be covered, rather than asking the participants to reflect on possibilities for particular aspects of the curriculum or care. This disregard for the debate surrounding pedagogy is a serious omission in terms of creating a thinking professional able to engage with debate and think creatively about solutions. This is why a higher-level degree course comes as such a shock to practitioners who are used to being told what to do and what to think and who have little agency or voice within their work. This disregard of pedagogical debate is not only recognised within specific early years programmes, but has been a common theme within teacher education over the past 20 years since the introduction of the National Curriculum in 1988. The Qualified Teacher (QT) and Early Years Professional (EYP) standards also seek to measure competencies, the QT standards being central throughout the duration of an undergraduate B.Ed. course, while the EYP standards, soon to be EYT (Early Years Teacher), only impinge upon the curriculum in the final year of an Undergraduate Practitioner Pathway (UPP) or Undergraduate Entry Pathway (UEP) programme. Thus a greater freedom to critically reflect on pedagogy is available for those on levels 4 and 5 of their programmes than is available on the B.Ed. course. If the Nutbrown (2012) recommendation is ever implemented fully, for undergraduates we could find the professional standards driving the content of the whole three-year degree programme. This may necessitate a change in lecturers' pedagogy that, although not legislated for, will probably emerge as the outcomes drive the agenda, as has happened throughout the rest of the educational system. Pedagogy is such a powerful concept and its development should be the result of critically reflective practice, which slowly adds to the effectiveness of the practice allowing it to be constantly refined. When pedagogy is taught as a specific set of skills to be mastered, the depth of the pedagogy is shallow and its ability to change and be refined with experience is limited. Pedagogy that is based on a set of deeply held values that are examined in light of self-awareness in terms of biased practice, and that allow new knowledge to be assimilated, provides the conditions for the practitioner to flourish and to support others in their own flourishing. A deep pedagogy based on critical reflective practice allows practitioners to confidently make and justify their own interpretation and implementation of policy and gives them agency to control and shape their practice.

The concept of flourishing has been a specific theme throughout the book and is something that the writing team feels strongly about. Most of us have been in practice in our various professions throughout the last 20 years and have seen policy agendas come and go all too frequently. The cynicism with which our ideas as NQTs (newly qualified teachers) were met by our more experienced colleagues lives with us, as do the comments that no ideas are new and, like fashion, they will come around again. Those established teachers who had started their careers prior to the introduction of the National Curriculum baulked at the performativity agenda that was being thrust upon them with the associated assessment routine. They kicked back against a prescribed curriculum and found ways to subvert the detail and make the targets workable; this had to happen to preserve the flow of the work they knew. These teachers were educated in the days before a specific teacher training curriculum existed, they knew what they were about, they had lived through the Plowden (1967) days and shaped their craft through engagement with the schools' council reflective practice model, and they engaged in school-based research supported by the aforementioned schools' council. They were confident in their own professionalism and flourished.

This is what today's early years graduates have. Their degree-level education is not as yet overly prescribed, the professional verification being a minor part of the educational process, and this is what we need to hold on to in the future development of policy. EYPs need an arena of participation in practice-based research to continue to support them in developing critical reflective practice through continuous professional development. In this way they are enabled to flourish and promote the best quality they can for the children and families with whom they work.

It is to be hoped that future government research-informed policy will recognise the need to continuously support the flourishing profession that has been created.

References

Field, F. (2010) *The Foundation Years: Preventing poor children becoming poor adults: The report of the Independent Review on Poverty and Life Chances*, London: Cabinet Office. Available online at www.nfm.org.uk/component/jdownloads/finish/74/333 (accessed 2 July 2013).

MacNaughton, G. (2005) *Doing Foucault in Early Childhood Studies: Applying poststructural ideas*, Abingdon: Routledge.

Nutbrown, C. (2012) *Foundations For Quality: The independent review of early education and childcare qualifications. Final report*, London: Department for Education.

Plowden, Lady B. (1967) *Children and their Primary Schools: A report of the Central Advisory Council for Education (England)*, London: HMSO.

Seligman, M. (2011) *Flourish: A visionary new understanding of happiness and well-being*, New York: Free Press.

Sylva, K., Melhuish, E., Sammons, P., Siraj-Blatchford, I. and Taggart, B. (2004) *The Effective Provision of Pre-school Education (EPPE) Project: Final report*, Nottingham: Department for Education and Skills.

Truss, E. (2012) 'Speech to the Daycare Trust conference', 4 December. Available online at www.education.gov.uk/inthenews/speeches/a00218139/daycare-trust-conference (accessed 11 April 2013).

Glossary

Agency: the ability to act; to have power to be able to participate.

Capitalism: an economic system that is based on private ownership and profit making.

Discourse: the formal treatment of a particular subject in both spoken and written formats.

Flourish: an approach to happiness and well-being that is underpinned by PERMA: Personal Enjoyment, Engagement, (Positive) Relationships, Meaning and Accomplishment.

Foucaultian (or *Foucauldian*): pertaining to the philosophy of Michael Foucault regarding situated power relationships.

Fundamentalist: a demand for strict adherence to a particular philosophical approach.

Globalisation: the emergence largely since the 1980s of a single world market in which companies can operate and compete internationally; this has led to the diminishing of the capacity of governments to fully control their economies. Globalisation can have a negative impact on those working at street level.

Hegemonic: the dominance of power or control; a particular approach gains hegemony or domination because it is underpinned by power. Therefore, approaches that are laid out in policy will be those that are supported by those who hold the power and hence approaches are seen to be hegemonic.

Ideology: a body of ideas that reflects the beliefs of a particular group, such as a nation, political party or class.

Modernist: relating to modern thought from the late nineteenth century onwards.

Neoliberal: ideas based on a free market economy with little political interference.

Paradigm: a general conception, or model, of social scientific endeavour within which a given enquiry is undertaken.

Performativity: a mechanism that reduces performance or practice to a measurement. Performance is measured against a predefined set of standards.

Positivist: a view that knowledge can only be gained through empirical experience.

Post-modern: the period that follows the modernist era, in which the ideas of the modernist era are rejected and a level of criticality is introduced.

Post-structural: recognising the power of thought and discourse in shaping reality.

Relativism: a theory that holds truth or moral value but is not universal and may vary between individuals or cultures.

Index

Abbott, L. 83
academies *see* free schools
accountability 15, 23, 29, 95–6, 100–2,
    202; tensions and challenges 33, 35,
    37–8, 40, 42, 45, 47, 49
Action for Children 75, 86
Adnett, N. 142
Africa 161
agency 49, 130; 'bounded' 104
Ailwood, J. 159
Albon, D. 50
Allen, G. 61, 87, 140
Ancient Greeks 153–4, 168
Apple, M.W. 16–18
assessment 56, 68, 86–7, 175, 178, 186
attainment 7, 48, 61, 95, 108, 110,
    126–7, 194, 216
auditing 37, 76
austerity 7–8, 125, 192, 209, 214
Australia 76, 124–5
autonomy 44–5, 52, 144

Baldock, P. 59, 70–1, 83, 193, 205
Ball, S.J. 33, 40, 44, 48, 136
Bamfield, L. 70
Bangura, A.K. 161
Bartlett, T. 162
Beck, U. 16
Belgium 108
Ben-Galim, D. 109
Bennett, L. 146
Berthelsen, D. 145

Bertram, A.D. 76, 193
Biesta, G.J.J. 38
Big Society, the 70–1
Birth to Three Matters 83
Blackmore, J. 33
Boddy, J. 132
Booth, R. 108
Bourdieu, P. 193, 197
Bowlby, J. 177
Boyd, A.D. 159
Boyle, E. 77
Brazil 119, 161
Broadhead, P. 161–3, 177
Brock, A. 49, 144
Bronfenbrenner, U. 58, 193–4, 197
Brooker, L. 85, 98, 100, 159, 161, 165
Brookfield, S. 51
Brownlee, J. 145
Bruner, J. 178–82, 185, 188
bureaucracy 75, 102, 123; street-level 14,
    16, 21, 23, 25

Callaghan, J. 62, 79
Cameron, D. 108
capitalism 28, 44
Carr, M. 68
child protection 137, 196, 205
child-initiated play 2, 56, 163, 165, 169,
    175
childcare provision 20, 65–6
childminders 66, 97, 109, 122, 145,
    165–6, 176

Children Act 80, 83, 137
children's centres 1, 40, 70–1, 131,
    192–3, 197–201, 205–6, 208
Children's Workforce Development
    Council (CWDC) 96, 121, 127–8
choice and voice 39–41
Clark, A. 164, 188, 198
Cleaver, H. 207
Climbié, V. 83, 137
Clough, P. 165
co-construction 84, 162, 179, 183
Coalition government (UK) 70–1, 88–9,
    129–30, 176, 214, 216; future policy
    101–2, 107, 109–10; impact on
    parents 201, 203–4, 209
cognitive development 26, 97, 120, 126,
    157, 161–2, 167, 178, 182–3, 186
Cole, M. 178–9
Collin, R. 16
Common Assessment Framework (CAF)
    137, 196–7, 207
common sense 34, 38–9, 143
communities 13, 70, 203; of practice 199,
    204
competition 17–18
Conservative Party, UK 39, 83, 111, 121
consumerism 17, 39
Corsaro, W. 153, 163
Cowes, S. 149
creativity 67, 82, 160, 182
critical engagement 33, 61, 88
critically reflective practice 27, 51, 124,
    132, 215, 217; future policy 100, 102,
    106–7; international policy 59, 61, 71;
    see also foundation degrees
Cromby, J. 50
Crook, D. 42
Csikzentmihalyi, M. 159
cultural differences 58, 160–1
curricula 27, 45, 48, 57, 65–9, 168, 196,
    200, 213, 215–17; EYFS 75–6, 79–84,
    86–8, 90–1; foundation degrees 136,
    144; sustained shared thinking 176,
    186

Dahlberg, G. 17, 26–8, 35, 41, 59, 143,
    183
David, T. 82
Daycare Trust 123, 126
De Lissovoy, N. 28

decentralisation 57, 70
democracy 25, 28, 30, 39, 104
Denmark 56, 58, 65–6, 68, 109, 118, 197
Department for Education (DfE) 71, 83,
    119, 121, 136, 165
Department for Education and Skills
    (DfES) 139, 174
deprivation 62, 71, 107, 109, 129
deregulation 45, 103, 111, 123–4, 174,
    176
desirable learning outcomes (DLOs) 82,
    136
developmentally appropriate practice
    (DAP) 162
Dewey, J. 16
dialogue 30, 64, 104
didacticism 64, 180
discourse 17, 20, 28, 39, 49, 51, 95,
    97–8, 107, 120, 144, 159, 215
discursion 28–9
domination 17, 28
Dowdell, K. 167
Down, J. 147
Dyer, M.A. 102

early childhood education and care
    (ECEC) 46–7, 59–60, 66, 70, 136,
    138, 147, 213
Early Learning Partnership Project
    (ELPP) 200
early years sector endorsed foundation
    degree (EYSEFD) 140, 148
Ebbeck, M. 50
economically viable units 39–41, 214
Edmond, N. 141
Education Reform Act (1998) 45
Edwards, R. 51, 159, 204
Effective Provision of Pre-school
    Education (EPPE) 85–6, 89–90, 97,
    117, 126–7, 206, 214; foundation
    degrees 135, 137, 139–40, 145,
    147–8; sustained shared thinking
    173–8, 183, 185–9
Einarsdottir, J. 164
Elfer, P. 83
emotional labour 60, 101, 106
empathy 132, 160
Enabling Environments 164, 166
Entry Pathway 131
epistemology 18, 28, 36

Epstein, J.L. 63, 193
Estola, E. 101
ethics 25–7, 61, 97, 100, 135, 192, 208
European Commission (EC) 61, 65, 71
European Union 61, 203
Every Child a Talker (ECaT) 200
exchange paradigm 101–2, 109

Fairclough, N. 17
Farrell, C. 166
feminism 97, 102
Field, F. 61, 87, 119, 125, 215
Finland 56, 58, 65–6, 68, 109, 118
Fjortoft, I. 167
flourishing 1–2, 14, 30, 136, 192, 206,
    208, 214–18; accountability 42, 52;
    changing environment 152, 154, 164,
    167–9; EYFS 88–9, 91; future policy
    101, 107, 111; international policy 59,
    61, 65, 71; research-informed policy
    177, 189; up-skilling 117, 123, 125,
    132
Forest Schools 66–7
Foucault, M. 39, 50
foundation degrees (FdA) 135, 147–8
France 108–9, 119, 123
free market see market-driven view
free schools 90–1, 201, 208
Freire, P. 194, 197
Froebel, F. 152, 154–6, 158–9, 168–9

Gasper, M. 192–209,
Gaunt, C. 89
gender 15, 18–19, 36, 97, 135, 140–1,
    160–1
General Certificate of Secondary
    Education (GCSE) 100, 106, 140, 142
gift paradigm 101–2, 107
globalisation 16, 18, 28, 34, 40, 57
Goldschmied, E. 83
Goncu, A. 178
Goouch, K. 159
Gosso, Y. 160
Gourd, J. 1–8, 56–72, 95–112, 117–33,
    213–18
Gove, M. 108
Graduate Entry Pathway (GEP) 128, 131
Graduate Practitioner Pathway (GPP)
    128–9
Greece 108

Grenier, G 89, 103
Grieshaber,S. 159–61, 169
Gutman, L.M. 201

Hadow, W.H. 77–8
Harcourt, D. 164
Hartas, D. 204
Head Start programme (USA) 62, 101,
    126, 194
healthcare 199, 201, 203
Hedges, H. 76
hegemony 20, 28, 38
Hendrick, H. 153
Hevey, D. 122
hierarchies 119, 195–6, 198
Higher Education Funding Council for
    England (HEFCE) 141, 148
HighScope programme 56, 63–5, 68–9,
    97, 120, 126–7, 194
Hill, T. 144–5
Hirsh-Pasek, K. 162
holism 60, 145, 161, 192, 197
Holland 194
Hoogsteder, M. 178
Howard, J. 84–5
Hungary 108

Iceland 56, 58, 65–6, 109, 118
ideology 18–19, 21–2, 34–9, 41, 46, 59,
    146
individualism 17–18
Industrial Revolution 152, 154–6,
    168
inequality 17, 27–8, 40, 56, 60–1, 72,
    108, 125, 148
international policy 21, 56–9
interventions 21, 24, 27, 30, 61, 111,
    196, 215
Isaacs, S. 152, 156–8, 168–9
Israel 108
Italy 58, 181–2

Jackson, S. 83
James, A.L. 153
Johnson, J. 59, 62
Jones, M. 165
Joseph, K. 79

Kelly-Byrne, D. 159–60
Kerr, J. 158

kindergarten 155–6, 159, 168
Kingdon, Z. 1–8, 75–91, 135–49,
    152–69, 173–89, 213–18
knowledge societies 57, 75–6

labour markets 18, 20
Labour Party, UK 39, 44–6, 61, 70–1,
    174, 192, 214; EYFS 82, 88–9;
    foundation degrees 135–6, 139, 143,
    145–6, 148–9; future policy 101–2,
    110–11; up-skilling 120–1, 127
Laming, H. 83, 135, 137–8
Langston, A. 87–8
Lea, S. 13–30
leadership 16, 29–30, 47, 67, 88–90, 97,
    103, 107, 196
league tables 16, 213
Lee, W. 68
legislative frameworks 96–7, 102
Levinas, E. 100
Lewin, K.Z. 182
Liberal Democrats, UK 109, 111
Lillard, A. 162
Lipsky, M. 16, 23
literacy 2, 82, 87
living contradictions 33, 37, 48–9
local authorities 70–1, 138, 144, 196–7,
    207
Local Government Association (LGA)
    199, 204–5
Locke, J. 153–4
Lord, P. 206
Louv, R. 68
Lyotard, J.F. 33, 50

McArdle, F. 159–61, 169
McGillivray, G. 97, 121, 138, 146
McMillan, M. 152, 157–8, 168–9
McMillan, R. 152, 157–8, 168–9
MacNaughton, G. 14, 28, 45, 61,
    123–4
Malaguzzi, L. 181–2
managerialism 17, 21, 28, 34, 45
market-driven view 16–18, 35–7, 40, 44,
    123, 213
Marxism 61–2
Maslow, A. 182
Mathers, S. 126
Maynard, T. 167
Mehan, H. 179

mental health 2, 157, 207
Mexico 108
micro-practices 14, 22–3
middle classes 71, 97–8, 121, 141, 147
Milbank, J. 136
Miller, L. 49, 67, 122
modernism 39, 41, 51
Montessori, M. 188
Morgaine, C. 45
Mosaic approach 188
Moss, P. 17, 26–8, 35–6, 60, 143, 164,
    183, 188
Moyles, J. 144, 163
Mugny, G. 182
multi-agency cooperation 200–2
Munton, T. 103, 118–20
Murray, J. 67, 122

Nairn, A. 60
National College of School Leadership
    (NCSL) 29–30, 90
National Curriculum 45, 65, 79–81,
    216–17
National Federation for Educational
    Research (NFER) 199, 205
national policy 18–19, 27
National Vocational Qualification
    (NVQ) 128, 195, 198, 215–16
nature-nurture debate 193–4
neoliberalism 14, 16–18, 20, 22–3, 28,
    34, 36–9, 41, 44–5
Neuman, S.B. 166
neuroscience 57, 76
neutrality 17, 21, 23–4
New, R. 70
New Zealand 76, 98, 104, 118, 129, 185,
    197
newly qualified teachers (NQTs) 217
Nguyen, T.X.T. 16
Nightingale, D.J. 50
Noise, W. 182
Nordic approach 4, 56, 65, 98
Norway 56, 58, 65–6, 68, 109, 118,
    197
numeracy 2, 82, 87
Nutbrown, C. 43, 47, 165, 176, 189,
    216; EYFS 76, 78, 88–9; future policy
    98–9, 104–6; up-skilling 119, 121,
    129–30
nutrition 158, 168

Oberhuemer, P. 56, 76
Ofsted 23, 48, 68, 81, 96, 126, 147, 165, 185, 213
Organisation for Economic Co-operation and Development (OECD) 56, 68, 71
Osborn, A. 136
Osgood, J. 45–7, 97, 138, 141, 144, 146–7, 149
O'Sullivan, J. 90
outdoor environments 67–8, 152–6, 158, 166–7
Owen, R. 77, 152, 155, 168

Palmer, S. 62
partnership with parents 192–3, 195–7, 199–201, 205–6, 208–9
Pascal, C. 76
Pea, R. 180
pedagogues 118–19
Pellegrini, V.D. 159
performativity 45, 47–9, 95, 103, 111, 213–15; international policy 56, 59, 61, 64, 70
Perkins, D. 180
Perry Pre-school Project 63, 139
personal development 135, 142, 177
Pestalozzi, J. 154–6
'philanthrocapitalism' 29
Piaget, J. 63, 69, 77, 182
Plato 153
play 15, 67–8, 80, 82, 84–6, 153, 156–7, 159–61, 168; playful pedagogy 65, 152, 161–4
Plowden, B. 19, 63, 77–9, 81, 90–1, 97, 136, 217
policy entrepreneurs 20, 24–6
policy interrogation 13–14, 18, 22
policy makers 16, 18–19, 21, 25, 85, 90, 127, 143, 159
political philosophy 16, 28
positivism 36, 39, 46, 51
post-structuralism 39, 50–1
PGCE (Postgraduate Certificate in Education) 106, 128–9
Pound, L. 63, 67, 126
poverty 15, 40, 87, 90, 125, 139, 148, 204
Powell, S. 26, 96, 143
power 15, 22, 24, 44, 194
Pre-school Learning Alliance 87

private sector 16, 18, 81, 107, 122–3
Professional Association for Childcare and Early Years (PACEY) 166
professionalisation 33, 36, 42–5, 47, 49, 131, 138–9, 141, 144, 213–14
professionalism 25, 103–4, 146, 149, 215, 217; accountability 38, 40–1, 46; up-skilling 119, 126, 132
Pugh, G. 137, 139

qualifications 47, 177–8, 184, 187, 198, 214–16; EYFS 78, 80–1, 88–9; foundation degrees 135–40, 142–6, 148–9; future policy 97–8, 104–6, 109–11; up-skilling 117–24, 127–9, 131
Qualified Teacher Status (QTS) 89, 98–9, 103–6, 119–21, 128–30, 140, 216

race 15, 40–1
Reay, D. 110
Reggio Emilia approach 56, 59, 64, 69–71, 178, 181–3, 188, 197
regulation 44–5, 49–50, 76, 86
relativism 50–1
research-informed policy 174, 189, 218
Researching Effective Pedagogy in the Early Years (REPEY) 85–6, 173, 175–6, 185–9
resistance 49, 51
rights of the child 20, 22, 25–6, 28
Rinaldi, C. 181, 183
risk aversion 67, 167
Roberts-Holmes, G. 84–5
Rogers, S. 159–61, 182
Romanticism 86, 153, 156, 159
Roopnarine, J. 62
Roskos, K. 166
Rousseau, J.J. 77–8, 152, 154, 168
Rumbold, A. 78–81, 136

Sachs, J. 33
Saunders, M.G. 193
Savage, C. 142–4
Schön, D. 44
school readiness 66, 87, 95, 118
Schuetze, H. 142
Schweinhart, L.J. 194
Scotland 25, 155

self-esteem 82, 142, 145, 154, 177, 198
self-governance 17, 29
Seligman, M. 2, 52, 110, 197, 214
Simpson, D. 49, 103–4
Siraj-Blatchford, I. 51, 173–4, 176, 185, 198
Slack, K. 142
Slowey, M. 142
Smith, P. 159
social constructivism 68, 178–82
social exclusion 90, 139, 176
social justice 18, 23, 26, 110
Social Services 195–6, 202
Socrates 153
Somalia 161
Spain 58, 60, 118
special educational needs (SEN) 203
Spencer-Woodley, L. 33–52
split-role workers 118–19, 121–2
staffing ratios 88, 103, 107, 109–11, 118,
    121–5, 176, 208
stakeholders 39, 57, 126
standards 23, 29, 33, 40, 43–4, 48–9, 95,
    106, 131, 136, 178
Statutory Assessment Tests (SATs) 100, 213
Strathern, M. 37
Straw, J. 108
Sure Start programme, (UK) 63, 192
sustained shared thinking (SST) 163, 173–89
Sutton-Smith, B. 159–60
Swarbrick, N. 89
Sweden 56, 58, 60, 65–6, 68, 109, 118, 197
Sylva, K. 82, 137, 139

Taggart, B. 139
targets 58, 69–70, 213
tax credits 122
Taylor, S.M. 102
Te Whariki approach 56, 59, 64, 68–9
Teather, S. 75, 86, 109, 119, 214
Thatcher, M. 78–9
Thompson, J. 187
Thomson, R. 87
Tickell, C. 75, 86–8, 129, 176, 178
Tobias, R. 43–5
top-down processes 33, 148
training 29–30, 120
Trevarthen, C. 178
Truss, E. 107, 109–10, 119, 123–4, 176, 214
Tyndale, W. 79

UN Convention on the Rights of the Child
    161–2
Undergraduate Entry Pathway (UEP) 128,
    216
Undergraduate Practitioner Pathway (UPP)
    106, 128–9
unemployment 192, 204, 208
unions 98–9
UKIP (United Kingdom Independence
    Party) 111
universal education 154–6
universal provision 71, 79, 127, 192
up-skilling 63, 97–8, 117, 120, 122, 130–1,
    138–9
Urban, M. 95, 130
USA 108–9, 119, 126, 155, 158, 161, 182;
    international policy 58–9, 61, 63, 68, 70,
    72

value for money 38, 125, 139
values 15–18, 21, 24–8, 50, 84, 95, 135, 143,
    146
Vaughan, G. 101
Vecchi, V. 183
Vincent, A. 34, 38
volunteers 142, 160, 195, 197–8, 203–4
Vygotsky, L. 63, 69, 85, 160–1, 177–9,
    181–2, 188

Wacquant, L. 197
Wales 75, 79, 82, 90–1, 136, 145, 147, 167,
    178, 183, 188
Walkerdine, V. 28
Waters, J. 167
Weikart, D. 63
welfare state 16, 18, 41, 66, 125, 202–3, 207
well-being 58, 61, 66, 76, 111, 194, 204
Wenger, E. 199, 204
White, J. 52
Whittington, C. 199
Whitty, G. 44, 46
Wood, E. 85, 161, 163
working classes 97–8, 141, 154–5
Wylie, C. 187

Yelland, N. 164

zone of proximal development 63, 179–80,
    182, 188